AutoCAD for Land Surveyors

Recommended to surveying students, engineers and employees, and cartographers

Harriet Mac Clarke

Javad Noormohammadi

Preface

Today, because of the development of electronic surveying systems such as Total Station instruments, we no longer use drawing papers, drafting tables, T-Square rulers, Curve rulers and other handy drafting tools for drawing a map, and land surveying software such as Land Desktop, AutoCAD, SDR maps have replaced them very well, because they can meet the user's needs with more precision and speed, less errors and lower costs in the best way possible. For example, if errors are made when handy drafting and the drawing paper becomes unusable, we must start drawing from the beginning and it requires more time and money. But now using drawing software, maps are printed out only when they are free of drawing and computational errors. When errors are made, it is easy to undo them and we can save time and money more easily. We can also print the map out in different dimensions and scales and map generalizations according to the user's opinion. Meanwhile, with its capabilities, AutoCAD drafting software helps the surveyors draw in the best way possible. It should be noted of course that AutoCAD has many other practical applications in various engineering and industrial fields such as civil engineering, construction, architecture, mechanical engineering and other engineering sciences, and given the breadth of this powerful software, each user benefits from parts of the AutoCAD commands and capabilities, depending on their needs and demands. This matter encouraged us to serve the land surveying community by amassing this collection so that we can summarize and teach the AutoCAD commands and capabilities that are used in land surveying and cartography and analyze practical examples. It helps the land surveyors stop spending their time studying books that contain general content about AutoCAD and start learning applied AutoCAD. Having many years of experience in the field of land surveying and cartography of research and executive projects, the author is eager to familiarize the land surveyors with applied, fully functional AutoCAD and to help them learn the AutoCAD commands and capabilities that are practical for map drafting. We have used a lot of examples in the book for the learners and specialized exercises have also been explained in the final chapters.

There is an important point to make about the presentation of the examples and exercises: It might be possible for you to find different solutions to solve the examples and exercises in the book and you might solve them using other software or methods. The purpose of presenting these examples and exercises is to help you master these commands. You can also use the commands for other purposes after mastering them.

In this set of tutorials, additional topics and other parts of the software that are used in other engineering fields have been avoided. It has simply been collected to help land surveyors and the learning process. There are also other sources that enthusiasts can study to learn other uses of AutoCAD.

I hope that you, dear readers, can meet your needs for conducting a land surveying project after reading this book carefully.

Tip:

To receive the attached files, email us at
javad_nm_aus@yahoo.com

Contents

Chapter 4: Professional settings for AutoCAD

Chapter 5: Professional Land Surveying Practices

Chapter 1:

Introduction to drawing area and AutoCAD capabilities

- Introduction to different sections of the software
- Introduction to LISPs and Macros
- Introduction to the professional approach of using AutoCAD
- Introduction to the most important and the most commonly used shortcuts

The word AutoCAD stands for Automatic Computer-Aided Design which means computer-aided drawing and design. This software is a product of the American software corporation Autodesk. Some important features worth mentioning about this software are drawing in 2D and 3D spaces, vectorization, the capability to update drawings, layering the objects in the drawing, support for the other land surveying software formats such as DXF software format (SDR map), the ability to connect to database software such as ArcGIS and its wide range of applications in other fields of engineering.

AutoCAD has 2D and 3D drawing spaces. But given the fact that computations and drawings of the third dimension (height) of land surveying projects are performed in other land surveying software, only the 2D space is taught here.

- **Different sections of the software**

1. Title bar

Like other Windows software, when you run AutoCAD, it has a bar at the top of it that is blue by default (version 2007) and in this bar, from left to right, you can see the name of the software program and its version number, and then the name of the currently running drawing file displayed in square brackets with the file extension. This name is optional and user-defined and if not defined, AutoCAD will automatically name the file Drawing1 and the drawing file extension also appears at the end of the file name which is the format and ID of each drawing file.

The file extension of this software is .dwg, but it also supports the other extensions like dxf, dwt and dws.

2. Menu bar

At the top of the window of this software and below the title bar, you will see a bar like the one in Figure 1-1 which is called menu bar.

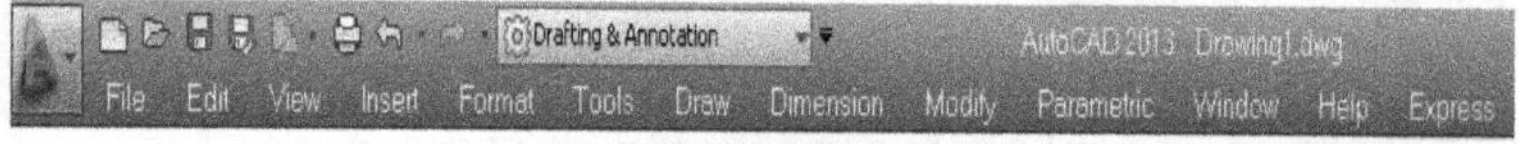

Figure 1-1

There are several menus in this bar and when you click on them, the corresponding drop-down menu opens. These menus contain different commands. In fact, most AutoCAD settings and commands are placed in this bar.

Introduction to the options available in the menu bar

File

This menu is the management center of the program and is able to run commands related to creating a new drawing, storing, opening, exporting, printing operations, and so on.

Edit

This menu is the hub for editing operations in the program and allows you to do things like copying, cutting, pasting, searching and more.

View

It is the hub for performing the image control task of the program and contains Zoom options to zoom in and Pan command to pan the view and Toolbars command which are used to manage the toolbars of the program.

Insert

This menu is responsible for importing and inserting drawings, images and files from other software such as Office and many others into the software environment.

Format

Allows the user to optimize and modify the appearance of the drawing area and objects in it.

Tools

With its various tools and options, this menu allows the user to modify files and projects and manage the software.

Draw

It is the hub of drawing and design sections in the AutoCAD software. When designing a project, knowing all the options and how they work will save you time and it ensures accurate execution of it.

Dimension

This menu has various commands to measure and give dimensions of the size of drawings.

Modify

Allows you to do things such as editing and modifying the project with functions like copying, deleting and rotating.

Window

Allows you to manage open windows with functions like closing and resizing and selecting windows in the drawing area.

Help

This menu provides a manual to familiarize users with the software features. This section is enabled by pressing F1 key in the software environment and Help window opens.

Express

This menu contains commands that do not always function properly and the software manufacturer does not guarantee that these commands will work correctly. If these commands are ran by users and then display their own capabilities and if they work well, in later versions of the software, they will be used as the main AutoCAD commands.

In pre-2008 versions, when installing the software, the user is asked if they want to install the Express menu as in Figure 1-2. If this option is checked, the menu will be installed and will appear at the bottom of the menu bar, otherwise it will not be installed.

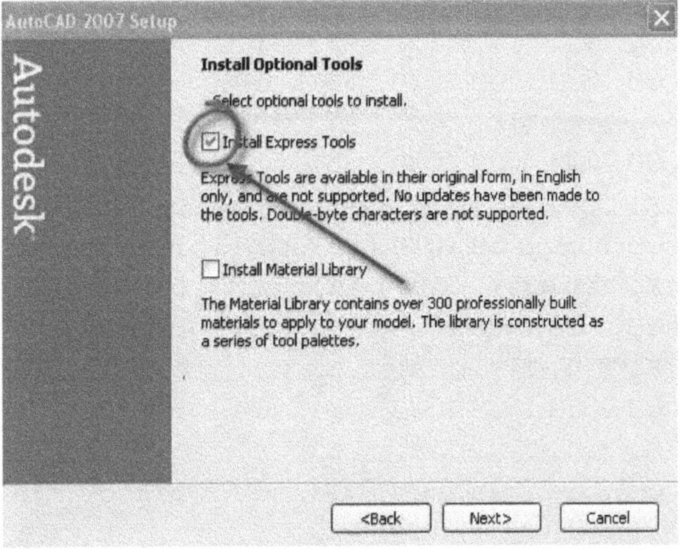

Figure 1-2

3. Toolbar

AutoCAD also has several toolbars, some of which are designed for 2D space and some are for 3D space and each of them has a set of commands. For example, you can find drawing commands in the Draw toolbar and the dimensions instructions in the Dimension toolbar. You can see the Draw and Dimension toolbars in the figure

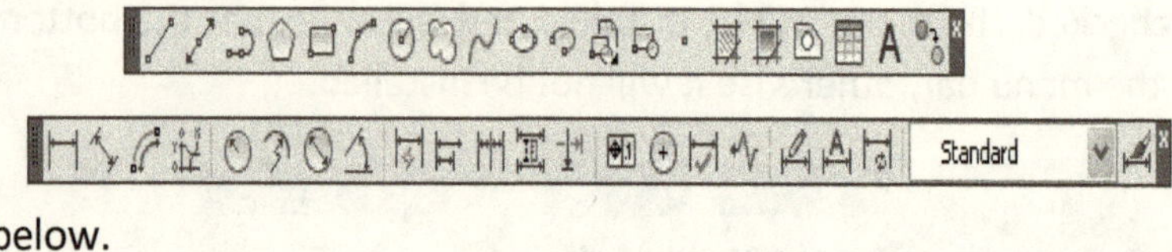

below.

Figure 1-3

When you right-click on one of the icons, you can view or select all the toolbars. Each toolbar that is checked on the left, is displayed on the AutoCAD page and will not be displayed if it is unchecked. For example, as shown in Figure 1-4, toolbars like Draw Order, Layers, Modify and Standard are checked, as a result, you will see these toolbars on the drawing area.

Dimensional Constraints
Draw
✔ Draw Order
Draw Order, Annotation to Front
Find Text
Geometric Constraint
Group
Inquiry
Insert
✔ Layers
Layers II
Layouts
Lights
Mapping
Measurement Tools
Modeling
✔ Modify
Modify II
Multileader
Object Snap
Orbit
Parametric
PointCloud
Properties
Refedit
Reference
Render
Smooth Mesh
Smooth Mesh Primitives
Solid Editing
✔ Standard
Standard Annotation

Figure 1-4

It depends on the user's choice whether or not to display these bars on the screen. Choosing all the toolbars will certainly make the work environment disorganized and consequently, limit the drawing space. This will not help to expedite the drawing process. It will only confuse the user in choosing the right tool. So, each user can customize the toolbar according to their needs and perform their tasks at any stage and in the end, if needed, hide them. You can see the most commonly used toolbars in land surveying drawings in Figure 1-5. Of course, other toolbars are also used in some stages of the drawing process, but these toolbars are among the most important and the most practical toolbars used in land surveying drawings.

Modify	Dimension
Modify⊓	Draw Order
Properties	Draw
Text	Inquiry
Zoom	Layers
	Lyaers⊓

4. Command bar

At the bottom of the AutoCAD page, a bar is shown called the command bar like the one in Figure 1-6 which the user must pay attention to when running the command and most of the errors and problems that occur when running the commands is due to ignoring the messages that appear in this bar.

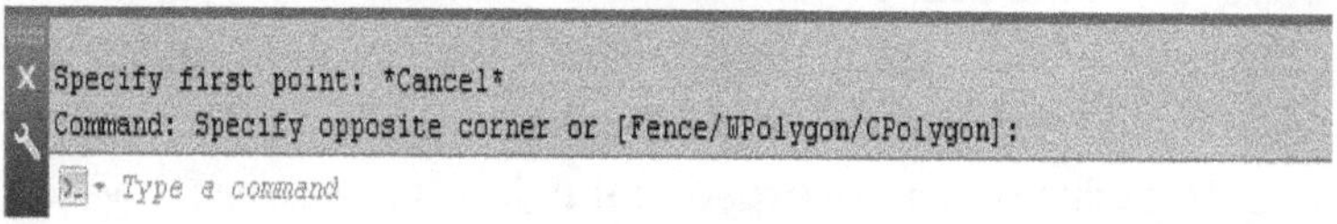

```
Specify first point: *Cancel*
Command: Specify opposite corner or [Fence/WPolygon/CPolygon]:
Type a command
```

Figure 1-6

The command bar has two modes:

Mode 1: Standby

If the command bar is the same as the one in Figure 1-6 and the expression "Type a command" is shown below it, the command bar will be in standby mode and only then can a command be ran.

Mode 2: Command Execution

If the command bar is not the same as the one mentioned and a text or phrase is shown below it, it means the command line is in Command Execution mode and you cannot run another command. If you want to run another command, you need to get the command bar into standby mode. If you want to change the command line from Command Execution mode into standby mode, you should use the Esc key in the upper left corner of the keyboard.

5. **Coordinate Display**

At the bottom of the command line, as shown in Figure 1-7, there is a small box called coordinate display showing the coordinates in the lower left corner of the AutoCAD page, which shows the coordinates of the mouse cursor position at any given moment.

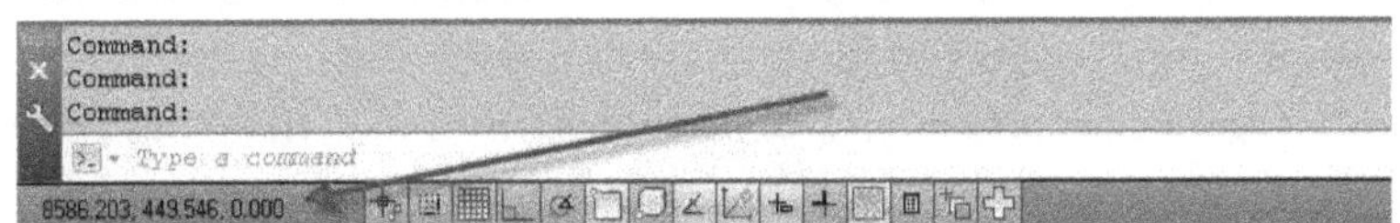

Figure 1-7

At what stage of drawing does AutoCAD help us?

You need to know that the steps in map preparation are as follows:

1. **Data collection**

At this point, start collecting the information needed to prepare a map with land surveying instruments. The information includes Total Station data, leveling data, traverse data and more.

2. Data Processing

Data collected in the previous step includes raw surveying data such as point coordinates, length, horizontal and elevation angles and so on which are not identifiable by AutoCAD. So, analyze this information with other editing/processing software like Excel in order to convert it to useful and identifiable information for surveying software such as SDR map, Land, and many others. If the software you are using is Land or Civil 3D, drawing and cartographic operations are performed in the same environment after analyzing the data. But if the software you are using is SDR map, due to its weaknesses in cartography, printing and map preparation, it is necessary to create a dxf file out of the drawings. dxf is one of the output formats of SDR map software that can be identified by AutoCAD.

3. Drawing and Cartography

In order to process and perform the initial drawings, you should type the data into the SDR map software. After performing the editing and drawing operations, you should store the data in the popular dxf format. Then open the dxf file in AutoCAD software and start performing cartography operations. In the drawing phase, operations such as editing contours are performed that can be done in the best way possible by AutoCAD.

- **LISP and Macro files**

What is Lisp?

Lisp is one of the programming languages invented in 1958 by John McCarthy and it is one of the easiest programming languages to learn. This language was intended for Artificial Intelligence research and its size is very small, due to the very simple rules it has. AutoCAD is one of the software that supports applications built on Lisp and this helps draftsmen a lot. Due to its generality and its many applications in other engineering and technical sciences, AutoCAD cannot help us in some very specialized operations. But the Lisp programming language covers this issue easily and you can write any command or request you have from AutoCAD in Lisp and run the program file built in AutoCAD.

What is Macro?

Macros are files that are created with the Visual Basic programming language and like Lisps, they can support us in operations that AutoCAD cannot perform.

The use of Macros and Lisps

As an example, AutoCAD software is not able to import data from Total Station instruments directly and you can do this by creating a Macro or a Lisp. And once the program is created, you can import it with AutoCAD and do your task.

How to become a professional draftsman

A very important matter in using AutoCAD is the speed in drawing and editing drawings and the most important factor here is the speed at which the command is ran. There are several ways to run the AutoCAD commands. For example, if you want to draw a line in AutoCAD, you can use the following methods:

1. Select Line from the Draw menu.
2. Click the icon in the picture from the Draw toolbar.

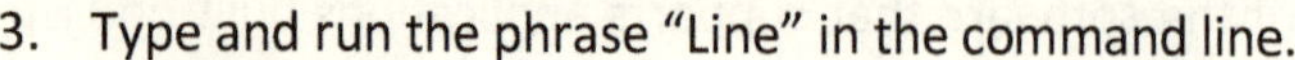

3. Type and run the phrase "Line" in the command line.
4. Use Shortcuts.

- **What is Shortcut?**

Shortcuts contain a letter or a combination of several letters, each of which runs an AutoCAD command. First, a list of the most important and the most used AutoCAD Shortcuts are shown with their uses in a table, which are very important to surveyors. They will be described in the following chapters.

Shortcut key	**Command Name**	**Command Description**
A	Arc	Drawing an arc
Aa	Area	Calculating the area
Al	Align	Moving, rotating and scaling objects all in one command
Ap	Appload	Running Visual Basic files
B	Block	Creating a block
Be	Bedit	Editing a block
Br	Break	Breaking objects in one or more points
C	Circle	Drawing a circle

Ch	Properties	Viewing and changing the properties of an object
Col	Color	Changing the default color of the drawings
Co	Copy	Copying
Cp	Copy	Copying
D	Dimstyle	Settings for creating dimensions
Dal	Dimaligned	Measuring the length
Dan	Dimangular	Measuring the angle
Dar	Dimarc	Measuring the radius of a circle or an arc
Dce	Dimcenter	Drawing the center of a circle or an arc
Di	Dist	Measuring ΔX and ΔY and the distance between two points
Div	Divide	Dividing a line into multiple lines
Dra	Dimradius	Measuring and inserting the radius of a circle or an arc
Dt	Text	Creating a text with desired angle and height
E	Erase	Erasing
Ed	Ddedit	Editing a text
Ex	Extend	Extending lines to other objects
H	Hatch	Creating a hatch
He	Hatchedit	Editing a hatch

J	Join	Joining two or more lines
L	Line	Drawing a line
La	Layer	Viewing the layers window
Le	Qleader	Drawing an arrow
Li	List	Displaying the properties of selected objects in a text file
Ls	List	Displaying the properties of selected objects in a text file
M	Move	Moving the objects
Ma	Matchproperty	Changing the properties of objects to properties of another object
Me	Measure	Dividing a line to multiple lines with desired dimensions
Ml	Mline	Drawing two parallel lines
O	Offset	Offsetting
Op	Option	Displaying the Option menu
Os	Osnap	Displaying the Osnap menu
Po	Point	Creating a point
P	Pan	Panning the map
Pe	Pedit	Advanced line editing
Pl	Pline	Drawing a Polyline
Pr	Properties	Viewing and changing the properties of objects

Re	Regen	Regenerating the drawings
Ro	Rotate	Rotation objects with a specific angle
Qselect	Quickselet	Quick selection of objects using their properties
Sc	Scale	Increasing and decreasing the size of objects using the scale value
T	Text	Inserting a text
Tr	Trim	Trimming objects relative to other objects
Un	Unit	Setting the length and angle units
X	Explode	Exploding objects and blocks
Z	Zoom	Zooming in and out
Ucsicon	Ucsicon	Setting AutoCAD coordinate system
Layoff	Layeroff	Turning off one or more layers
Layon	Layeron	Turning on all the layers
Layiso	Layer isolate	Isolating the desired layers from the rest of the layers
Layuniso	Layerunisolate	Contrary to the action of Layiso
Id	Identity	To list the X, Y and Z values of the specified point
U	Undo	Go back to the previous state

Figure 1-7

The items in the first column of the table that you see in Figure 1-8 are the most important shortcuts used in land surveying drawings. Using these shortcuts will speed up working with AutoCAD. Most professional users of AutoCAD use shortcuts to run commands. It is suggested to do so. At first, it may seem a little bit difficult, but when you master it, you will no longer use icons and you will see the benefits of using shortcuts. One of the advantages of using shortcuts is not having to display all the toolbars on the drawing area. If you want to run your commands using toolbars, you need to have all the toolbars that contain the required commands on the page and this will make the drawing area disorganized and limit the drawing window. But using the keyboard and shortcuts, you don't need to have all the toolbars and you can hide most of them. Another advantage of using a shortcut is that you can define your own custom shortcut for each command, which will be explained below.

To use shortcuts, you can type the shortcut of any command in the command line and run it by pressing the Enter key. The software developer has chosen the Space key to run the command for the convenience of users who use a keyboard, so that the Space key performs the same function that the Enter key performs. So, whenever this book refers to command execution, it means using the Space key.

AutoCAD users work with AutoCAD in two ways. The first group are the ones who use a mouse and icons to run AutoCAD commands. When they want to run any command, they use the mouse and click on the icon and run that command. As you know, every set of commands is in one particular toolbar. So, this may seem simple at first glance, but if the range of commands you use becomes broad, you need to display all the toolbars that contain your commands on the AutoCAD page and also keep in mind the location of each icon. As it turns out, this process slows the user down and it also blocks the user's view of the drawing page by displaying various toolbars. If you want to change the version of your AutoCAD software, you need to adapt ourselves to the new icons.

The second group are the ones who use shortcuts. Working with shortcuts may seem a bit difficult at first, but in fact, it is not true. The reason is that most of the times, the shortcut of any command is the first letter or first letters of that command. Shortcuts speed up the command execution process and they also reduce the number of tasks that you do with a mouse. A mouse has limited capabilities due to its small number of keys and by reducing the range of using it, the process of working with AutoCAD will speed up. When you use a keyboard and shortcuts to run commands, you will be actually using the mouse less than before and the use of the mouse will be limited to selecting objects and clicking on the drawing are and this will play a significant role in speeding up the use of AutoCAD.

Note 1

A command may have two shortcuts, but a shortcut cannot run two commands. For example, the CP and CO shortcuts run the copy command.

Note 2

To run a command, the command line must be in standby mode, otherwise press Esc to get the command line into standby mode.

Another advantage of using shortcuts is that all shortcuts are the same in different versions of AutoCAD and if you have worked with AutoCAD 2007 and want to change your version of AutoCAD to 2013, you can use the same shortcuts. The only thing is that the icon display format is not the same in different versions of AutoCAD.

It is strongly suggested that you practice the contents of this book as stated here. Do not use the icons to run commands at all, so that you will soon become one of the AutoCAD professional users.

It should be noted that these shortcuts also apply to the other land surveying engineering software such as Land and Civil 3D that run under AutoCAD.

Chapter 2: AutoCAD General Settings

- Drawing area display settings
- Drawing units settings
- Setting coordinate systems in AutoCAD
- Settings for saving drawings

- **Changing the background color of the drawing area**

To change the background color of the drawing area, select Options from the Tools menu. Then enable the Drafting or Display tab in the open window. In the left box, click on the Color key to open the Drawing Window colors window. Now set the Context box to 2D model space and the Interface element box to Uniform background. Then select the desired color for the background of the drawing area and finally, confirm the work done with the Apply & Close option. The steps are schematically shown in Figure 1-2. In this window, you can also change the color of other items like the mouse cursor color, color of grids and so on.

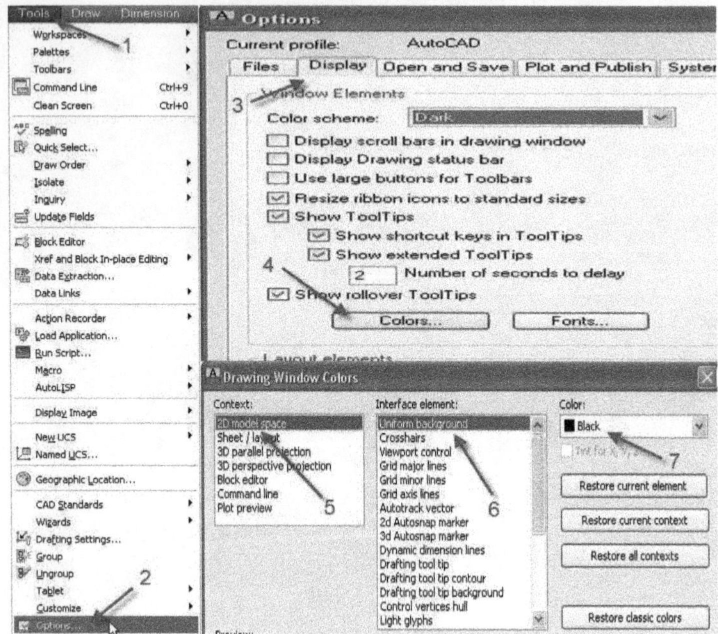

Figure 2-1

- **Setting AutoCAD default font**

If a font is used in a drawing by another person and that font is not available in the system, when you open the drawing file, the software will automatically replace that font with one that is defined in the system. You can select the replaced font. In order to do this, select Options from the Tools menu and display the Files tab, and after selecting the + sign on the left side of the Text Editor option, click on the Alternate Font File option. Then click on Browse key from the box on the right and select and confirm the desired font.

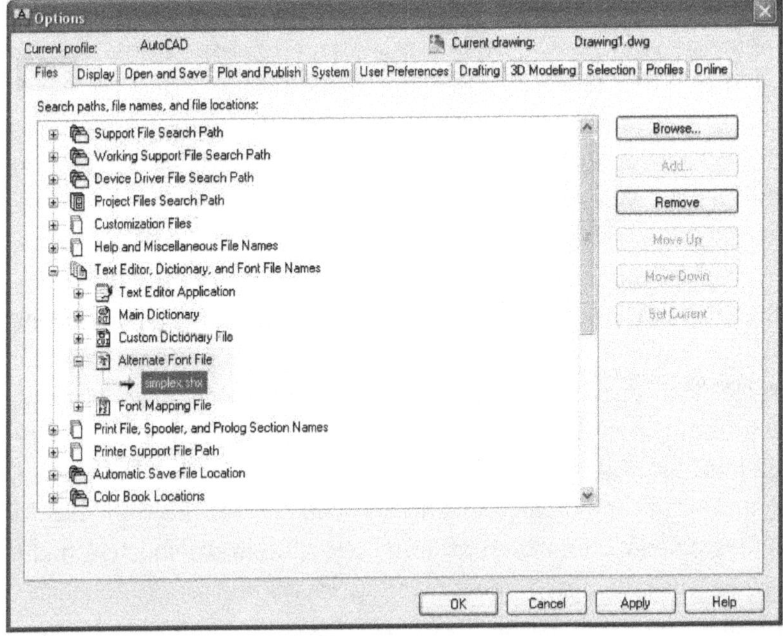

Figure 2-2

- **Right-click settings**

By default, a shortcut menu will appear if you right-click on the drawing area as in Figure 2-3. It contains edit and display commands and AutoCAD users use them. But the right-click action can be adjusted in three modes: Standby Mode, Edit Mode, and Command Execution Mode. This means that when AutoCAD is in Standby Mode, a right-click will perform an action and it will also perform different actions in Command Execution Mode and Edit Mode.

At this stage, to understand better, select Options from the Tools menu or use the OP keyboard shortcut to display the Options window. Then select the User Preferences tab and click the Right-click Customization option in Windows Standard Behavior section to display a window with the same name as in Figure 2-4. You can see the Default Mode, Edit Mode and Command Mode in this window and you can define a right-click action for any of the above-mentioned modes. The Default Mode is actually the standby mode that has two options. The first one is the Repeat Last Command option that re-runs the last command ran by the user in the previous stage. The second one is the Shortcut Menu option, which displays the above-mentioned shortcut menu. These two options can be defined for the Edit Mode. The third mode is a mode in which AutoCAD is running a command and you can set the right-click to either perform the action of Enter key or to make shortcut menu appear. But the best mode for land surveyors and cartographers is a mode in which you can perform the action of the Enter key by right-clicking when running a command and re-run the last ran command in Standby Mode and Edit Mode.

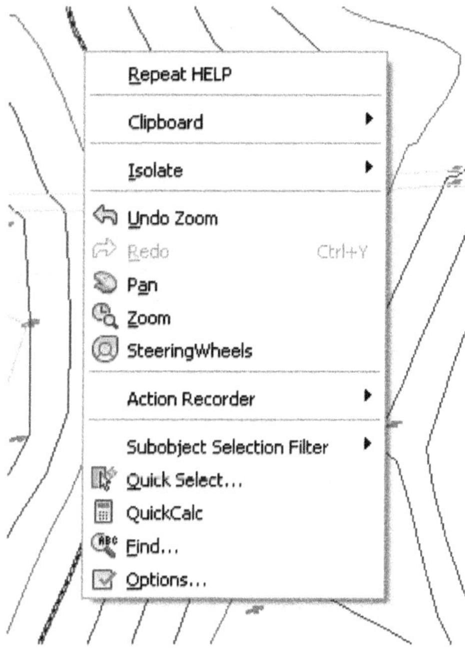

Repeat HELP
Clipboard
Isolate
Undo Zoom
Redo
Ctrl+Y
Pan
Zoom
SteeringWheels
Action Recorder
Subobject Selection Filter
Quick Select...
QuickCalc
Find...
Options...

Figure 2-3

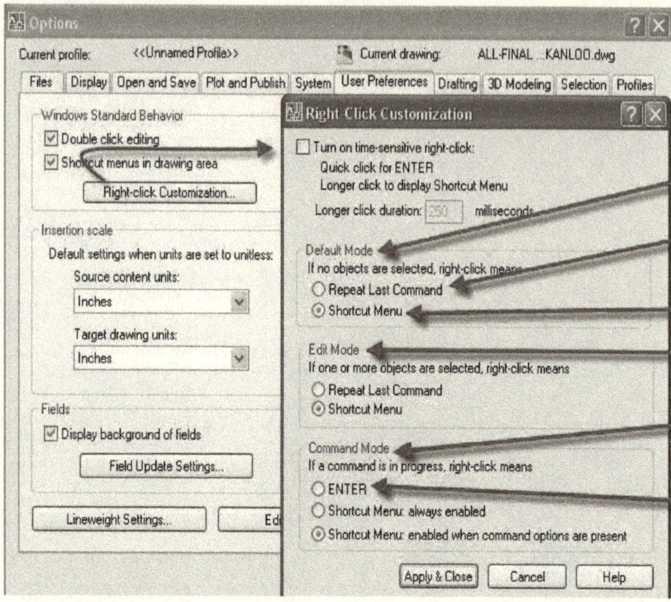

Figure 2-4

- **Setting drawing units**

To set the length and angle units in this software, select the Unit option from Format menu or use the UN keyboard shortcut to make the Drawing Units window appear like Figure 2-5. Now select Length Unit in Length section and Angle Unit in Angle section. In land surveying, select the Length Unit with the accuracy of three decimal places and the Angle Unit (Grads) with the accuracy of four decimal places. If you check the Clockwise option in the Angle box, the angle will increase clockwise and, if unchecked, the angle will increase counterclockwise. The Insertion Scale box is also used to specify drawing units for blocks or other external references that you intend to draw on the drawing area. To specify the base angle direction, the

Direction key is used at the bottom of the window and set this axis in the north side of the drawing area. However, in this box, you can set the north axis on the desired axis by using Other option and this will be used to draw a traverse using AutoCAD, which will be elaborated on in the next sections of the book. Now, after making the above adjustments, save the changes by clicking OK.

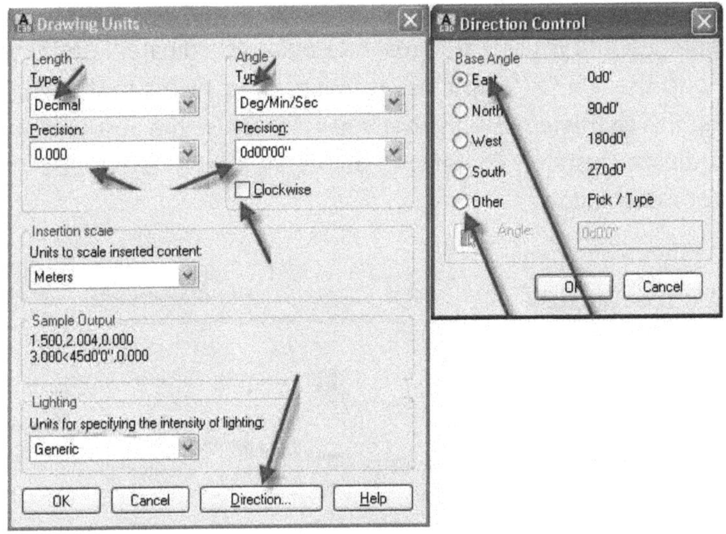

Figure 2-5

- **Setting the AutoCAD Coordinate System**

Before getting into the topic of Setting the AutoCAD Coordinate System, you need to know AutoCAD's coordinate systems. In general, the coordinate systems in this software are divided into four different types.

A) Absolute polar coordinate system

In this type of coordinate system, the position of each point with the parameters of length and angle are specified relative to Origin (0,0).

It means that the length of the point represents the distance from that point to Origin (0,0) and the angle is specified relative to the angle measurement point. For example, in Figure 2-6, point A is displayed with coordinates (43.9970, 67.7930) and point B is also displayed with coordinates (46.6010, 30.2037). The numbers 43.997 and 49.601 represent the points A and B in Origin (0,0), and the numbers 67.7930 and 30.2037 represent the angles of the OA and OB axes relative to origin axis respectively. Now if you want to type in points A and B using the absolute polar coordinate system, you need to use the ">" character. It means after typing in the length, using this character, specify that you want to use the absolute polar coordinate system. Therefore, points A and B are typed into AutoCAD as follows.

A: 43.997 < 67.7930

B: 49.601 < 30.2037

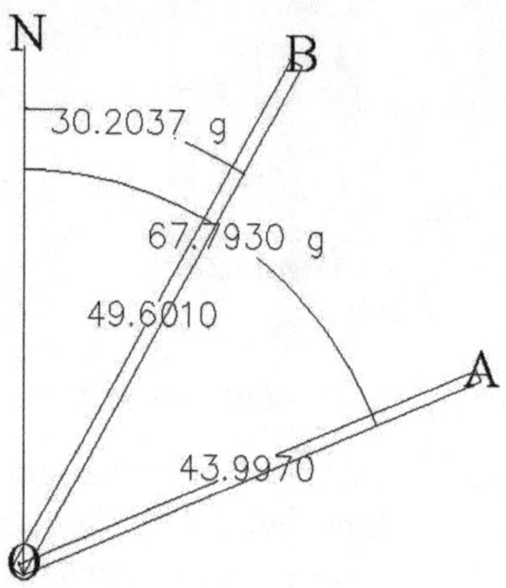

Figure 2-6

B) Relative polar coordinate system

In this type of coordinate system, like the absolute polar coordinate system, the coordinates of each point are specified by the parameters of length and angle. The difference is that, the base point coordinates for determining the length and angle is the preceding point, not Origin (0,0). For example, in Figure 2-7, point B is defined with parameters (9.196, 36.0954). The first parameter related to the length and the second parameter related to the angle are specified relative to the defined axis, which was defined in the Unit section and also relative to its preceding point. By this definition, the coordinates of points C and D are as follows.

C(9.304 , 140.4620)
D(6.976 , 236.6580)

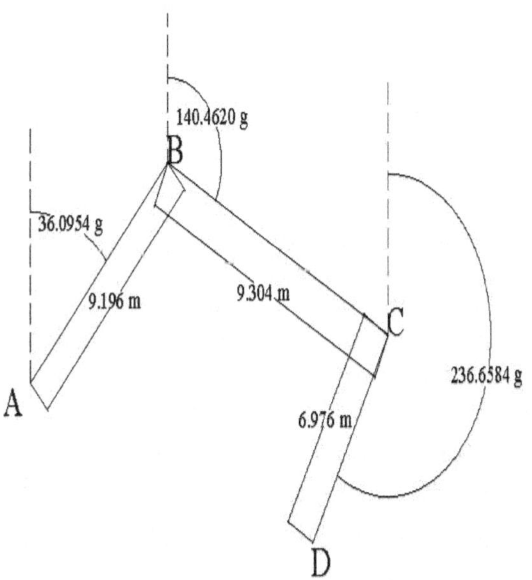

Figure 2-7

It is necessary to explain that to define point A, which is the starting point, and there is not any point before that, the parameters that you specify are absolute polar and follow Origin (0,0). This type of coordinate system is used to draw a traverse. To draw these points using the relative polar method, the characters @ and > should be used. So, at first, by using the @ character, specify that the point coordinates are relative. Then type in the length of the point and then using the character < type in the angle of that point relative to the previous point. For example, to type in points B, C, and D using the relative polar method, do as follow.

B: @9.196 < 30.0954

C: @9.304 < 140.4620

D: @6.976 < 236.6584

C) Absolute Cartesian coordinate system

In this type of coordinate system, the position of each point is specified by parameters X and Y relative to Origin (0,0) and is most useful for land surveyors, because surveying data is collected either UTM-based and universal or Locally, which is also measured relative to Origin (0,0). For example, to type in a point with coordinates like A (500, 320), just type the numbers 320,500 that are separated by a comma "," in the command line while running the command.

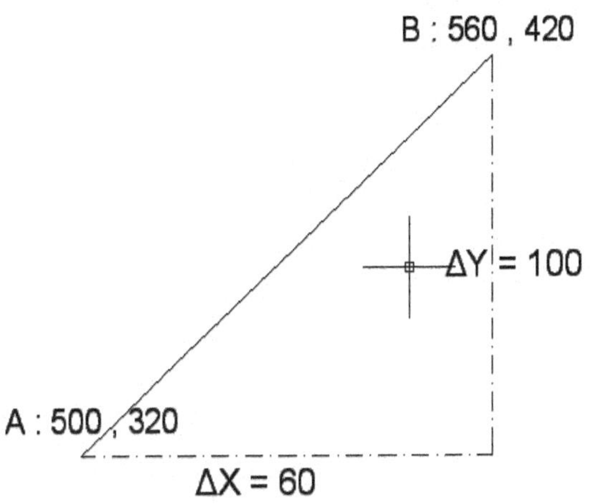

Figure 2-8

D) Relative Cartesian coordinate system

In this coordinate system, like the absolute Cartesian coordinate system, the position of each point is specified by parameters X and Y. The difference is that in this system, the values of X and Y are not measured relative to Origin (0,0), but rather, these measurements are done relative to the previous point. For example, you want to specify a point with coordinates B (420, 560) that is ΔX=560-500=60 to the right of point A and is ΔY=420-320=100 above point B. What you need is to simply type in the coordinates of point B relative to point A as follows.

B: @60, 100

Now it is the time to set up AutoCAD's coordinate system. In order to do this, select the Drafting Settings option from the Tools menu or use the DS keyboard shortcut to display the Drafting Settings window.

In this window, select the Dynamic Input tab, then in the Pointer Input section, click on the Settings option to display the Pointer Input Settings window as in Figure 2-9. As you can see, the user can choose from two types of coordinate systems: Cartesian format coordinate system that means right-angled coordinates and Polar format coordinate system. These two systems can be used in two modes: Relative coordinates and Absolute coordinates. To set up the software in Absolute Cartesian coordinate system mode, you need to enable the Cartesian format and Absolute coordinate radio buttons.

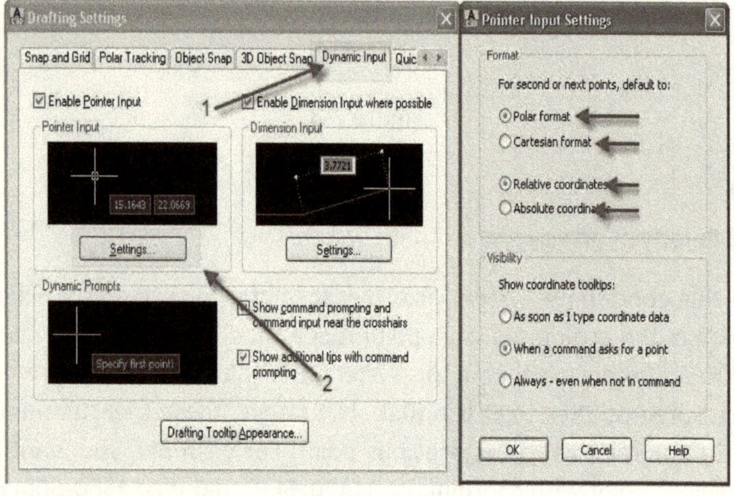

Figure 2-9

Switching the workspace from 2D to 3D

As you know, AutoCAD has two separate workspaces and you cannot enable both spaces simultaneously. To enable your workspace, select Workspace option from the Tools menu. This will display a submenu in front of the Workspace option. You can enable the 2D model space by selecting the AutoCAD Classic option and the 3D model space by selecting the 3D Modeling option in the software.

- **Switching the drawing area to Clean Screen mode**

The Clean Screen is a mode where all the toolbars are hidden, except menu bar, command bar, status bar and coordinate bar. Some professional draftsmen, especially those who work with keyboards and shortcuts, usually set AutoCAD to this mode to have more workspace for drawing. To make that possible, you can select the Clean Screen option from the Tools menu or use the Ctrl+0 keyboard shortcut.

- **Display/hide the command bar**

To show or hide the command bar, select the Command Line option from the Tools menu. Selecting this option will hide the command bar. If you want to display the command bar, repeat the instructions. You can also use the Ctrl+9 keyboard shortcut.

- **Resizing the mouse cursor**

To resize the mouse cursor, select Options from the Tools menu to open the Options window as in Figure 2-10. Then select the Display tab from this window. After that, resize the cursor to the desired size in the Crosshair size section and finally, confirm the changes by clicking OK.

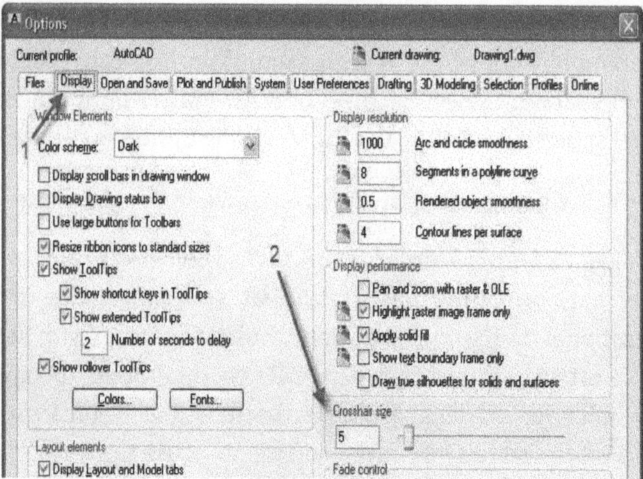

Figure 2-10

- **Saving the drawings automatically**

AutoCAD can be set to automatically save work progress steps after predetermined amounts of time so as not to lose the work progress if the drawing operation is interrupted or in case you forget to save the work progress for any reason. For this purpose, select Options from the Tools menu, then enable the Open & Save tab. After that, check the Automatic Save option from the File Safety Precautions section and enter the desired time in the box. For example, by selecting the number 10 in this section, you specify that the drawing will be automatically saved every 10 minutes by the system.

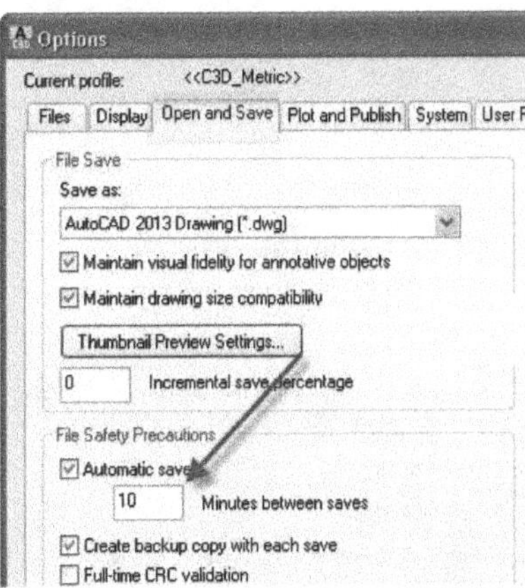

Figure 2-11

- **Setting the multi-drawing mode**

In pre-2000 versions of AutoCAD, you could only work on one drawing at a time. In this case, if you want to open another drawing file, you need to close the drawing file that is already open. This is very difficult when a user wants to compare and edit multiple files simultaneously, because they have to run AutoCAD as many times as the number of drawings. For example, if you want to draw and edit five drawings simultaneously, you need to run AutoCAD five times. This will take up a lot of space on your computer's storage and consequently slow the system down. But in post-2000 versions, it is possible to work on several drawings at the same time and it is adjustable. This means that the software can be set to the single drawing mode or multi drawing mode. To do this, select Options from the Tools menu and then enable the System tab. And uncheck the Single Drawing Compatibility Mode option from the General Options section to use the multiple drawing mode and if this option is checked, the single drawing mode will be enabled. It should be noted that this option is not available in AutoCAD after the 2008 version.

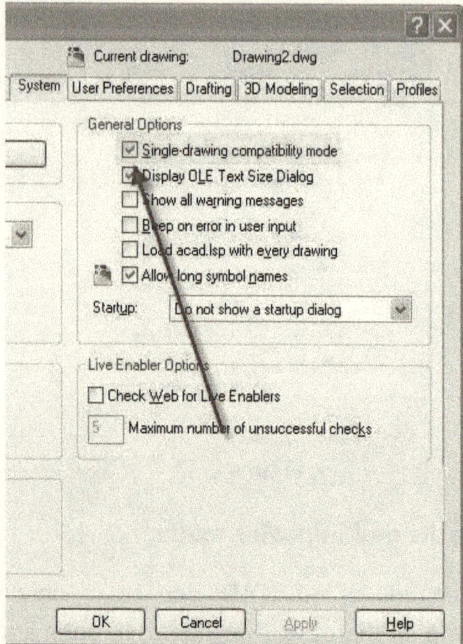

Figure 2-12

- **Changing the default color of the drawings**

Select the Color option from the Format menu to open the window. In this window, select a color from the AutoCAD color library and press OK to confirm it. By doing so, from now on, all the objects will be painted in that color.

By Layer Mode

If you set the AutoCAD default color to this mode, the color of the objects in the drawing will change to the color of their own layer. For example, if an object is in layer 7 and the color of layer 7 is blue, all the objects in that layer will also turn blue.

Chapter 3: Important and useful commands

- Introduction to important drawing commands
- Introduction to editing commands
- Introduction to measuring and dimensioning commands
- Introduction to useful shortcuts
- Introduction to the professional operation of working with layers
- Introduction to group selection tools

1. Line command with L shortcut

This command is used to draw a line segment and the shortcut is L. If you type the letter L in the command line and then run it by pressing the Space key on the keyboard, the "Specify first point" message will appear in the command line as in Figure 1-3. You can now specify the first point in two ways:

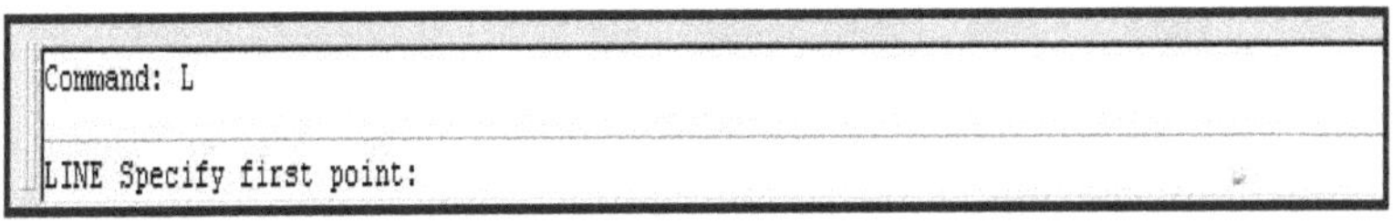

```
Command: L

LINE Specify first point:
```

Figure 3-1

The First Method:

You can do it with the mouse click and the AutoCAD drawing area. It means you can specify a point on the drawing area with a left-click. Then the "Specify next point or [Undo]" message will appear in the command line. Likewise, you can select other points on the other parts of the drawing area using the left-click. Finally, close the command by pressing the Esc or Space or Enter key on the keyboard. For example, suppose you want to draw that side of Figure 2-3 which has not been drawn. For this purpose, after running the command, left-click on the start and the end of the not drawn side to draw it.

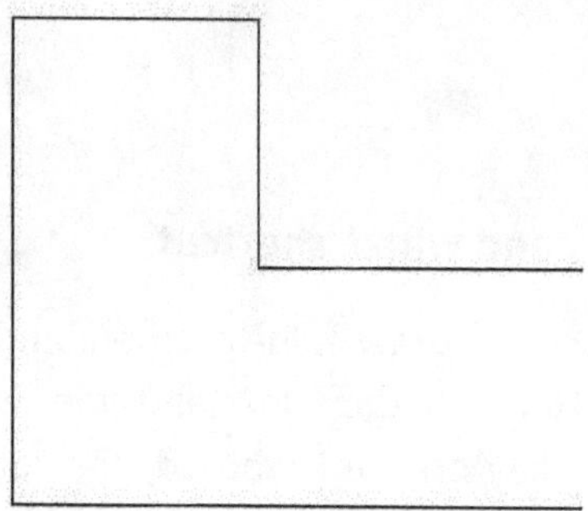

Figure 3-2

The Second Method:

Using the coordinates to draw lines. You can use this method to draw lines that cross the desired coordinates. This method will be explained using an exercise.

Exercise 1

A building has been drawn with 6 corners. You can see the coordinates of its 6 corners in Figure 3-3. Draw this building using the Line command. To draw this building with the Line command, type the letter L in the command line and press the Space key on the keyboard to run the command. After running the command, AutoCAD is ready to receive the first point coordinates.

Point Number	X	Y
1	1000	1000
2	1100	1000
3	1100	1050

4	1075	1050
5	1075	1125
6	1000	1125

Figure 3-3

Question:

How can we type X and Y separately?

Answer:

To do this, you need to use comma (,) after typing in the X coordinate number to get AutoCAD ready to receive Y. Then also type in the Y coordinate number and press Enter. After running the Line command, first type in the first point's X. Then, using a comma, type in the first point's Y and press Enter. Now AutoCAD is ready to receive the second point. Likewise, type in the second point coordinates as well and after typing in the coordinates of each point, use the Enter key to get the software ready for the next point.

```
Command: L
LINE Specify first point: 1000,1000
Specify next point or [Undo]: 1100,1000
Specify next point or [Undo]: 1100,1050
Specify next point or [Close/Undo]: 1075,1050
Specify next point or [Close/Undo]: 1075,1125
Specify next point or [Close/Undo]: 1000,1125
Specify next point or [Close/Undo]:

Command:
```

Figure 3-4

After typing in the coordinates of the sixth point, you can connect the sixth point to the first point in three ways.

The First Method:

After typing in the coordinates of the sixth point, you can then type in the coordinates of the first point as the seventh point and press Enter to connect the sixth point to the first point.

The Second Method:

After typing in the sixth point, you can click on the first point using the mouse and connect the sixth point to the first point.

The Third Method:

In this method, you can use the C shortcut (stands for Close) to connect the last point to the first point by typing in the letter C and pressing Enter after typing in the coordinates of the sixth point.

Question:

If you type in the coordinates of a point incorrectly and run it, how can you edit it?

Answer:

There are two methods to deal with this situation and you should learn two more commands to learn how to use these two methods.

2. UNDO command with U shortcut

This command undoes the drawings and corrections you have made, step by step, to the previous state. The shortcut for this command is the letter U.
Now to solve the problem using this method, after typing in the coordinates of the point incorrectly, close the command. Then type in and run the letter U to undo the drawing. And if you want to go back to the previous step, type in and run the letter U again. You can also use the Ctrl+Z keyboard shortcut to run this command. The REDO command does the opposite. This means if you go back to the previous step using the UNDO command, you can come back to the step you were in before performing the UNDO command using the

REDO command. You can also use the Ctrl+Y keyboard shortcut to run this command.

But the important point is that most commands that have multiple steps also have the UNDO command when running in their submenus. That means you can type in U and Enter to go back to the previous step without closing the command and continue your work.

3. Erase command with E shortcut

The Erase command with E shortcut that is one of the Modify toolbar editing commands, is used to erase objects. You can use this command in two ways.

The First Method:

Before you run the command, select the objects you want to erase by clicking the left-click button or by using other methods of selecting the objects that will be explained below. Then type and run the E shortcut in the command line. This will erase the selected objects.

The Second Method:

In this method, type and run the E shortcut before selecting the objects. Then select the objects that you want to erase, and erase them by pressing the Enter key at the end. It can be said that these two modes are applicable to most commands that perform actions on objects. This means that you either select the objects first and then run the command, or you run the command and then select the objects.

It should be noted that the first method in which you select the objects first and then run the command, is customizable.

As shown in Figure 3-5, if you select Options from the Tools menu and then uncheck the “Noun/verb selection” option in the Selection modes box from the Selection tab, this method will be disabled and from now on, if an object is previously selected, by running each command, you will unselect the objects and in fact, no action will be taken on the previously selected objects.

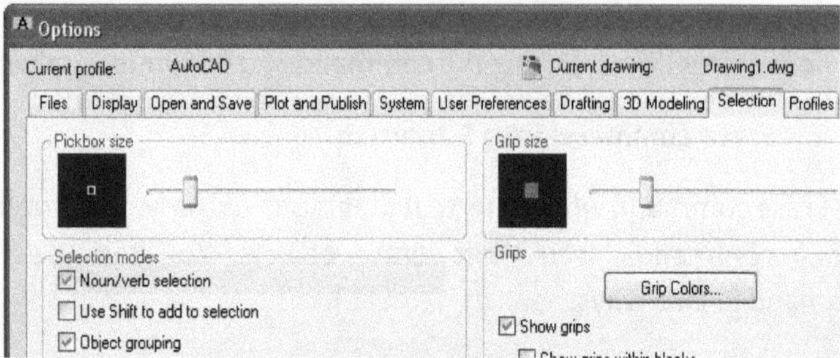

Figure 3-5

Now to answer the previous question using this method, after typing in the coordinates of a point incorrectly, close the command using the Esc key on the keyboard. Then erase the line that was incorrectly drawn using the E shortcut and redraw the line.

4. Polyline command with PL shortcut

Polyline is a set of interconnected lines that are all considered as one object. It means by choosing one of them, they will all be chosen together. The shortcut for this command is PL. This command is used more frequently in land surveying drawings to draw lines. One of the advantages of Polyline over Line is having many connected lines just in one object, which makes the work much easier for cartographers, because although Polyline has many vertexes, you just need to select one part of it to select all the lines. For example, if you have a piece of land on a cadastral map that has 20 sides and want to erase or do any other editing actions on it, if the piece of land is drawn using the Line command, you need to click on and select all the sides to erase the land which is time consuming. But if the piece is drawn using the Polyline command, you just need to click on one of its sides to select the whole piece. Another advantage of Polyline over Line is that it is possible to easily join two linear features using the Join command which will be explained in the following sections. But if those lines are of the Line type, they must first be converted to Polyline and then become joined.

Of course, in 2012 version and above, this problem has been resolved, and in these versions, the lines can also become joined. So, it is suggested that you use the Polyline command to draw lines. Now, as an exercise, draw the building given in the previous example using the Polyline command. One of the modes of drawing a line with the Polyline command is to draw lines of a certain line weight. There are cases where the user intends to draw lines whose line weights are different from those of other lines or draw a line with a desired line weight. For example, you intend to draw a line that has a 5-cm line weight. To do this, type and run the PL shortcut in the command line, then specify the first point, and then type and Enter the letter W. As you can see, the "Specify starting width" message appears in the command line asking you for the line weight of the start of the line. So, type and Enter 0.05. Then the "Specify ending width" message appears in the command line asking you for the line weight of the end of the line. So, type and Enter 0.05 again. From now on, every line you draw using this command has a 5-cm line weight.

```
Command: PL
PLINE
Specify start point:
Current line-width is 0.0000
Specify next point or [Arc/Halfwidth/Length/Undo/Width]: W
Specify starting width <0.0000>: .05
Specify ending width <0.0500>: .05
Specify next point or [Arc/Halfwidth/Length/Undo/Width]:
Specify next point or [Arc/Close/Halfwidth/Length/Undo/Width]:
Specify next point or [Arc/Close/Halfwidth/Length/Undo/Width]:
Command:
```

Figure 3-6

5. Rectangle command with REC shortcut

This command is used to draw a rectangle. The most common method for drawing a rectangle is to select the two lower left and upper right points using the mouse. But to draw a rectangle, you can use other methods which will be explained with some exercises.

Exercise 2

Draw a rectangle with the lower left corner coordinates (100,100) and the upper right corner coordinates (120,105).

Answer:

Type and run the REC shortcut in the command line, then type in the coordinates (100,100) using the keyboard as the bottom left corner of the rectangle, then type in the coordinates (120,105) as the coordinates of the next point of the rectangle, meaning the top left corner and press the Enter key to draw the rectangle.

```
Command: REC
RECTANG
Specify first corner point or [Chamfer/Elevation/Fillet/Thickness/Width]:
100,100
Specify other corner point or [Area/Dimensions/Rotation]: 120,105
Command:
```

Figure 3-7

Exercise 3

Draw a rectangle with the coordinates of the lower left corner (100,100) and dimensions of 80 by 50.

Answer:

Type and run the REC shortcut in the command line, then type in the coordinates (100,100) using the keyboard as the bottom left corner of the rectangle. Now, to draw a rectangle using its dimensions, type D in the command line and press the Enter key.

As you can see, the "Specify length for rectangles" message appears in command line, meaning you should type in the length of the rectangle. So, type 80 and press the Enter key. Now the "Specify width for rectangles" message appears which means you should type in the width of the rectangle. So, type 50 as the width of the rectangle and press the Enter key to draw the rectangle with the desired dimensions.

```
Command: REC
RECTANG
Specify first corner point or [Chamfer/Elevation/Fillet/Thickness/Width]:
100,100
Specify other corner point or [Area/Dimensions/Rotation]: D
Specify length for rectangles <80.0000>:
Specify width for rectangles <50.0000>:
Specify other corner point or [Area/Dimensions/Rotation]:

Command:
```

Figure 3-8

Exercise 4

Draw a rectangle with the corner coordinates (100,100) and (150,150) which makes a 25° angle with the horizon line.

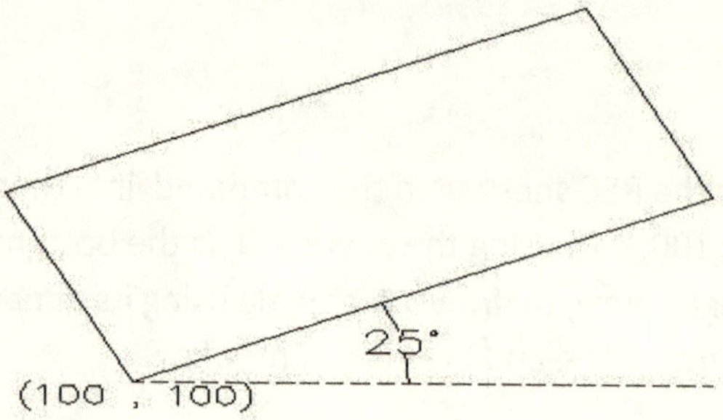

Figure 3-9

Answer:

Type and run the REC shortcut in the command line, then type in the coordinates (100,100) using the keyboard and press the Enter key. To apply a 25° angle to the horizon line, type the letter R and press the Enter key, then also type 25 and press the Enter key. Now type in the next point coordinates to draw the desired rectangle.

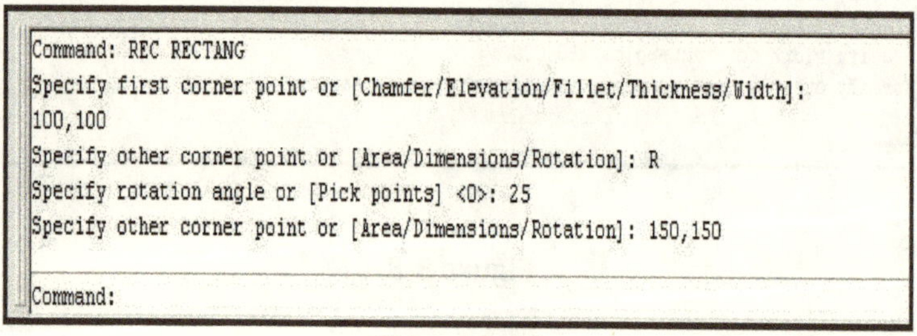

```
Command: REC RECTANG
Specify first corner point or [Chamfer/Elevation/Fillet/Thickness/Width]:
100,100
Specify other corner point or [Area/Dimensions/Rotation]: R
Specify rotation angle or [Pick points] <0>: 25
Specify other corner point or [Area/Dimensions/Rotation]: 150,150

Command:
```

Figure 3-10

Exercise 5

Draw a rectangle with a fixed area of 500 square meters and a width of 17 meters with the coordinates of its starting point as (180,180).

Answer:

Type and run the REC shortcut in the command line. Then type in the coordinates of the first point as (180,180) and select the Area mode by typing the letter A and type 500. After pressing the Enter key, the "Calculate rectangle dimensions based on [Length/Width]" message appears which asks if the rectangular calculations should be based on length or width, and since in this example you have the rectangle width, type the W letter and press the Enter key and type 17 as the rectangle width to draw the desired rectangle.

```
Command: REC
RECTANG
Current rectangle modes:  Rotation=25
Specify first corner point or [Chamfer/Elevation/Fillet/Thickness/Width]:
180,180
Specify other corner point or [Area/Dimensions/Rotation]: A
Enter area of rectangle in current units <500.0000>: 500
Calculate rectangle dimensions based on [Length/Width] <Length>: W
Enter rectangle width <17.0000>: 17
Command:
```

Figure 3-11

6. EXPLODE command with X shortcut

The main function of this command is explosion, and the shortcut is the letter X. One of its most important uses is to decompose a Polyline into separate lines and change them to Lines. To further understand this command, consider a Polygon drawn using polyline. Now if you type and run the letter X in the command line and click on the Polygon and press the Enter key, you will see that the Polygon sides are exploded into separate lines and the Polyline changes to Line. Of course, the EXPLODE command has many applications that will be explained when necessary.

7. Properties command with PR shortcut

Properties means features and has the same meaning in AutoCAD. You can use it to view or modify the properties of an object. One of the properties of any object is its type. As an example, you can use this command whenever you want to know if the type of a line is Line or Polyline.

The shortcut for this command is PR. To use this command, left-click on the object you want to select, then type and run the PR shortcut in the command line. After running the command, you will see a window like Figure 3-12 appears on the left side of the software window and this window will display all the properties of that object.

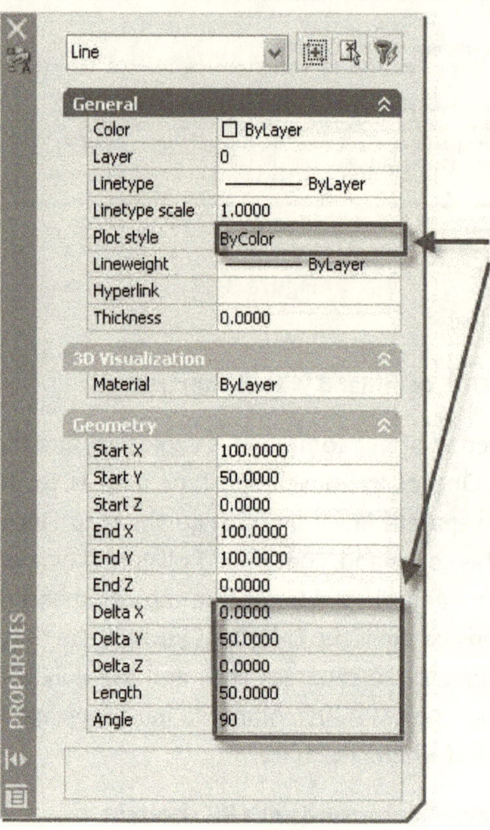

Figure 3-12

The type of the selected objects is displayed at the top of it. The other properties of the object such as color type, layer name, line type, line weight, and other corresponding descriptive properties of that object are displayed in the box below. The second box is for the 3D properties of the object. The third box displays the geometrical properties of the object such as the starting point coordinates, the ending point coordinates, ΔX, ΔY, line length and line slope angle.

This command displays all the properties associated with the object depending on the type of the selected object. For example, if the object is a circle, it will also display its other properties such as area, perimeter, radius and diameter. Some of these properties such as layer name, line type and more are changeable, and some others are unchangeable. In this window, those properties that are unchangeable have a gray highlighted background. Like the boxes specified in Figure 3-12, the unchangeable properties depend on the selected object and vary from object to object.

It should be noted that to run this command, other than the PR shortcut, you can also use the CH shortcut or the Ctrl+1 keyboard shortcut.

Another one of the most useful and important features that this command displays of objects is that if you select a Polyline, the Misc window will display whether it is closed or open as in Figure 3-13. This option is used to control whether the parcels should be close or not in cadastral maps.

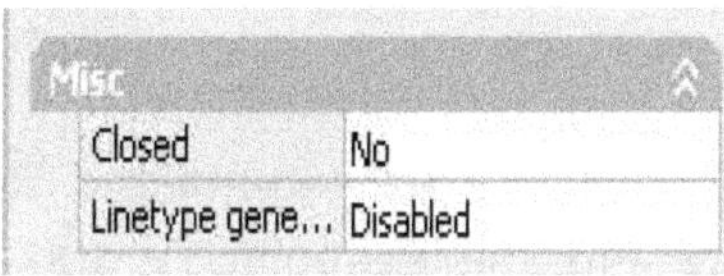

Figure 3-13

8. Arc command with A shortcut

This command is used to draw arcs. After typing A shortcut and running it, the "Specify start point of arc or Center" message appears in the command line, which means specify the first point of the arc or the center of it. If you want to draw an arc that crosses three specified points in the drawing, after running the command, select those three points with the left mouse button one after each other. But the case in which you want the arc to cross through three points with specified coordinates will be explained in the following exercise.

Exercise 6

Draw an arc that crosses points with the following coordinates.

Point Number	X	Y
1	100	100
2	150	170
3	300	70

Figure 3-14-1

Answer:

To do this, type A shortcut in the command line to run the Arc command, then type X for the first point, i.e. 100, and type Y for the first point using a comma and press the Enter key. Then type X and Y for the second point and press the Enter key again. Do the same to specify the third point.

```
Command: A
ARC Specify start point of arc or [Center]: 100,100
Specify second point of arc or [Center/End]: 150,170
Specify end point of arc: 300,70

Command:
```

Figure 3-14-2

Exercise 7

Draw an arc with the center coordinates (123.26, 204.82) that crosses the points with the coordinates (199.05, 228.84) and (125.08, 53.08).

Answer:

First, type and run the shortcut A in the command line, then type C in the command line and press the Enter key. After that, type in the coordinates of the center of the arc and then type in the coordinates of the two points that you want the arc to cross and press the Enter key.

```
Command: A
ARC Specify start point of arc or [Center]: C
Specify center point of arc: 123.26,204.82
Specify start point of arc: 199.55,228.84
Specify end point of arc or [Angle/chord Length]: 125.08,53.08

Command:
```

Figure 3-15

9. Zoom command with Z shortcut

As the name of the command implies, it is used to zoom in and zoom out on the objects in the drawing and there are various ways to do this. The shortcut for this command is the letter Z. To use it, type and run the letter Z in the command line. But if you run this command, you will notice that after running it, there will be no change in the drawing and only the following message will appear in the command line:

All/Center/Dynamic/Extents/Previous/Scale/Window/Object <real time>

Each of the above options runs one of the Zoom modes. To run any of them, after running the Zoom command, just type in and run the letter or letters of that word in the upper case.

All

This mode is used to zoom in on all the objects in the drawing. The shortcut is the letter A, and to use it, type and run the letter Z and then type the letter A and press the Enter key. It is the most used mode among Zoom modes. One way to use this command is to not observe the object on the drawing area after drawing it and you can see all the drawings with the Zoom All command.

Center

This mode is used to zoom in on specific coordinates and is widely used in land surveying drawings; for example, when trying to find a point with specific coordinates on a map with a lot of details. To use this mode, after running the Zoom command and selecting the Center mode, the “Specify center point” message appears in the command line asking you to specify the center of the Zoom. Do this by typing in your desired coordinates. After that, the "Enter magnification or height" message will appear asking us to specify the magnification level. Type in the magnification level number as needed and press the Enter key.

Dynamic

This mode is used to zoom in on a section of the drawing.

Extents

This mode of Zoom restricts the objects in the drawing to the side boxes of the drawing area and it slightly enlarges the objects in the drawing so that they reach the sides of the AutoCAD drawing area.

Previous

This mode is used to restore the Zoom action to the previous state. If you have zoomed in and intend to go back to the previous state, type and run the Z shortcut in the command line, then type the first letter of this mode, i.e. P and press the Enter key.

Scale

This mode is used to zoom in with a specific scale, so if you want to view the objects in the drawing with a 2x magnification, type and run the letter Z in the command line. After that, type the letter S and press the Enter key, then type 2 as the magnification level number.

Window

This mode is used to zoom in on a specific window. To do this, type and run the letter Z in the command line, then type the letter W and press the Enter key. Then select the window you want to zoom in on the AutoCAD drawing area using the mouse.

Object

This mode is used to zoom in on a particular object. For example, if you want to zoom in on a circle, type and run the Z shortcut in the command line, then type the O letter and press the Enter key. After that, click on the circle using the mouse and press the Enter key again.

10. Pan command with P shortcut

This command is used with the P shortcut to pan the map. To run this command, type and run the P shortcut in the command line, and then pan the map using the mouse.

11. Using the mouse instead of the Pan & Zoom commands

These commands are two of the most commonly used AutoCAD commands. But the important point is that these two commands are more efficient and faster when ran simultaneously. In this particular case, using the mouse is recommended. As for zooming in, scroll up the scroll wheel, and for zooming out, scroll down. The Zoom Extents command is ran by double-clicking the scroll wheel consecutively, and you have ran the Pan command if you click and hold the scroll wheel on one part of the map and move it.

12. Circle command with C shortcut

As the name implies, this command is used to draw a circle. There are two methods to draw a circle: The first method is to use the mouse, and the other one is to type in the coordinates of the center of the circle and its radius, which will be explained below.

Using the mouse

For this purpose, type and run the C shortcut in the command line. Then, using the left mouse button, select a point as the center of the circle and the circle will be drawn by moving the mouse to the sides and left-clicking to select the radius.

Suppose you intend to draw an equilateral triangle with a side length of 50.

To do this, first draw a line with a length of 50 using the Line command, then run the Circle command and click on the start of the line as the center of the circle and after that, click on the end of the line to use the line as the radius of the circle and draw a circle with a radius equal to the line length (in this example, 50). Do the same thing to the end of the line to draw the desired shape.

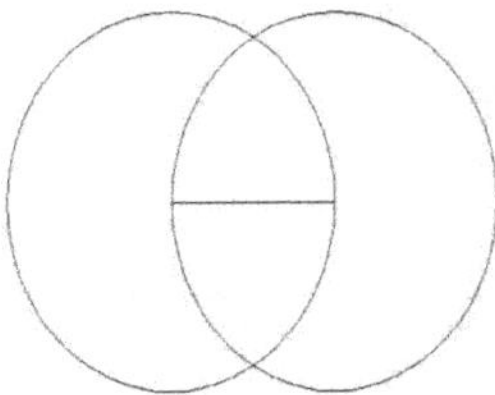

Figure 3-16

Now if you draw a line from the start of the drawn line to the intersection of the two circles, the second side of the triangle is also drawn. Do the same to draw the third side, then erase the two circles using the Erase command.

Using the coordinates

In this method, type and run the letter C in the command line, then type in the coordinates of the center of the circle and press the Enter key. Then type in the radius of the circle and press the Enter key again to draw the circle with the specified center and radius.

Exercise 8

Draw a circle with the center point O with coordinates (200,100) and a radius of 50 meters.

Answer:

To do this, type and run the C shortcut in the command line, then specify the center of the circle as follows: Type 100 as the X for the center of the circle, then type comma after that and type 200 as the Y for the center of the circle and press the Enter key. Then by typing 50 and pressing the Enter key, the desired circle with the center with specified coordinates and radius will be drawn. If you can't see your circle on the screen, you can see it by using the Zoom All command or by double-clicking the scroll wheel consecutively.

```
Command: C
CIRCLE Specify center point for circle or [3P/2P/Ttr (tan tan radius)]: 100,200
Specify radius of circle or [Diameter] <50.0000>: 50

Command:
```

Figure 3-17

But apart from this simple method for drawing a circle mentioned above, AutoCAD also allows the user to draw the circle in various other ways. As you can see, when you run the Circle command, the "CIRCLE Specify center point for circle or [3P/2P/Ttr (tan tan radius)]" message appears in the command line, which shows the different modes for drawing a circle inside the sign [ ]. 3P is a mode with which you can draw a circle that crosses three desired points. The 2P mode is also useful when you want the circle to cross two points. Ttr is also a mode with which you can draw the circle with the desired radius so that it is tangent to two tangents or two lines. To further understand this, each mode mentioned will be explained with an exercise.

Exercise 9

Draw a circle that crosses the points with the following coordinates.

Point Number	X	Y
1	1000	1000
2	1050	1070
3	1150	1070

Figure 3-18

Answer:

To do this, first type and run the C shortcut in the command line to run the Circle command, then type the 3P shortcut and press the Enter key to enable the three-point crossing mode. As you can see, the "Specify first point on circle" message appears in the command line which means specify the first point of the circle. So, do this by typing in the coordinates of point A. Then the command line asks for the coordinates of the second point. So, type in the coordinates of point B and press the Enter key. Finally, type in the coordinates of point C and press the Enter key again.

Figure 3-19

```
Command: C
CIRCLE Specify center point for circle or [3P/2P/Ttr (tan tan radius)]: 3P
Specify first point on circle: 1000,1000
Specify second point on circle: 1050,1070
Specify third point on circle: 1150,1070

Command:
```

Exercise 10

Apply a simple curve with a radius of 100 meters between the AB and BC tangents. The coordinates of the start, end and the third point are as follows:

A (1000 ,1000)
B (1300 ,1000)
C (1150 ,1200)

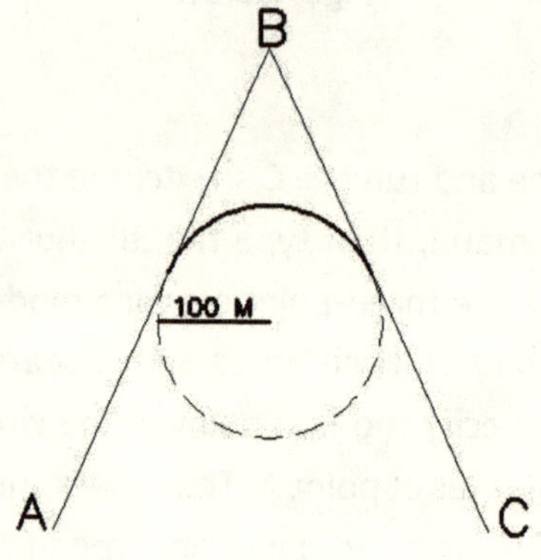

Figure 3-20-1

Answer:

To do this, first draw the AB and BC lines using one of the line drawing commands, such as Line or Polyline. Then type and run the C shortcut to run the Circle command, and type the letter T to select the Ttr drawing mode and press the Enter key. After that, click on the AB and BC lines respectively, and then type 100 as the radius of the curve. As you can see, a circle with a radius of 100 meters is drawn tangent to tan AB and tan BC. The steps are as follows:

Command: **L**
LINE Specify first point: **1000,1000**
Specify next point or [Undo]: **1150,1200**
Specify next point or [Undo]: **1300,1000**

Specify next point or [Close/Undo]:

Press the Enter key once more to close the command

Command: **C**

CIRCLE Specify center point for circle or [3P/2P/Ttr (tan tan radius)]: **T**

Select the Ttr mode

Specify point on object for first tangent of circle

Click on one of the tangent lines

Specify point on object for second tangent of circle

Click on the other tangent line

Specify radius of circle: **100**

Type in the radius of the circle

Drawing a hypotenuse with the desired size on the perimeter of a circle

Sometimes you want to draw a hypotenuse with the desired size on the perimeter of a circle. For example, in Figure 3-20, you have a circle with a radius of 30 meters and want to cut a 40-meter length on its perimeter.

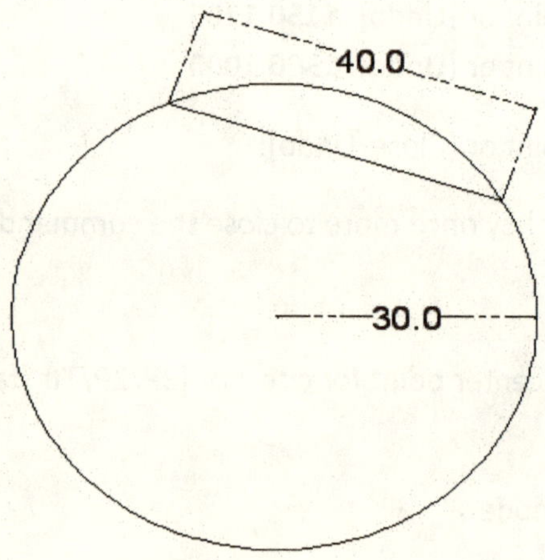

Figure 3-20-2

For this purpose, after drawing the circle, again using the Circle command, select the center of the circle at the starting point of the 40-meter hypotenuse, then consider the radius of the circle as 40 meters and draw a line from the center of the second circle using the Line command with the end point being the center of the two circles' intersection.

This will draw a 40-meter hypotenuse on the perimeter of the circle.

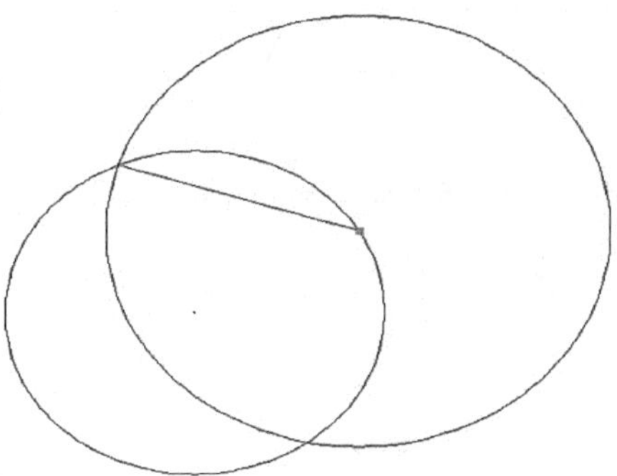

Figure 3-21

Now if you have questions about how to cut a 40-meter length on the perimeter of a circle in a way that its arc is 40 meters, follow the command number 40.

One of the modes for drawing a circle is a mode where you draw a circle that is tangent to three lengths or tangents, as in Figure 3-22.

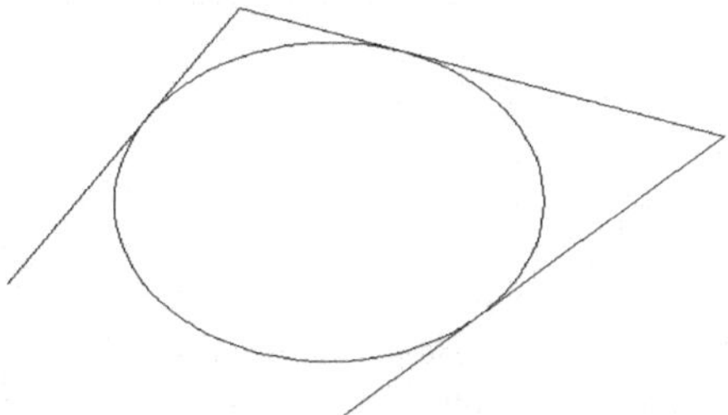

Figure 3-22

This mode of drawing a circle is not done with the help of the Circle command through the command line. To use this method, you should select the Circle option from the Draw menu and then select the "Tan, Tan, Tan" option from the submenus provided as in Figure

3-23. Then left-click on the three desired tangents respectively, to draw the circle.

Note that the shortcut for this command is AI_CircTan.

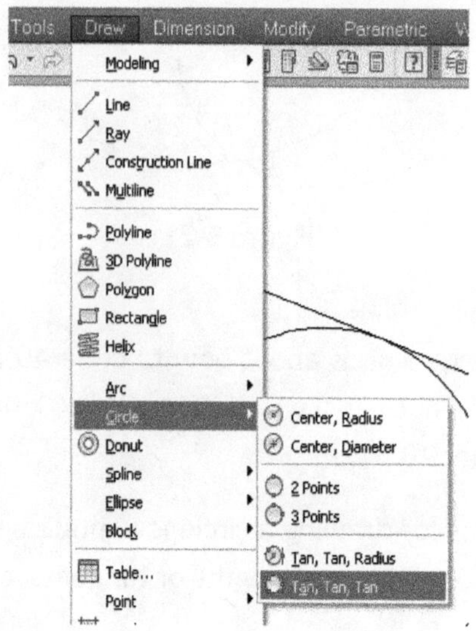

Figure 3-23

13. Join command with J shortcut

This command is used to connect two lines and join them. This command is used when you want to connect two linear features, both of which have been drawn using Polyline and intersect each other at one point. To further understand this command, consider a drawn dirt road that has two Polylines on one side and three

Polylines on the other. To turn each side of the dirt road to a Polyline, click on the first polyline, then type and run the J shortcut in the command line. Then click on the second and third parts of the Polyline and press the Enter key at the end. Now if you click on it, you will see that it has become a Polyline.

14. Color command with COL shortcut

This command is used to change the default drawing color. To do this, type and run the COL shortcut in the command line. Running this command will open a window that allows the user to select the color as in Figure 3-24. Any color you select and confirm in this window will then be the default color in your drawings. You can also set the default color for your drawings, either ByLayer or ByBlock. In these modes, the color of each object, the color of the layer, or the color of the object's block will be applied.

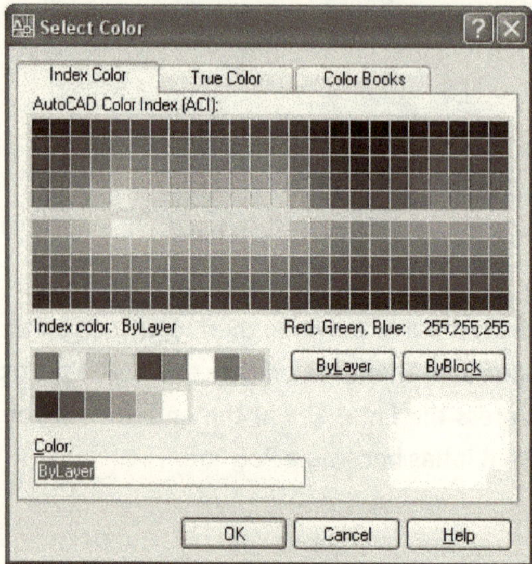

Figure 3-24

15. Area command with AA shortcut

This command is used to calculate the area of drawn shapes in AutoCAD. The two methods of calculating the area are explained below.

The First Method:

To calculate the area of the shapes that are not joined and are composed of separate lines, type and run the AA shortcut in the command line, then click on each corner of the shapes and after selecting the last corner, close the command by pressing the Enter key. Now you can see the perimeter and area of the shapes in the command line.

Important Note:

Remember, the corners you click on should be in order and you should start from a specific corner and move in one direction to reach the same corner of the shape.

The Second Method:

In this method, the area is calculated faster than the first method, if the shape you want to calculate the area of is a close Polyline or is Region. If the shape is made of broken regular lines of Polyline and is actually made of a Polyline, calculate the area as follows:
Type and run the AA shortcut in the command line, then type the letter O to select the Object mode and press the Enter key. Now click on the closed shape and then you can see its area in the command line. To calculate the area of the shapes made up of one Polyline, follow the command above and do as mentioned, but if you want to calculate the area of a shape consisting of two or more Polylines, you must first convert it to a Polyline, then calculate its area. To convert them to a Polyline, use the Join command with the J shortcut. So, type and run the J shortcut in the command line, then click on the Polylines of the shape to convert them to a Polyline. After that, type and run the AA shortcut in the command line and then type the letter O in the command line and press the Enter key and click on the shape to see its area in the command line.

Calculating the total of areas of multiple shapes

When you have multiple shapes and want to calculate the total of their areas, after running the Area command, simply enable the Add option by typing the letter A and pressing the Enter key. Then select your multiple shapes in order and see their total area.
But if your shape consists of several shapes of different types, such as Figure 3-25, which consists of a Polyline, two arcs and a line, it must be converted to a Region to calculate its area. In the next command, you will learn how to form a Region, then you can calculate the area of the shape.

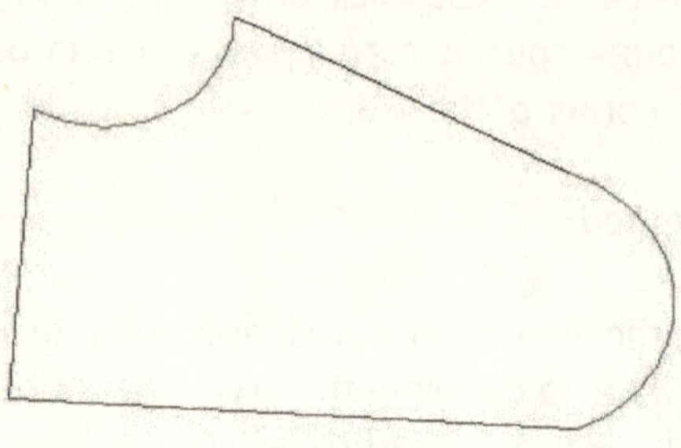

Figure 3-25

16. Region command with REG shortcut

Region means a region and an enclosed area. The components of a region can consist of any shape. One of the applications of Region is calculating the area of the shapes made up of several different object types.
To do this, type and run the REG shortcut in the command line. After that, left-click on all the components of the region to select them and then press the Enter key to convert the shape to a Region.

Important Note:

Only the shapes can be converted to a Region that are closed.

17. Boundary command with BO shortcut

This is one of the most important and applicable commands in land surveying drawings, especially in drawing cadastral maps, which is very useful.
The general function of this command is to convert a region composed of different shapes to a Region or Polyline, and ultimately has the most utility in calculating the area of particular shapes. This command will be explained with an example.

Suppose you intend to calculate the area of the section with the hatches in Figure 3-26. As you can see, this shape is the result of the intersection of a rectangle with a circle, and by itself, is not a shape with a specific area that can be calculated using the Object submenu in the Area command. It is therefore necessary to first convert this shape to a joined Region or a closed Polyline. But if you want to use the Region command to convert this shape to a Region, first you need to cut the circle from its intersection with the rectangle in a way that its arc is separated and also cut the rectangle from its intersection with the circle. Then convert them to a Region using the Region command.

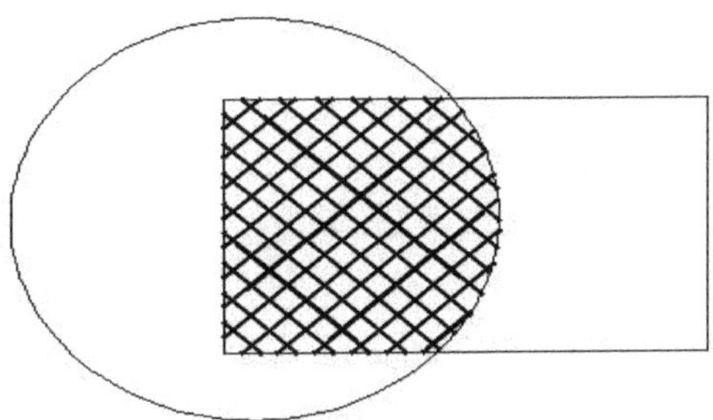

Figure 3-26

But AutoCAD offers the users a faster and easier way to do this, and that is using the Boundary command. This command works as follows: After running the command, if you click anywhere on the drawing area, it forms a user-defined area with Region or Polyline object type that is enclosed with other objects around its center.

To further understand it, take a glance at Figure 3-26. Now if you want to create a new region out of the section with the hatches, just run the BO shortcut in the command line to open a window as in Figure 3-27. In this window, first choose the type of conversion in the Object type section. For example, if you want to convert the shape into a Polyline, select the Polyline option. Then click on the Pick Points icon. Now this window will be closed and the drawing area will be enabled. Now click inside the section that you want to create hatches in and press the Enter key. As you can see, a new shape is created that contains parts of the rectangle and the circle. Now you can calculate its area using the Object submenu in the Area command.

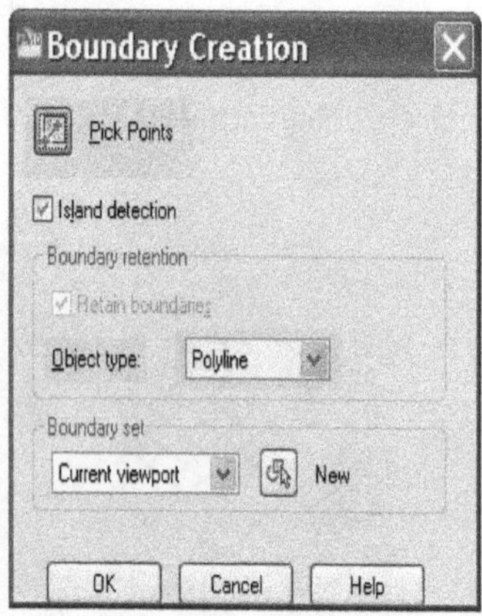

Figure 3-27

One of the most important uses of this command is forming separate parcels of Polyline object type. As you know, in cadastral maps, each piece of land must be drawn separately without any common sides. For example, in Figure 3-28, parcel 1 should form a Polyline passing through points A, B, E and D. And other parcels should likewise form a Polyline passing through the points in their region. But these parcels have not been drawn like this and these four parcels consist of the lines AC, CI, GI, AG, BH and DF. In order to make each parcel to be formed by a Polyline, you should either run the Polyline command and redraw the parcel which is a very time-consuming task, or use the Boundary command. To do this, run the BO shortcut in the command line and from the opened window, select the Polyline shortcut and then click on the Pick Points icon. Then click inside the parcels respectively, so that each of them forms a separate Polyline.

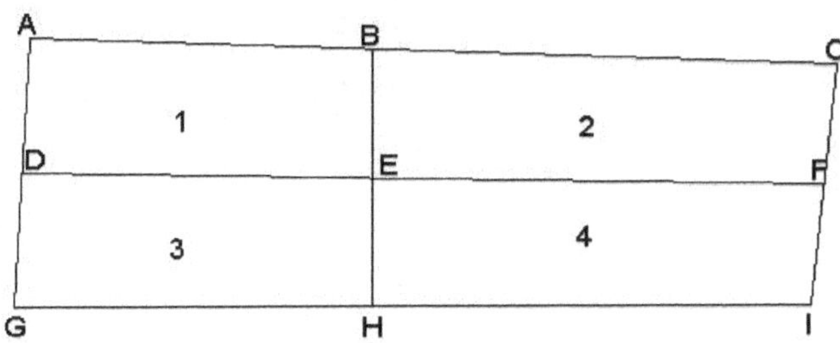

Figure 3-28

Important Note:

Area can also be extracted from the hatches. You can do this by considering the hatches as the Object.

18. List command with LI shortcut

This command is used to get a property report on an object. The properties that you can see of an object after running the List command are:

The coordinates of the points that the shape crosses, the area of the shape, the perimeter of the shape, name of the layer, type of the line, the radius of an arc or a circle, the 2D and 3D length of the line, and so on.

To run this command, left-click on any object that you want to get the properties of to select it, then run the LI shortcut in the command line. After that, a window opens that displays all the technical and descriptive specifications of that object. For example, if you get the properties of a circle, a window like the one in Figure 3-29 which is related to the geometric and descriptive specifications of that circle will be displayed. This window displays the name of the

layer, the drawing space, the center point coordinates of the circle, the radius, the perimeter and the area of the circle respectively.
It should be noted that also the LS shortcut runs the List command.

```
AutoCAD Text Window - Drawing1.dwg
Edit
Command:
Command:  LIST 1 found

                  CIRCLE    Layer: "0"
                            Space: Model space
                   Handle = c0
            center point, X=  56.6380  Y=  26.4842  Z=   0.0000
            radius    10.1985
     circumference    64.0789
              area  326.7533

Command:
```

Figure 3-29

19. Copy command with CO shortcut

This command is used to copy objects in the drawing in different parts of the drawing area. To do this, left-click on the object you want to copy to select it, then run the CO shortcut in the command line. Then left-click on the point on the drawing area where you want the copy to be based on, then left-click on the desired point to paste the object or objects wherever you want. For example, if you want to draw a circle with a radius of 3 meters on each corner of Figure 3-30, draw a circle with a radius of 3 meters on one corner of the shape in order to save time and do the task faster, then copy_the circle and paste it on the other corners.

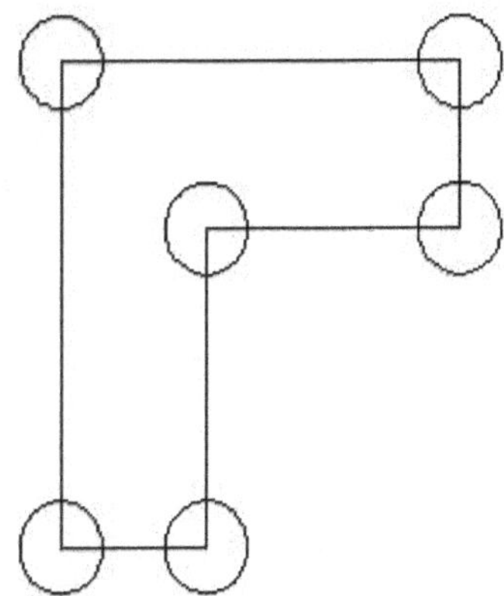

Figure 3-30

This command has many applications not only in land surveying drawings, but also in all Engineering and Technical fields. In land surveying drawings, by combining this command with other commands, many of your needs are met, which will be described in more detail below.
It should be noted that also the CP shortcut runs the Copy command.

One of the modes of the Copy command is using its Array submenu. If you notice the options in the command line when copying an object after specifying the base point, you can see that the Array mode can be selected by typing the letter A. Consider the following example to understand the application of this mode.
You want to copy a lot of circles with desired (organized) distances on a desired direction. For this purpose, you do not need to create the points first, then copy and paste the circles in those points using the Copy command. You just need to draw the first two circles, then copy the first circle. After specifying the base point which is the center of the first circle, type the letter A and press the Enter key to select the Array mode. As you can see, the "Enter number of items to array" message appears in the command line which asks the user for the number of copies. After typing in the desired number, AutoCAD asks for the second point for copying, and in fact, you

specify the distance between the circles by specifying the second point. In this exercise, you should click on the center of the second circle. After this, the defined number of circles will be copied along that direction.

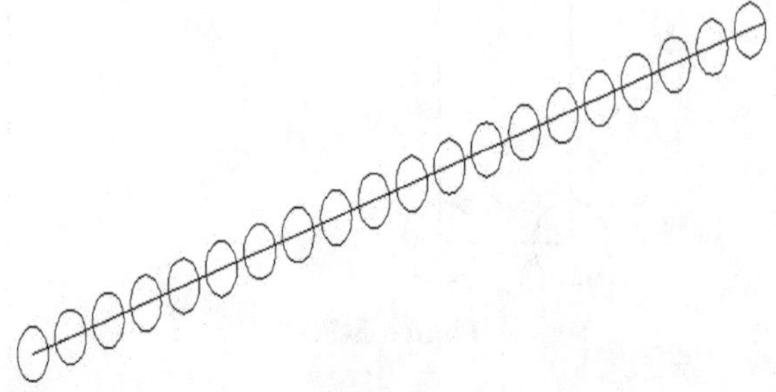

Figure 3-31

Another way to use this command is to copy and paste a number of circles at a certain distance in a particular direction so that AutoCAD can calculate and display the distance between them. For example, copy and paste 85 circles on a 1234-meter long straight line.
To do this, simply copy the first circle after drawing it, and after defining the base point, select the Array mode and type 85 and press the Enter key. By doing this, before specifying the second point, the Fit mode appears in the command line, and you must type the letter F and press the Enter key to select this mode. Now click on the end of the line to paste 85 circles along that line in this distance.

20. Array command with AR shortcut

This command is used to duplicate one or more objects with horizontal and vertical distances relative to each other, in two different modes, with the desired angle of array. It is very handy and allows you to create a number of objects equally and very quickly. After running this command, a window opens as in Figure 3-32.

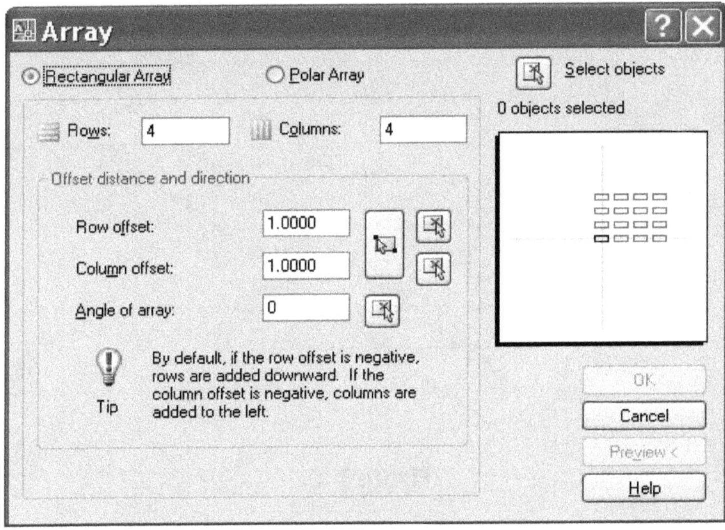

Figure 3-32

At the top of the window, you can choose between Rectangular Array and Polar Array modes. The Rectangular Array mode is related to the rectangular Matrix Array, and the Polar Array mode is related to the Angular Array based on a rotation point.

In the first mode, which is more applicable, first select the desired object or objects using the Select Objects icon and press the Enter key to display this window again. Then type in the number of rows in the Rows box and the number of columns in the Columns box. Type in the distances between rows and columns in the Row offset and Column offset boxes. The Angle of array box is also related to the angle of rotation relative to the horizon line and you can see the results of your work after clicking OK.

For example, suppose as shown in Figure 3-33, you want to install 12 light poles, each 10 meters away from the other along an asphalt road which has a 42° angle with the horizon line 15 meters away from the road.

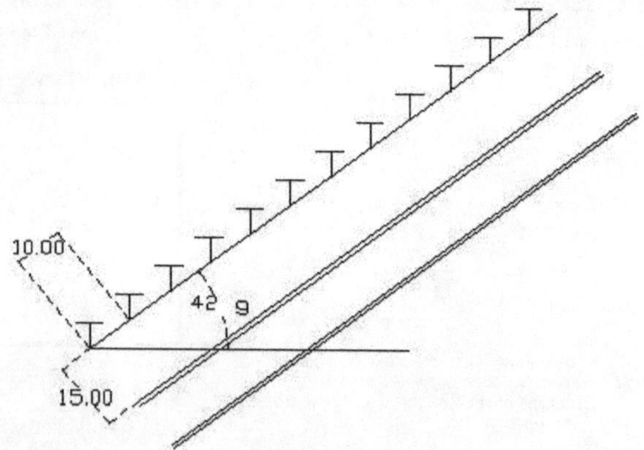

Figure 3-33

First, it is necessary to calculate their coordinates and then specify their position on the ground using land surveying equipment. The Array command can be used to expedite this process. This is how it works:

First, specify the position of the first light pole using other drawing commands. Then use the Array command to specify the position of and draw the other 11 light poles.

Now type and run the AR shortcut in the command line, then select the first drawn light pole using the Select Object option and set the window as in Figure 3-34. Finally, click OK to draw the desired light poles. Now you can extract their coordinates using other methods of drawing and getting properties. The Polar Array mode is not usually explained.

It should be noted that in AutoCAD versions 2010 and above, you should use the Arrayclassic command to run the Array command and view the corresponding window.

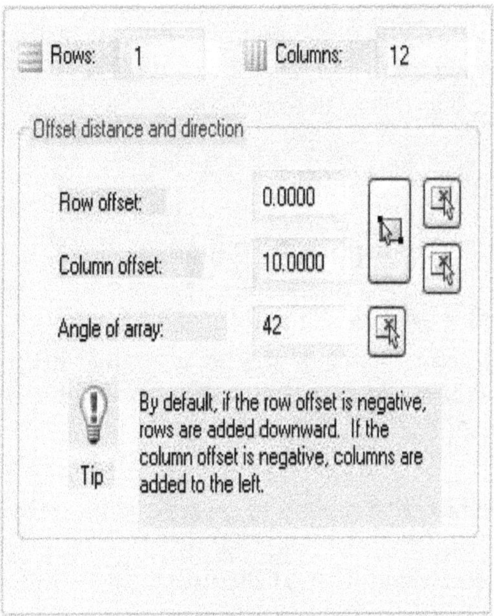

Figure 3-34

21. Text command with T shortcut

This command is used to insert text into the drawing area. So, run the T shortcut in the command line. By doing so, the mouse cursor on the drawing area gets ready to select the box in which you want to insert your text. Do this by left-clicking on one corner of the box and holding and dragging the box to the last corner and clicking on that corner. After selecting the text box, the Text Formatting window opens as in Figure 3-35.

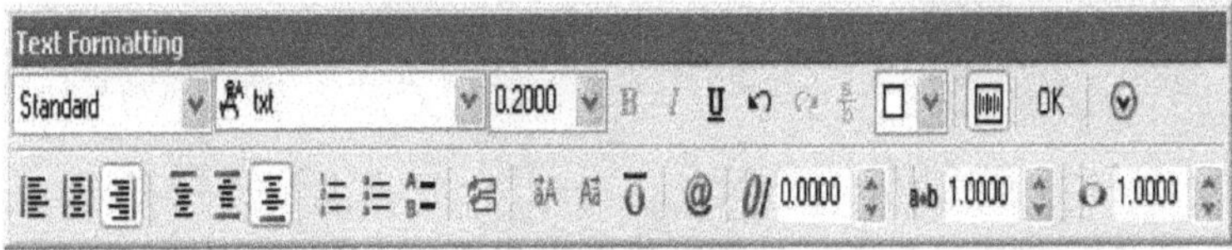

Figure 3-35

In the bottom box, you can type in the desired text and in the top box, you can adjust the settings for text type, text format, size and other settings. Then click OK to finish.

How can we edit a text?

22. DDEDIT command with ED shortcut

This command is used to edit a text. To do this, select any text you want to edit by left-clicking on it, then type and run the ED shortcut in the command line. As you can see, the Text Formatting box opens and lets the user edit that text.

An easier and faster command to create and insert text

23. Text command with DT shortcut

The DT command is used in land surveying drawings to create and insert text more than any other command, because it is faster than other text creating commands and has the ability of defining the direction.
For this purpose, type and run the DT shortcut in the command line. After running this command, the command line is ready to receive the starting point of the text and by clicking on the first point, the command line asks for the text height and you can type it in using the keyboard. After typing in the height, the command line asks you for the angle of the text relative to the horizon line. By typing the angle and pressing the Enter key, you can type your text. Then to finish the command, click on another part of the drawing area and press the Esc key.

Exercise 11

Insert a text on the drawing area with a height of 2 and an angle of 15°.

Answer:

Command: **DT**
Command:Specify start point of text or [Justify/Style]:

After this message is displayed, click on a point on the drawing area.

Specify height <0.2000>: **2**
Specify rotation angle of text <0>: **15**

How to convert uppercase and lowercase letters in a text into one another?

24. Textcase command with TCASE shortcut

This command is used to convert uppercase and lowercase letters in a text into one another. For example, if you want to convert a text that is typed in lowercase letters into a text with uppercase letters, type and run the TCASE shortcut in the command line. Then click on the desired text or texts and press the Enter key. As you can see, a window opens like Figure 3-37 whose options are as follows:

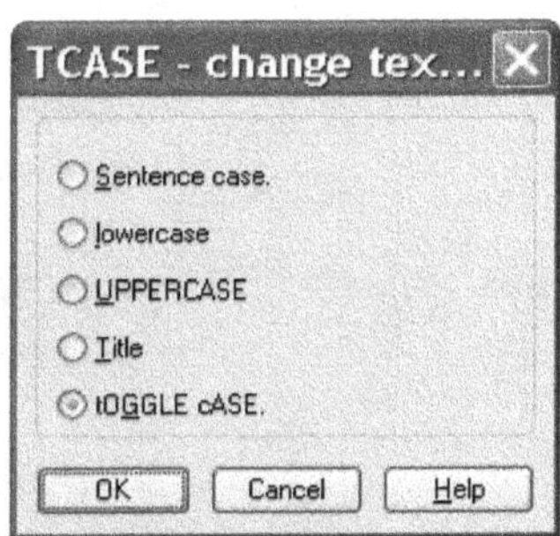

Figure 3-37

The Sentence case option only converts the first letter of any number of paragraphs to uppercase and converts the rest of the letters to lowercase letters.

The lowercase option converts all the letters to lowercase.

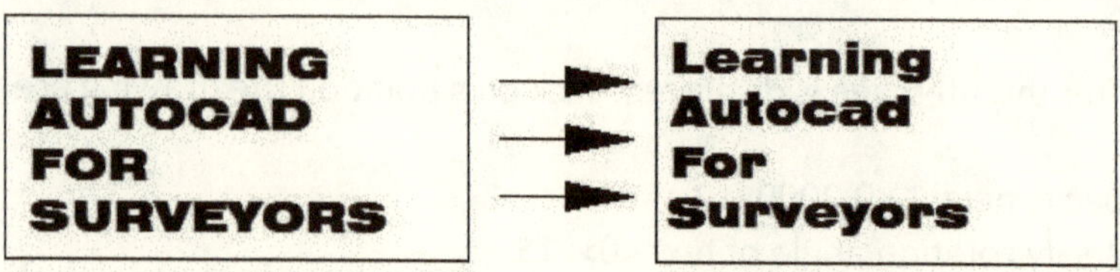

The UPPERCASE option converts all the letters to uppercase letters.

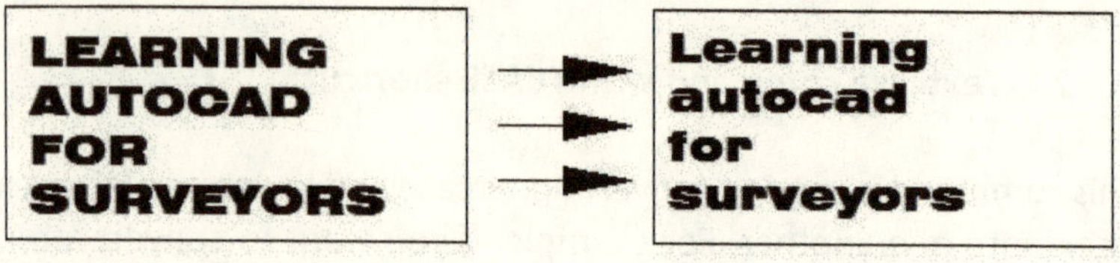

The Title option converts the first letter of each paragraph to uppercase, and converts the rest of the letters to lowercase letters.

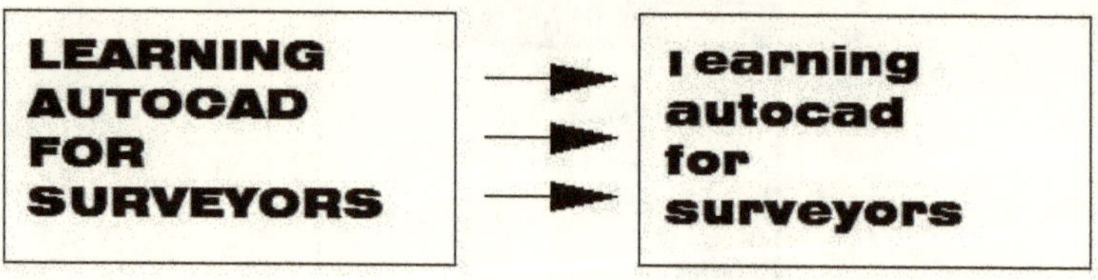

The tOGGLE cASE option does the opposite, by converting the first letter of each paragraph to a lowercase letter and the rest of the letters to uppercase letters.

Inserting a text along an arc

25. Atext command

This command is used to insert a text along an arc. To do this, type and run the Atext shortcut in the command line. Then, in response to the "Select an Arc or an ArcAlignedText" message that appears in the command line, click on a drawn arc using the mouse. By clicking on the desired arc, a window will appear for selecting and settings the text as in Figure 3-38.

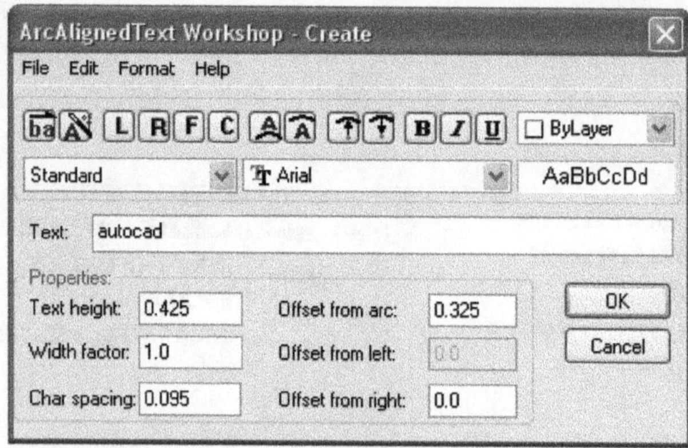

Figure 3-38

In this window, type the desired text in the Text box and make other adjustments to options such as font type, text size, left and right offset relative to the arc and so on, and finally click OK to insert the desired text along the arc as in Figure 3-39.

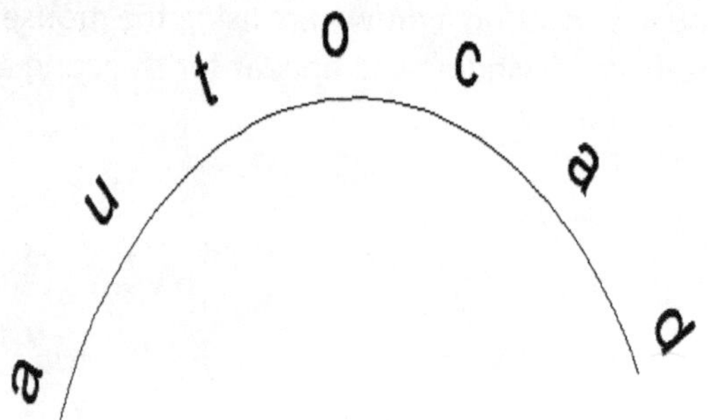

Figure 3-39

26. Move command with M shortcut

This command is used to move objects in the drawing to another part of the drawing. This is also one of the most important AutoCAD commands. To move the objects in the drawing, click on them to select them, then type and run the M shortcut in the command line.

Then click on one point as the base point and move those objects to another point based on the base point that you have just specified. Now if you want to move the objects in the drawing as desired on the X-axis and Y-axis, first select your objects, then type and run the M shortcut in the command line. Then type the letter D and press the Enter key to select the Displacement submenu. You can now type in the values of ΔX and ΔY to move the desired objects as much as you want.

For example, suppose you have the coordinate file that you have drawn, then you notice that the station adjustment is 2 mm to the west (-2 mm) and 7 mm to the north (+7 mm). As you know, the station adjustment should be applied to all the coordinates. So, select all the objects, including points, lines and so on, and type and run the M shortcut in the command line. Then type the letter D and press the Enter key and type in the station adjustment values respectively and press the Enter key again.

Command: **M**
MOVE
Select objects:
Select objects:
Specify base point or [Displacement] <Displacement>:**D**
Specify displacement <0.0000, 0.0000, 0.0000>:**-.002,+.007**

27. Rotate command with RO shortcut

This command is used to rotate objects around a point with a desired angle. To do this, select the objects you want to rotate, then type and run the RO shortcut in the command line. After that, the command line asks you for the rotation base point, which you can specify by clicking on a point on the AutoCAD drawing area or by typing in the rotation base point coordinates. After doing this, the command line wants the rotation angle. This can also be specified by typing in the rotation angle or by clicking on a point on the AutoCAD drawing area along the rotation angle.

One of the practical uses of the Rotat command is to rotate an object so that one side of it is positioned in a particular direction. For example, you want to rotate the triangle in Figure 3-40 around point A with an angle so that the AB side overlaps the AD line.

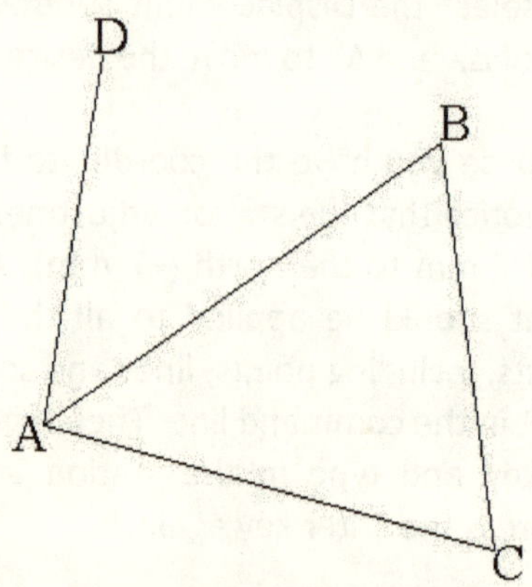

Figure 3-40

Generally, this is done as follows: First, measure the angle between the AD and AB sides, then apply the Rotate command to the triangle. After that, specify the angle as the rotation angle. But the problem is that it does not make it possible for the AB side to fully overlap the AD line and the overlap accuracy depends on the angle measurement accuracy.

But AutoCAD offers a faster, simpler, and more accurate way to do this without the need of measurements. To do this, first click on the triangle to select it and type and run the RO shortcut in the command line. Then the software asks you for the rotation base point, which you can specify by clicking on point A. Then in order for the AB line to overlap the AD line, type the letter R in the command line and press the Enter key and click on points A, then B, and finally D respectively. As you can see, the rotation angle is applied in a way that the AB side overlaps the AD line.

Command: **RO**
ROTATE
Current positive angle in UCS: ANGDIR=counterclockwise
ANGBASE=0

At this point, click on the triangle or any desired object and press the Enter key.

Select objects: 1 found
Select objects:
Specify base point

Click on point A as the rotation base point.

Specify rotation angle or [Copy/Reference] <0>: **R**

Type the letter R to select the Reference mode and press the Enter key.

Specify the reference angle <0>:

Click on point A.

Specify second point:

Click on point B.

Specify the new angle or [Points] <0>:

And finally, click on point D.

How to place an object in parallel with another object?

The *Rotate* command can be used to rotate an object such that one of its sides becomes parallel to a line or a side of another object.

For example, suppose that in the drawing of Figure 3-42, you want to rotate the triangle ABC about the point A such that the side AB becomes parallel to the line DE.

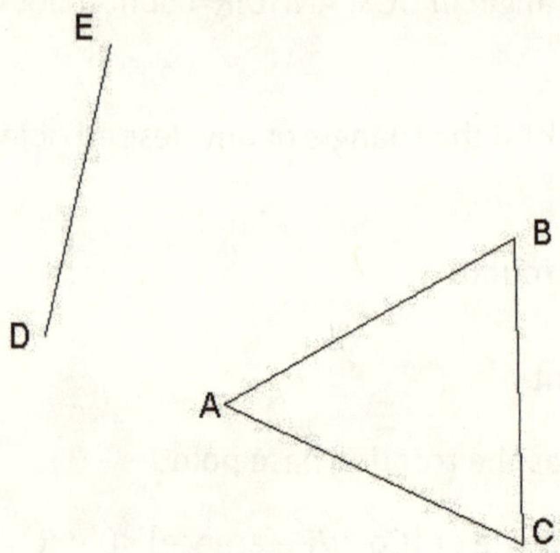

Figure 3-42

For this purpose, type the shortcut command *RO* in the command line and press enter. Then click on the triangle and press enter. Next, click on the point A as the base of rotation. The next step is to type *R* and press enter (to select the *Reference* option). Then you have to click first on the point A and then on the point B to designate the side AB as the origin side. Next, type *P* and press enter (to select the *Points* option). Then, click first on the point D and then on the point E to designate the line DE as the destination side. After pressing enter, the triangle ABC should rotate such that the side AB becomes parallel to the line DE. This form of the *Rotate* command has extensive use when working with survey drawings.

To practice, open the file Rotate2.dwg file and follow the instructions given below.

Type RO.

- Command: RO

- ROTATE

- Current positive angle in UCS: ANGDIR=counterclockwise ANGBASE=0

In this step, you must click on the target triangle or any object you want rotated and then press enter.

- Select objects: 1 found

- Select objects:

- Specify base point

Here, you must click on point A as the base of rotation.

- Specify rotation angle or [Copy / Reference] <0>: R

Now type *R* to select the *Reference* option and press enter.

- Specify the reference angle <0>:

Click on the point A.

- Specify second point:

Click on the point B.

- Specify the new angle or [Points] <0>: P

Here, you must type P to select the *Points* option and press enter.

- Specify first point:

Click on the point D.

- Specify second point:

Click on the point E.

28. SCALE command with SC shortcut

As the name implies, this command is used to increase or reduce the size of the objects in the drawing by entering a scale number. For example, if you want to double the size of an object on the drawing area, select the object and then type and run the SC shortcut in the command line. The command line then asks you for the base point, which you can specify either by typing in the base point coordinates or selecting a point on the drawing area. After specifying the base point by one of the two methods mentioned above, the command line now asks you for the scale number, and if you want to double the size of the object, type 2 and press the Enter key. One way to use this command is using the specific length. This will be explained using an example.

For example, suppose you have a map containing Longitudinal and Cross sections of an alignment, but these sections do not have real scales. In the cross section in Figure 3-42, the distance between the center line of the alignment to the left end of it has been inserted as 20 meters on the section. But when you measure the length between these two points using the measuring commands, the length is 5 meters.

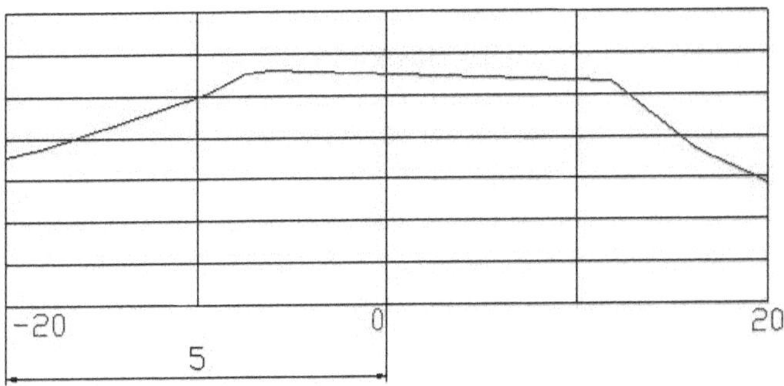

Figure 3-42

If you want to convert this section to its real size, you need to use the SCALE command. First, run the SC shortcut in the command line. Then select the desired section using the mouse. Then specify a point as the base point by left-clicking on the drawing area and typing the letter R in the command line and pressing the Enter key to select the Reference mode and then left-click on the start and end of the desired length. As you can see, the "Specify reference length" message appears in the command line, which means enter the new length, and you should type 5 as the new length so as to resize the section with the rate scale of 20:5.

Important Note:

Before doing this, you need to make sure that the scale factor is the same in all the sections you want to change the scale of, and that the scale factor is equal in both vertical and horizontal exaggerations.

29. Trim command with TR shortcut

This command is used to cut off extra parts of objects. To fully learn how to use this command, take a good look at Figure 3-43.

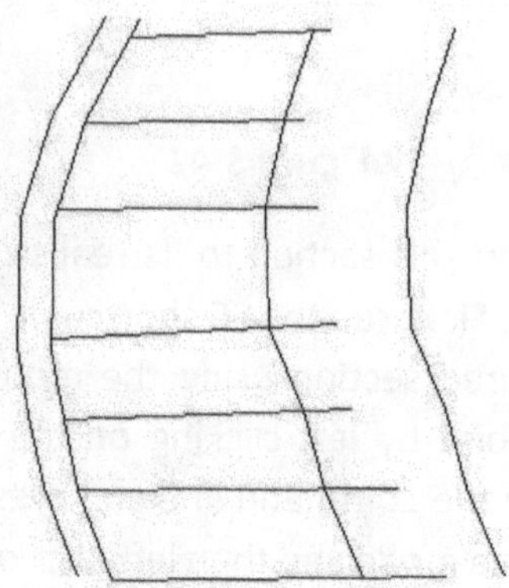

Figure 3-43

In this drawing you can see a number of parcels that have a dirt road on their left and a large canal on their right. As you can see, the lines that determine the parcels' borders have even passed the canal line a bit. The Trim command is used to cut and omit the extra parts of the lines based on the left line of the canal.

To do this, run the TR shortcut in the command line and left-click on the left line of the canal to select it. Then specify this line as the cutting base line by pressing the Enter key. Then click on the extra lines respectively to cut those lines based on the cutting line.

30. Extrim command with Extrim shortcut

This command is used when you want to cut all the objects in the drawing relative to a reference object from the inside or outside. For example, suppose you want to cut the contours and all the objects in Figure 3-44 relative to the box drawn in it in a way that only the objects remain in the box.

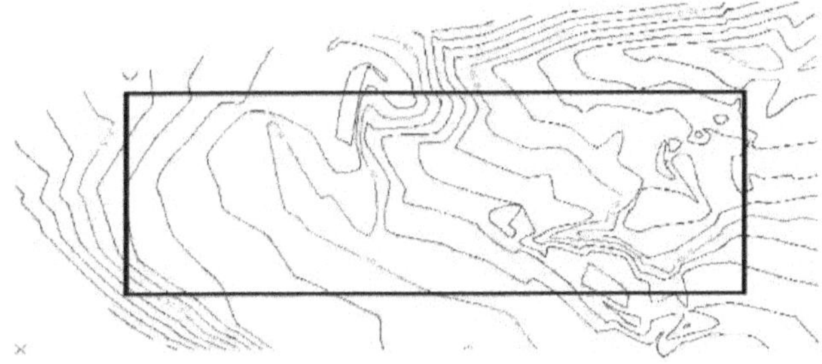

Figure 3-44

To do this, just type and run the Extrim shortcut in the command line. Then click on the desired box and to cut external references, click on a point on the drawing area outside the box. As you can see, all the objects that passed through this box were cut relative to the box. This command is used to create sheet layout grids for the cadastral and topographic maps.

31. Regen command with RE shortcut

This command is used to regenerate the map. Sometimes due to overactivity on the map, the drawings are not as they should be. For example, Figure 3-45 is a circle which is displayed like this as a result of overactivity on the drawing. To fix this, you need to regenerate the map by running the RE shortcut in the command line.

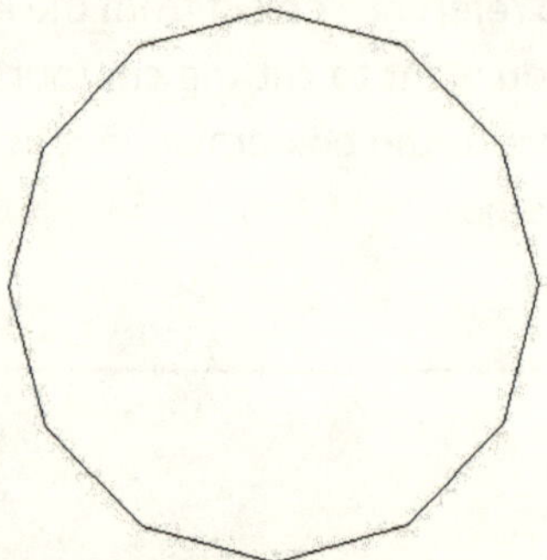

Figure 3-45

32. Break command with BR shortcut

This command is used to break objects only at one or two points. In order to do so, type and run the BR shortcut in the command line, then left-click on the object you want to break to select it. Then left-click on the point where you want the object to break, in order to break the object from the defined location.

If you want to break an object in two points, after running the command, type the letter F to select the First point mode and press the Enter key. Then click on the two points in order and press the Enter key.

For example, suppose in Figure 3-46, you want to break the AB line from its intersection spot with two other parallel lines at points c and d.

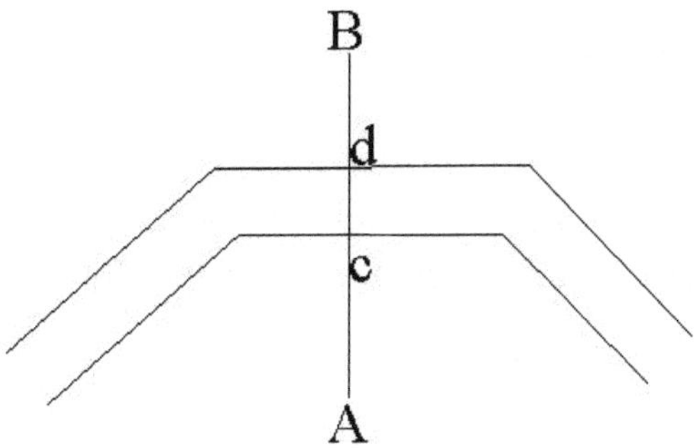

Figure 3-46

To do this, type and run the BR shortcut in the command line and click on the AB line to select it. Then type the letter F and press the Enter key. Then click on points c and d to break the AB line at those two points.

33. EXTEND command with EX shortcut

This command is used to extend one or more lines to other lines. For example, on the left part of Figure 3-47, you can see parcels that are restricted on the right to a dirt road, but for whatever reason, their lines have not reached this road. To solve the problem, use the EXTEND command with the EX shortcut.

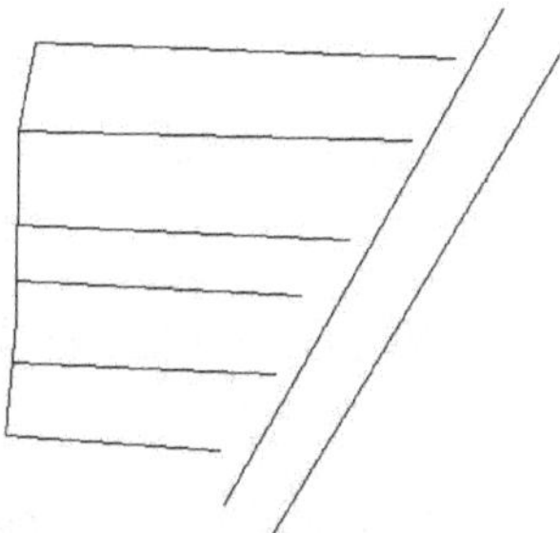

Figure 3-47

Run the EX shortcut in the command line. The software now asks you for the line that the other lines need to reach. So, select the line on left-hand side of the dirt road by left-clicking it, then confirm it by pressing the Enter key. Now you can connect any of the land boundary lines to the dirt road by clicking on them.

34. HATCH command with H shortcut

This command is used to create hatches in different regions. The important note is that you can create hatches only in regions that are closed. For example, in Figure 3-48, you can only create hatches in the two shapes on the left, and you cannot create hatches on the shape on the right, because it is open. The hatches are symbols that are used to identify the regions faster and better.

Figure 3-48

As you know, in land surveying, the features include the following three categories:

1. Point features such as light poles, single trees and others, that are symbolized in the drawings and a specific symbol is defined for each feature.

2. Linear features such as roads, tree rows, canals and so on. To identify these features, colors and line symbols such as dashed lines are used in the drawings.
3. The third category of features are Area features, such as buildings, gardens, farmland and pastures, which are identified more easily when they are drawn with hatches. There are a number of standards that apply to all maps that make these hatches known the same way throughout the world and each area feature has a particular type of hatch.

But first, you need to learn how to create a hatch. For example, if you want to create hatches in the two upper left shapes, type and run the H shortcut in the command line to open the hatch window as in Figure 3-49.

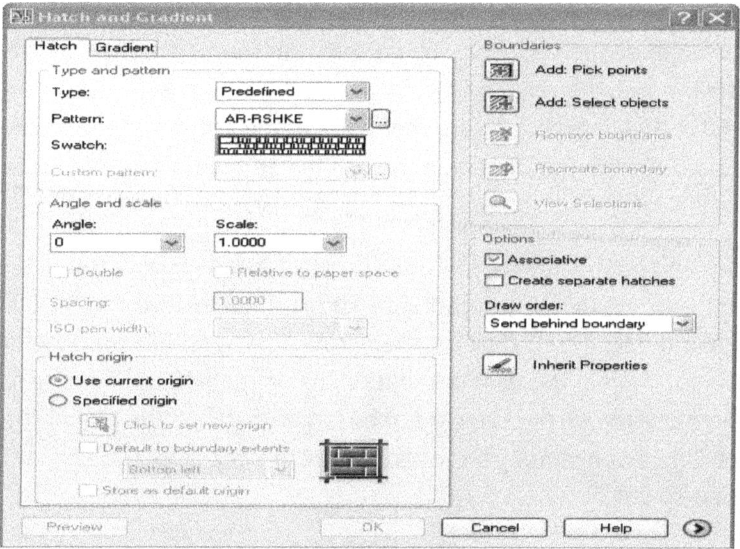

Figure 3-49

Now you should select the regions you want to create hatches in. To do this, click on the "Add: pick points" icon in the right-hand side of the window, then click on a point inside that region and press the Enter key to open the window again to select the type and settings for creating hatches. Now in the left-hand side of the window, choose the type, size and angle for creating hatches, and then press OK to finish.

35. HATCHEDIT command with HE shortcut

This command is used to edit hatches. For example, if you want to change the type, size or angle for creating hatches, click on the desired hatch and run the HE shortcut in the command line to open the hatch window for that hatch and adjust your settings.

36. QLEADER command with LE shortcut

This command is used to create an arrow and insert a text at the end of the arrow. For example, you should use this command if you want to create an arrow on the side of an asphalt road and write (toward the village) at the end of it. To do this, run the LE shortcut in the command line, then click on a point on the drawing area as the arrow tip. After that, left-click on another point as the bottom of the arrow and then right-click. Then type the desired text and press the Enter key.

If you can't see the arrow tip, it is because of its small size. To enlarge it, left-click on the arrow and type and run the PR shortcut in the command line. Then, click on the Arrow Size option in the Line & Arrows section in the window that opens on the left and enlarge it. Remember, the arrow size cannot be larger than half the size of the arrow line. For example, if the arrow is 20 cm, the arrow size cannot exceed 10 cm.

37. Mline command with ML shortcut

This command is used to draw two parallel lines with desired distance. For example, if you want to draw a dirt road about 5 meters wide, run the ML shortcut in the command line and to define the width, type S in the command line and press the Enter key. Now type 5 as the width and press the Enter key and then start drawing using the methods explained about drawing Line and Polyline.

Exercise 12

Draw a road 7 meters wide that crosses the points with these coordinates: (100, 900), (1200, 1600), (2200, 1500)

Answer:

To draw this road, run the ML shortcut in the command line and type S and press the Enter key. Then type 7 and press the Enter key again. After that, type 1000 as X and after typing the comma, type 900 as Y for the first point and press the Enter key. Then enter the coordinates of the next two points in the same way and then press the Enter key after entering each point. As the last step, close the command by pressing the Enter key again.

```
Command: ML MLINE
Current settings: Justification = Top, Scale = 1.00, Style = STANDARD
Specify start point or [Justification/Scale/STyle]:  S
Enter mline scale <1.00>:  7
Current settings: Justification = Top, Scale = 7.00, Style = STANDARD
Specify start point or [Justification/Scale/STyle]:  100,900
Specify next point:  1200,1600
Specify next point or [Undo]:  2200,1500
Specify next point or [Close/Undo]:
Command: '_.zoom _e
Command:
```

Figure 3-50

38. Offset command with O shortcut

When surveying urban and rural regions, land surveyors familiar with AutoCAD, do not fully survey linear features (features that are in fact parallel lines with fixed width along the whole of these features, such as driveway drain, roads and canals) to survey them faster. They only survey one side of it with its width and draw the other side of it in AutoCAD using the Offset command. For example, a land surveyor has surveyed a canal as in Figure 3-51.

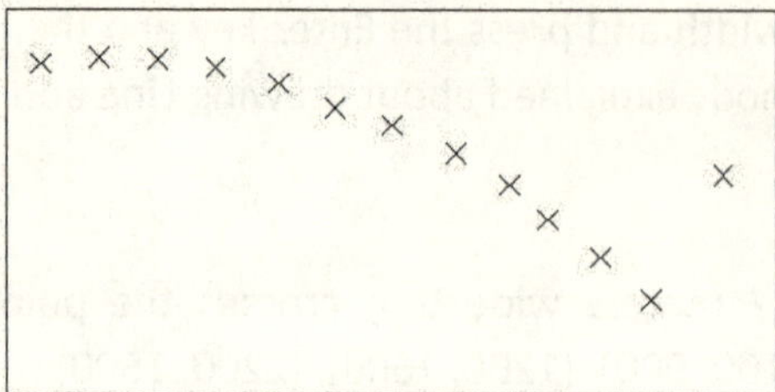

Figure3-51

As you can see, the land surveyor has surveyed one side of the canal completely and has surveyed only one point on the other side to specify its width. Now draw the other side of it using the Offset command.
To do this, first draw the side that has been surveyed using the Polyline command. Then left-click on the drawn line to select it. Then type and run the O shortcut in the command line to run the Offset command. Then click on the first point on the left and then click on the point on the right to enter the Offset width. Then if you click on the right side of the drawn line, the right side of the canal will also be beautifully drawn. In fact, you have offset the left side of the canal to the right side of it.

Offsetting is actually the action of drawing parallel lines while keeping all the changes of the shape with the desired width on the sides of the lines.

39. Point command with PO shortcut

This command is used to draw points. To do this, run the PO shortcut in the command line. Then you can draw the desired point using the coordinates or by left-clicking on the drawing area.

Important Note:

You can only draw one point using this command, and you need to run the command again to draw the next point. But if you want to draw a lot of points consecutively, you can select the Point option from the Draw menu and then select the Multiple Point submenu.

40. Setting point symbols with DDPTYPE command

Point symbols in AutoCAD are usually points. But if you want to change this symbol and view it as a special sign, select the Point Style option from the Format menu in the menu bars or type the DDPTYPE shortcut in the command line and press the Enter key to open the point symbols selection window as in Figure 3-52.

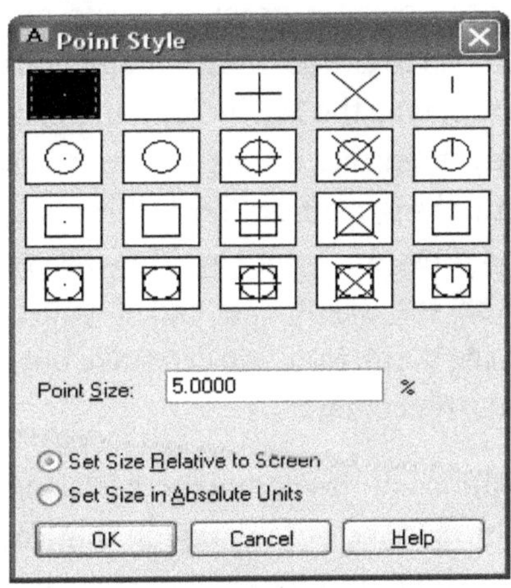

Figure 3-52

In this window, you can select one of the symbols and specify its size in the middle box. You can also specify whether the entered size is absolute or relative in the last section. Actually, the "Set Size Relative to Screen" option adjusts the symbol size relative to the screen and the "Set Size in Absolute Units" option adjusts the symbol size Absolutely.

41. Measure command with ME shortcut

This command is used to create points with desired distances on a line or a curve. For example, if you want to create points on a 1000-meter line with 50-meter distances, you should use this command. In order to do this, left-click on the line and select it, then type and run the ME shortcut in the command line. Then type the 50-meter distance in the command line and press the Enter key.

One of the applications of this command is to create horizontal reference points in order to grade an alignment, and extract the coordinates and stake them out. For example, you want to create horizontal reference points in order to grade an alignment in 25 meters. First, you need to extract the 25-meter coordinates from the alignment. To do this, type the ME shortcut in the command line and press the Enter key, then click on the alignment and in response to the "Specify length of segment or [Block]:" message, type 25 in the command line and press the Enter key. This will create points in 25-meter distances on the alignment, and if you change the point symbols, you can see them. Now you can stake out their coordinates by using the properties commands.

One of the applications of this command is staking out regions. For example, you want to stake out the region that you want to survey using Handy GPS without making a gap or collecting data more than needed. To do so, draw the region using the Polyline command, and type and run the ME shortcut in the command line. Then click on the desired region and type the desired distance, which is often 150 meters for flat regions, and press the Enter key. After that, extract the coordinates of the created points and stake them out in the desired region.

Drawing an arc with specific length on the perimeter of a circle

If you want to draw an arc with a specific length on a circle, first you should create its points using this command, then draw the corresponding line using those points.

For example, assume that you want to draw a 40-meter arc on a circle with a radius of 30 meters like Figure 3-53.

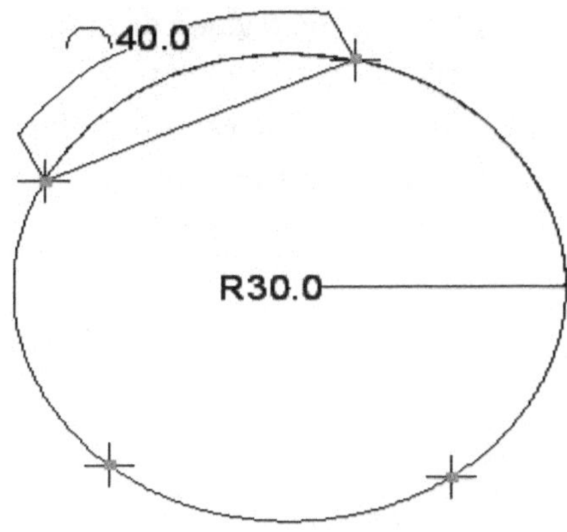

Figure 3-53

To do so, after drawing the circle, type and run the ME shortcut in the command line, then click on the desired circle and in response to the "Specify length of segment or [Block]:" message which appears in the command line, type 40 as the distance between each two points. After that, AutoCAD will create points in 40-meter distances on the circle. If you are not able to see the points, you need to change the display format of the points. Then draw a line between two created points using the Line command. After that, you can cut the circle relative to the drawn line using the Trim command.

But if you want to draw the arc in a way to specify its starting point, first you should draw a line at the specified point and cut the circle using the Trim command at that point, then use the Measure command.

42. Divide command with DIV shortcut

The application of this command is similar to that of the Measure command, except that it divides the selected line into a desired number and creates points at the divided distances. For example, if you have a 1000-meter line and want to divide the line into 25 sections, run the DIV shortcut in the command line, then select the desired line and type 25 and press the Enter key. As you can see, it creates points in 40-meter distances on this line.

1000/25 = 40

Setting drawing aid tools

AutoCAD has tools that speed up the drawing and editing process. For example, it can intelligently display the center of the circle, the start of the line, the end of the line, the middle of the line, the center of the point, the tangent points to the circle, etc. You can customize them as desired according to your task. To do this, you need to learn another shortcut.

43. OSNAP command with OS shortcut

If you type and run the OS shortcut in the command line, a window like the one in Figure 3-54 will pop up. This window has a number of drawing aid tools that help you when choosing objects while you are running drawing or editing commands. This means when you are running the command, if you move the mouse cursor close to the desired object, the shape of the snap will be displayed on that object.

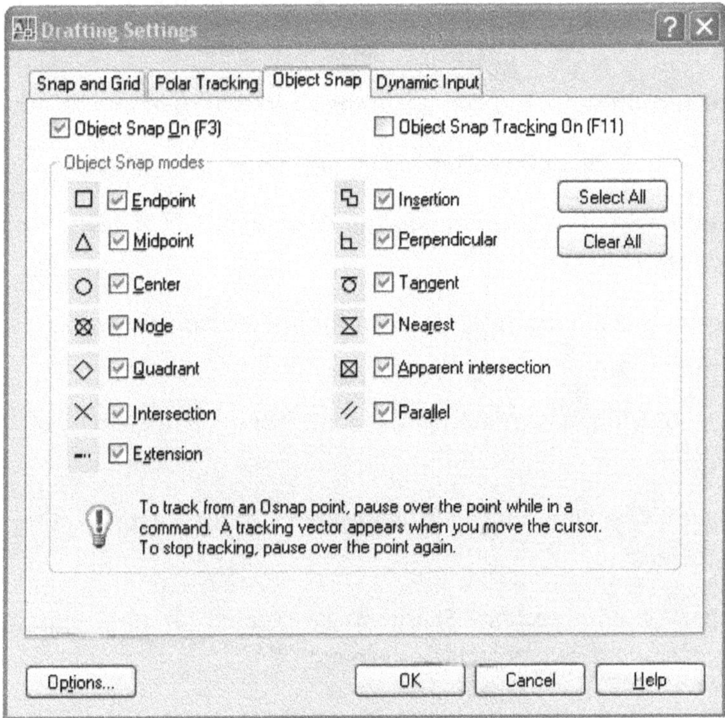

Figure 3-54

The exact location of the desired point on the object can then be selected by left-clicking. It should be noted that the shape of the snap created on the object is unique for each of these tools. Now each of these snaps will be explained.

Endpoint Snap: It is created at the start and end of each line segment.

Midpoint Snap: It is created in the middle of the line segment.

Center Snap: It is created at the centers of the circles and arcs.

Node Snap: It is created on the points.

Quadrant Snap: It is created at the locations of 0°, 90°, 180° and 270° angles, on the perimeter of a circle or an ellipse.

Intersection Snap: It is created at the intersections of two objects.

Extension Snap: It is created along the lines.

Insertion Snap: It is created at the creation points of texts, blocks and regions.

Perpendicular Snap: It is created at the intersection of two axes with right angles.

Tangent Snap: It is created at the point tangent to the circle, on the circle.

Nearest Snap: It displays the nearest point to the cursor location on the object.

Apparent Intersection Snap: It is created at the apparent intersection of two objects.

Parallel Snap: It appears when drawing lines, on the parallel line to the line that is being drawn.

Note:

The F3 key turns the OSNAP mode on and off.

44. Align command with AL shortcut

This command is used to match objects relative to the specified sizes. Consider the following example for a better understanding of this command.

Figure 3-55 shows a region that has been drawn like this after the initial surveying and drawing.

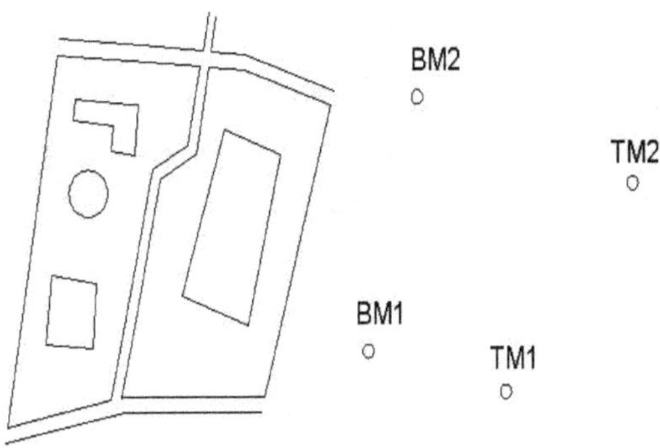

Figure 3-55

This region has been surveyed based on the BM1 and BM2 points located next to the region. But after the surveying finishes, you can notice that the coordinates of the points have been entered in the Total Station instrument incorrectly and the exact location of the points on the AutoCAD drawing area are points farther away. In order to correct this error, use the Align command and move the entire map to its actual location.

To do so, select all the drawings, then type and run the AL shortcut in the command line. After that, click on BM1 and set it to TM1. Also, click on BM2 and set it on TM2. Now transfer the whole map by pressing the Enter key and selecting “Yes”.

It is necessary to explain that using the “Yes” option will also apply the scale change. But if you use the “No” option, the scale change will not be applied.

In fact, it can be said that the Align function runs the Move and Rotate commands at the same time, and the SCALE command will also be applied if you use the “Yes” option. It is also worth noting that if the third point is used, the Scale function will be applied inevitably.

This command has many applications. One of the most practical applications of this command is to convert maps with Local coordinates to ones with UTM coordinates. In fact, this command performs the transformation operations.

Important Note:

Using this command, you can perform the transformation operation with three points at most. But if you want to perform the transformation operation with more than three points, you cannot do it using this command and you have to use the Adersheet command that can be ran by Civil 3D software.

45. Block command with B shortcut

This command is used to create a block. Blocks are a set of objects that are entered in the software in an integrated manner relying on a known point, and are used in different locations. For example, to display a light pole, create a symbol and enter it in the software as a block. Then place it wherever you want and this helps you draw each symbol only once. You can also use them in drawings for other projects too. For example, assume you intend to represent the symbol in Figure 3-56 as a symbol of radio masts.

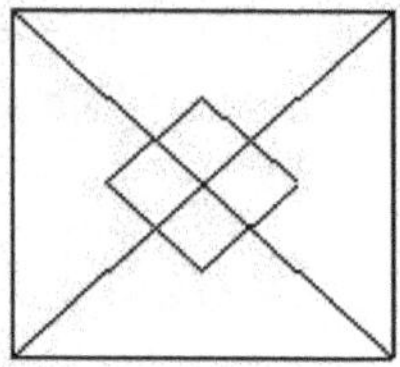

Figure 3-56

To do so, first you need to draw this symbol using drawing tools. After drawing it in standard dimensions, type and run the B shortcut in the command line to open the Block Definition window as in Figure 3-57.

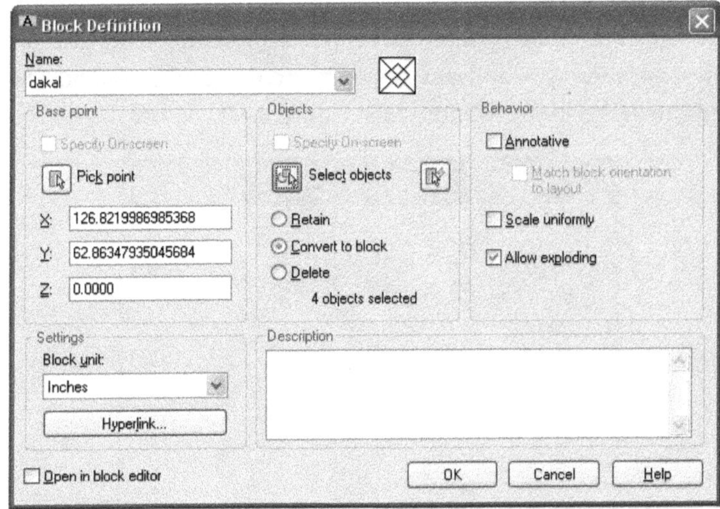

Figure 3-57

In this window, in the Name section, type in the name of your desired block and select the objects you intend to block using the Select object icon. Then, using the Pick point icon, set specific coordinates for the center of the block. The best way to set the coordinates of each symbol is clicking on its center, because in land surveying, symbols are used to display point features. After that, click OK in this window to save the block with a desired name.

Do not forget to set the Objects box to the Convert to block option, and if you check the Allow exploding option in the Behavior box, you will be allowed to explode it when inserting it; otherwise, it cannot be exploded.

46. Write Block command with W shortcut

This command is used to save a block with a desired name, which can be used wherever you want. For example, after drawing the above block, you want to save it as a block with a desired named.

To do so, first create a block with a desired name using the block command, then type and run the W shortcut in the command line to open the Write Block window as in Figure 3-58.

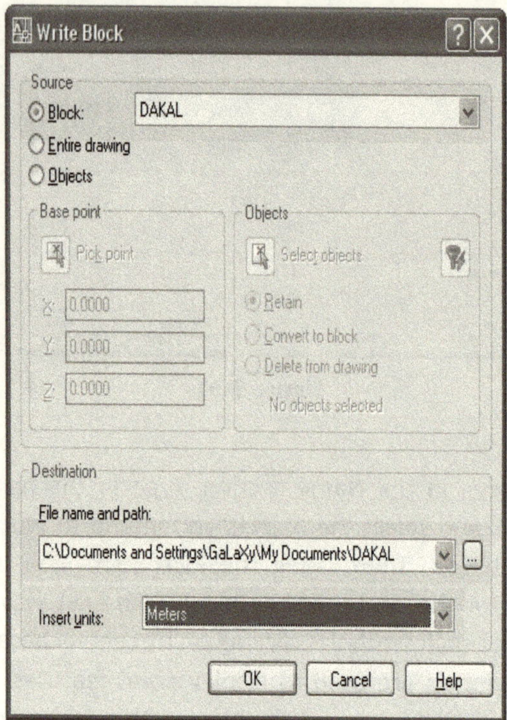

Figure 3-58

Select the Block mode in the Source section of this window and select the name of the desired block that was created in the previous section in the box in front of it.

In the Destination box, and in the "File name and Path" section, select the path and the name of the block, and in the Insert Units section, select the block insertion unit. Usually this unit is set on meter. After completing the steps above, click OK on the window to save the block. In the next section, after learning the Insert command, you will learn how to insert a block into other drawings.

47. Insert command with I shortcut

This command is used to insert the desired block or another file into the drawing. For example, assume that you have surveyed a region where there is a mast, now you want to insert the symbol of the mast that you made for the block in the previous exercise. To do so, type and run the I shortcut in the command line to open the Insert Block window as in Figure 3-59.

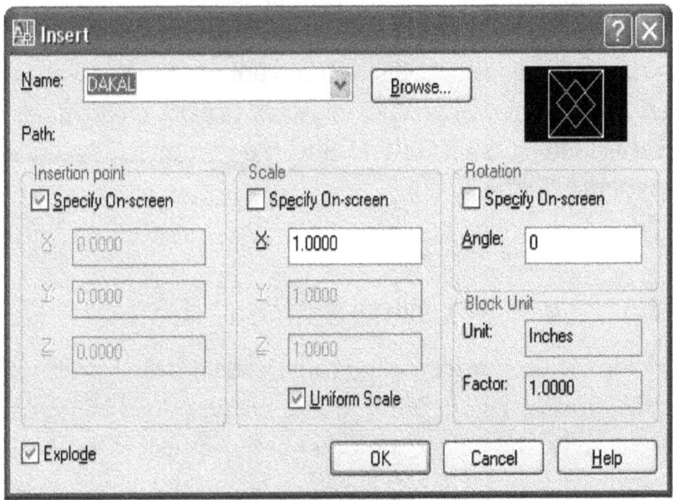

Figure 3-59

In this window, using the Browse option, find the desired block or file in the save path and insert it into the desired location using the

OK option. If you check the Explode option before inserting it, the block will be inserted in an exploded manner.

What is a Layer?

When there are many features in the drawings and the drawings are complex and contain too much details, in order to make them tidier, easier and more efficient to work with, the objects in the drawing are moved to different layers, and depending on the need, each type of object is located at a different layer so that you can turn it off or unable it when not needed. Layers also provide the user with additional capabilities and conveniences that will be discussed later. If you have different types of features in the drawing such as roads, canals, land, buildings or trees, you can put any type of feature into a layer. For example, when you only want to work on buildings, turn the corresponding layer on and turn the rest of the layers off. It makes it much easier to draw.

Now how can you create a layer?

48. Layer command with LA shortcut

By running the LA shortcut in the command line, the Layers window will pop up as in Figure 3-60. In this window, you can create or remove a layer and adjust the other settings related to the layers such as the color of the layer, line weights, turning the layer on and off, making the layer current and the other layer settings.

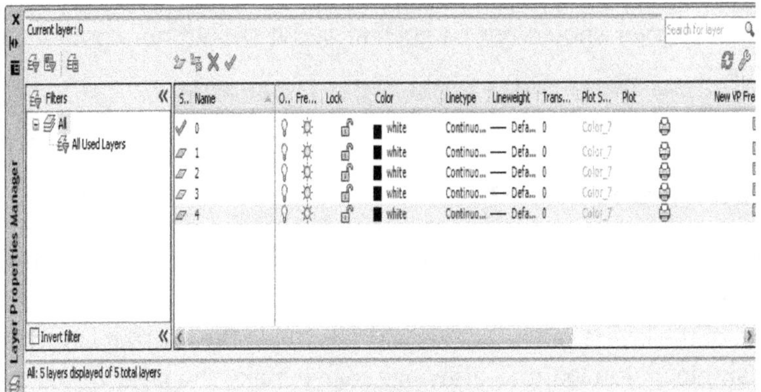

Figure 3-60

How to create a new layer

To create a new layer, click on the icon on the left side of the figure in the Layers window, or use the Alt+N keyboard shortcut. After doing this, you can choose the desired name for the layer, and you can adjust the other settings such as turning it off and on, freezing, locking, the layer color, the line type and the other settings in the opposite sections, respectively.

Setting the Plot mode is one of the most important settings. If this option is off, some of the objects in that layer will not be printed when plotting.

How to delete a layer

In this figure, a layer can be deleted using the third icon (from the left side). To do this, select the desired layer, then click on the icon to delete that layer. It should be also noted that the layer should not be current and it should not contain any objects.

What is a current layer?

You may have a drawing made up of multiple layers. Among these layers, you can only work on one layer at a time. In other words, only one of the layers can be active, which is called the Current Layer. For example, if you want to draw dirt roads, make the layer of the dirt road current and all the drawings will be in that layer as long as it is current.

How to make a layer current

To make a layer current, you just need to click on the layer you want to work on. Then click on the icon on the right side of this figure to make the layer current. As soon as you make the desired layer current, the name of the current layer will appear at the top of the layers window as in Figure 3-61.

Current layer: 4

Figure 3-61

How to move objects from one layer to another one

If you have forgotten to draw a feature in a layer, or if you intend to move objects to another layer, for example, if you have drawn the dirt road features in the canal layer and now want to move them to the dirt road layer, do as follows.

First, select those features, then as shown in Figure 3-62, click on the layer icon at the top of the page in the Layers toolbar to open the list of the layers. After that, click on the desired layer so as to move the selected features to this layer.

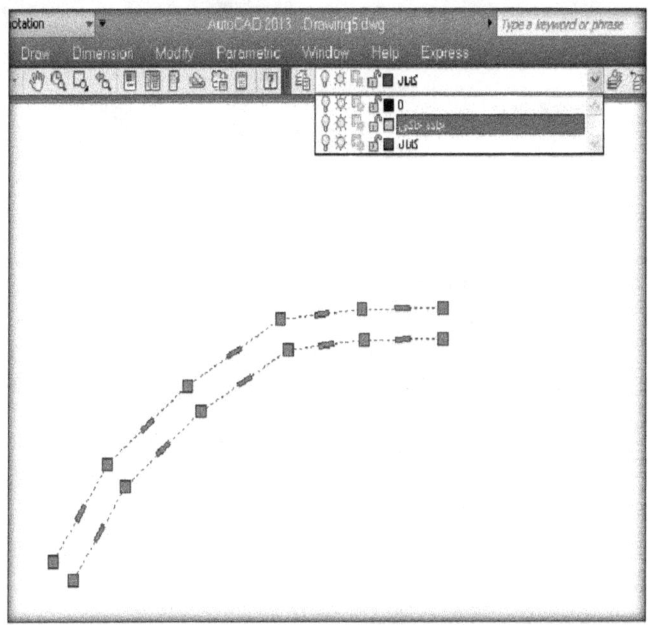

Figure 3-62

To find out that each feature is in which layer, click on the desired object or feature on the drawing area to display its layer name in the Layers toolbar at the top of the page.

Another way to move objects from one layer to another is to use the Properties window. In order to do so, after selecting the desired objects, run the PR shortcut in the command line so that the Properties window appears as in Figure 3-63. In this window, click on the Layer option in the General section to open the list of the layers. Then click on the layer that you want to move the desired objects to.

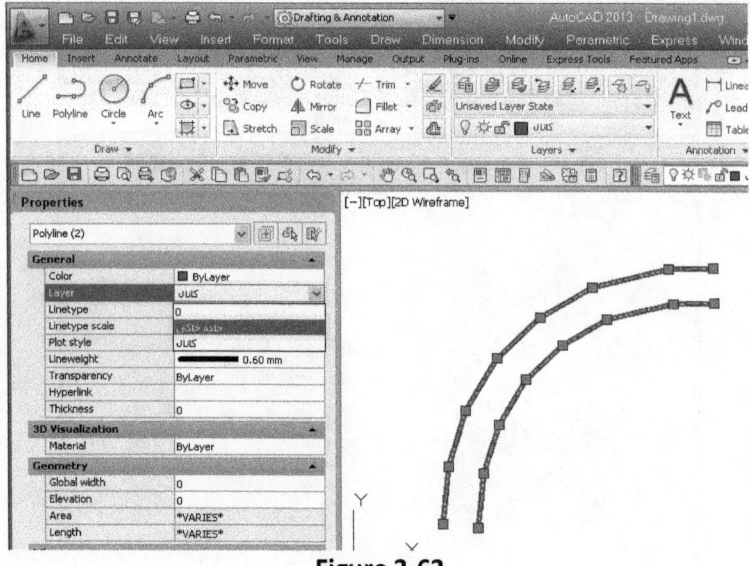

Figure 3-63

How to quickly turn layers off

49. LAYOFF command

If you want to turn a layer off in a drawing full of features and details, normally you should first open the layers window, then click on the desired layer. But the designers of AutoCAD have assigned commands to do the job faster. One of these commands is the LAYOFF command. So, click on one of the objects in that layer, then type and run the LAYOFF command in the command line. As you can see, the layer turns off faster without having to open the layers window.

How to quickly turn all layers on

50. LAYON command

This command is used when trying to turn all the layers in the drawing on. To do this, run the LAYON command in the command line. If you want to use another method to turn all the layers on, you should open the Layers window and turn each layer on one by one. As you know, it will take more time and using the LAYON command is much faster and easier.

51. LAYISO command

If you want to work on just one of the layers in a drawing with multiple layers, and want to temporarily turn off or lock the rest of the layers to have more control and focus over the drawing, as you may know, using the Layer Window and turning on or off each individual layer is very time consuming, but it can be done quite easily using the LAYISO command. You should click on one of the objects in that layer to select it, then run the LAYISO command in the command line.

Of course, sometimes you also need to have a fade view of the rest of the layers other than the only layer you want to keep turned on.

As you can see in Figure 3-64, the Channel layer is turned on, but the rest of the layers are not turned off; they are locked and a fade view of them is visible.

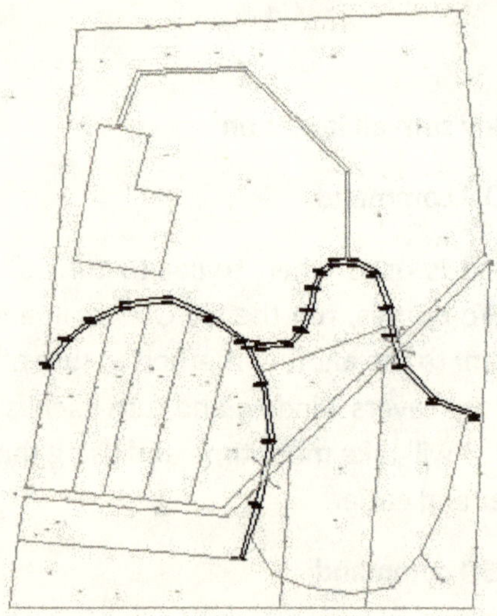

Figure 3-64

To do this, after running the LAYISO command, select the Settings mode by typing the letter S and press the Enter key, then select the Lock and fade option by typing the letter L and pressing the Enter key. After selecting this option, the command line asks you for the fading value, which you can provide by typing a number from 0 to 90. The closer this number is to 90, the greater its degree of fading would be.

It is necessary to know that this mode of the command is operative in AutoCAD 2008 version and above.

To practice more, try it with different layers and different degrees of fading.

52. LAYUNISO command

This command is used when you want to go back to the initial mode after running the LAYISO command and making changes and drawing on the desired layer. So, run the LAYUNISO command in the command line to go back to the previous mode.

Difference between the commands Layon and Layuniso

Some users think that the commands *Layon* and *Layuniso* do the same thing, but obviously this is a wrong misconception. To understand the difference of these commands, consider the following example.

A drawing contains 20 layers, of which 17 are enabled and 3 are disabled. Now, after enabling one of the enabled layers with the *Layiso* command, we will have 1 enabled layer and 19 disabled layers. Note that of these 19 disabled layers, 3 were disabled from the beginning, and the remaining 16 were disabled by the *Layiso* command. Now, if we use the *Layuniso* command, only the 16 layers that got disabled by the *Layiso* command will be re-enabled. In contrast, using the *Layon* command will enable all the layers, including those three that were originally disabled.

How to quickly make a layer current

53. LAYMCUR command

This command is used to quickly make a layer current. In order to do so, run the LAYMCUR command in the command line, then click on one of the objects in the desired layer so that the layer becomes current.

How to quickly delete a layer

54. LAYDEL command

So far, you have learned how to delete a layer using the Layers window, but now a quick way to delete a layer will be introduced that is using the LAYDEL command. To do so, type and run this command in the command line. By running this command, the following message will be displayed in the command line:

Select object on layer to delete or [Name]:

This message tells you to click on one of the objects in the layer or enter its name. So, by clicking on any object, its layer will be deleted and if you want to enter the name of the layer, type the letter N and press the Enter key. This will open a window that displays the list of all the layers in the drawing as in Figure 3-65. If you click on any layer in this window and then click OK, that layer will be deleted. However, before it gets deleted, a message will be displayed asking you to make sure that you want to delete the layer and you should select OK.

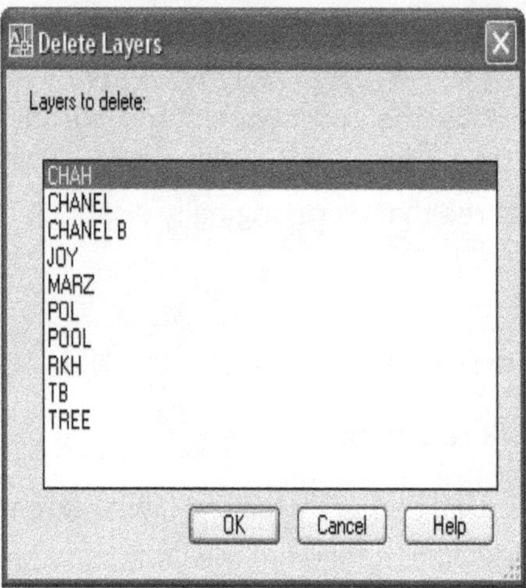

Figure 3-65

How to lock a layer

55. LAYLCK command

A locked layer is a layer that is visible on the drawing area, but no editing operations such as moving, rotating or deleting can be performed on it. This feature of layers is widely used in drawings. Sometimes in drawings, some of the commands affect a series of objects due to negligence and carelessness, like deleting objects that you do not want to delete. Therefore, it is suggested to lock the layer when drawing if you are not working on it.

To do so, run the LAYLCK command. By doing that, the message below will appear in the command line:

Select an object on the layer to be locked:

This message asks the user to click on an object from the layer you want to lock. After clicking on any object, the corresponding layer will be locked and a message will appear as shown below:

Layer "MARZ" is already locked.

56. LAYULK command

This command is used to unlock layers. To do so, run the LAYULK command in the command line, then click on one of the objects in the locked layer to unlock the layer.

57. LAYCUR command

This command is used to move the objects to the current layer. To do so, run the LAYCUR command in the command line. The following message will appear in the command line after running the command:

Select objects to be changed to the current layer:

This message asks the user to select the objects intended to be moved to the current layer. Once you have selected all the objects, press the Enter key and the objects will be moved to the current layer.

58. LAYMCH command

This command is used to move objects to a desired layer. To do so, type and run the LAYMCH command in the command line. By performing this action, the "Select objects" message will appear in the command line. So, select the desired objects and press the Enter key. The following message will appear:

Select object on destination layer or [Name]:

You can now select the destination layer by clicking on one of the objects in that layer or typing the letter N and pressing the Enter key. Then, enter the name of the destination layer.

Merging two or more layers

59. LAYMRG command

This command is used to merge two or more layers. To figure out the widespread applications of this command, see the following example.

Figure 3-66 shows a part of a map of a region that includes a dirt road, a gravel road and an asphalt road, and each one is in its own layer. Now you want to have all of these roads together in a new layer named Road.

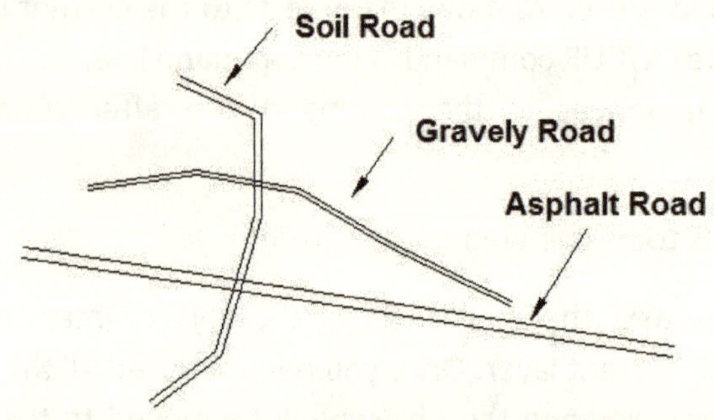

Figure 3-66

To do so, first create a layer named Road, then run the LAYMRG command in the command line so that the message below shows up:

Select object on layer to merge or [Name]:

This message asks you to select the layers you want to move. So, you can click on one of the objects in those layers, or type the letter N in the command line and press the Enter key to display the layers window and select them (You can select multiple layers by holding the ctrl key).

After selecting all the three layers of dirt road, gravel road and asphalt road using one of the two methods mentioned above, press the Enter key to display the following message:

Select object on layer to merge or [Name/Undo]:

This message asks you for the destination layer, the layer you want to move these three layers to. This can be done using one of the two methods mentioned above. That is, either click on one of the objects in that layer, or type the letter N in the command line and press the Enter key and click on the desired layer in the window that appears. The important point in this command is that all the three initial layers will be deleted.

60. Match Properties command with MA shortcut

Whenever you want to change all the properties of an object such as layer type, line type and color to the properties of another object, use this command. Although there are other methods, this shortcut does it much faster. For example, if there are lines in a dirt road in a drawing and you draw the dirt roads again, if the features that you have drawn later are not in the dirt road layer and you want to locate those features in that layer, there would be two methods to do the job:

The First Method:

As mentioned before, select the desired objects and features, then click on the icon next to the toolbar to open the list of the layers. Then select the desired layer to locate the selected objects into that layer. You can also use the LAYCUR command.

The Second Method:

The second method is using the MA shortcut. So, click on one of the objects in the desired layer, then type and run the MA shortcut in the command line. Now if you click on any object from any layer, that object will be moved to the desired layer. Of course, as mentioned before, this command not only changes the object layer to the desired layer but also changes all of its properties.

It is important to know that the customizable properties can be adjusted. For example, it can be adjusted in a way that this command only changes the line weight.

To adjust this command, after running it and clicking on the desired object, just type the letter S in the command line and press the Enter key so that the Property Settings window pops up as in Figure 3-67.

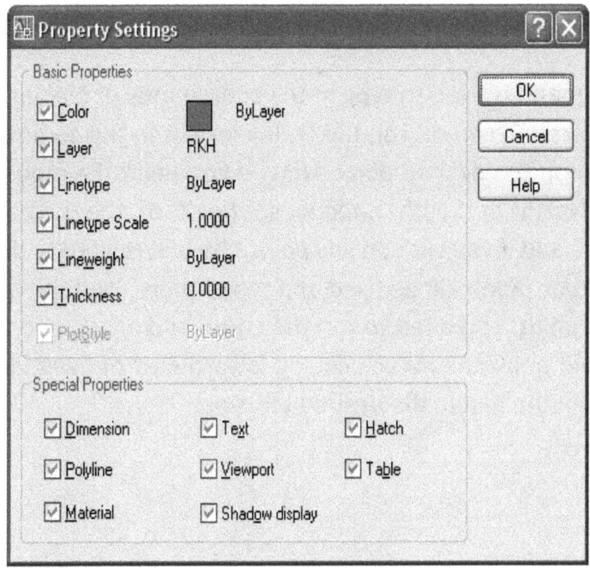

Figure 3-67

In this window, you can adjust the command in order to specify which type of object properties should change into properties of another object. For example, if you only want to change the color of the objects using this command, just check the Color option in this window and if you only want to make sure that the line weights will not change by this command, just uncheck this option.

Measuring point coordinates

61. Identity command with ID shortcut

This command is used to measure the coordinates of a point. To do so, after typing the ID shortcut in the command line and running it, if you click anywhere on the drawing area, the coordinates of that point appears in the command line as you can see below:

Command: **ID** Specify point: X = 9064.4397 Y = 4034.0243

Typing in point coordinates into the drawing area

62. DIMORDINATE command with DOR shortcut

This command is used to type in the coordinates of a point into the drawing area. To do so, run the DOR shortcut in the command line, then click on the desired point. Now, if you point the mouse cursor toward North or South directions, the X of the point will be displayed, and if you click on any point, the text related to displaying the X of that point will be fixed and typed there. And to type in the Y of that point, you need to run the command again, and this time you should point the mouse cursor toward East or West directions and type in the text in the desired location.

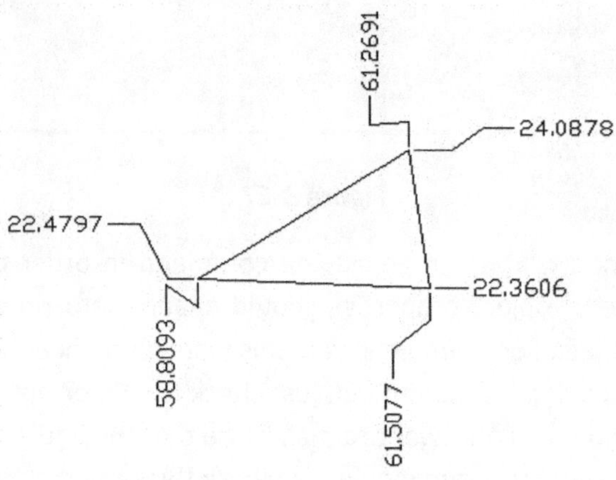

Figure 3-73

Measuring dimensions of a line

63. DIST command with DI shortcut

This command is used to measure ΔX and ΔY and the distance between two points. To do this, simply run the DI shortcut in the command line and click on the two desired points respectively. Then ΔX and ΔY and the value of the distance between the two points will appear in the command line. It should be noted that this command does not insert the measurements, but only calculates and displays them in the command line.

Command: **DI** DIST
Specify first point:

After this message appears, click on the first point:

Specify second point or [Multiple points]:

Now click on the second point:

Distance = 707.11 , Angle in XY Plane = 59.033g , Angle from XY Plane = 50.000g

Delta X = 300.00 , Delta Y = 400.00 , Delta Z = 500.00

Items reported by running this command:

Distance: The distance along the slope

Angle in XY Plane: The horizontal angle between two points

Angle from XY Plane: The right angle between two points

Delta X: The distance between two points along the X-axis

Delta Y: The distance between two points along the Y-axis

Delta Z: The difference in elevation or distance between two points along the Z-axis

One of the applications of this command is measuring the distances that have more than two vertexes. For example, if you want to calculate the length of the line drawn in Figure 3-74, there are several methods to do the job such as using the List command. But this command can be used when the lines are Polylines. You can also use other methods, but the fastest method is using the DIST command.

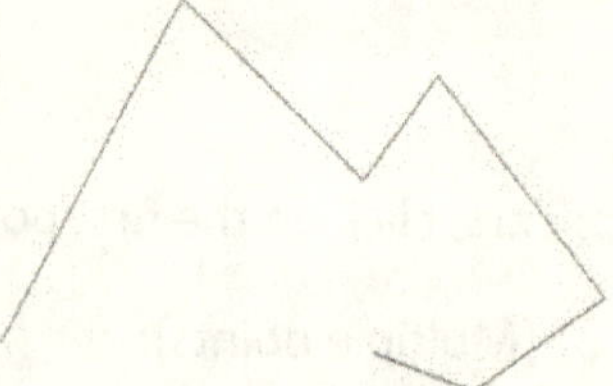

Figure 3-74

To do so, type the DI shortcut in the command line and press the Enter key, then click on the starting point of the line, and type and run the M shortcut in the command line to select the Multiple points mode and press the Enter key and then click on the other points respectively. Anywhere you click, the software reports the total of the distances relative to that point.

Creating dimensions of a line

64. DIMLINEAR command with DLI shortcut

This command is used to insert the dimensions of a line into the drawing area. As shown in Figure 3-75, type the DLI shortcut in the command line and press the Enter key, then click on the two points at the start and the end of the desired line respectively, and hold the mouse cursor on the desired point and click again to insert it into that point. And to insert the other dimension of the line, run the command again and repeat the operation.

In fact, by using this command, the values of ΔX and ΔY between two points will be inserted on the drawing area.

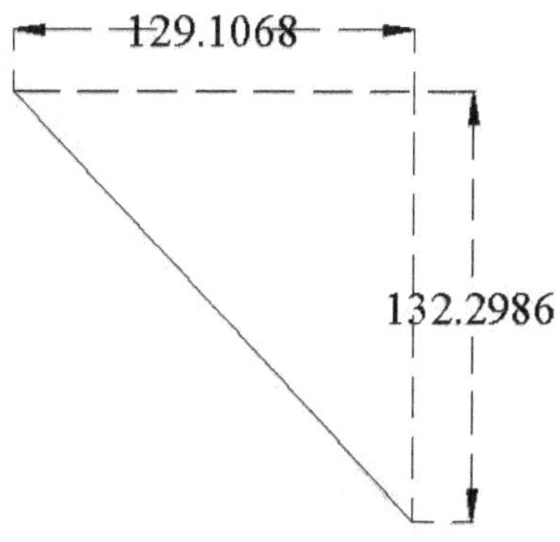

Figure 3-75

Measuring and creating dimensions of the length of a line

65. DIMALIGNED command with DAL shortcut

This command is used to measure and create dimensions of the lengths of lines. Use this command whenever you want to know the length of a drawn line and insert the value of its length next to it. For this purpose, type and run the DAL shortcut in the command line. After that, click on the two points at the start and end of the lines respectively and then insert the length value wherever you want.

It should be noted that this command inserts the horizontal distance between two lines.

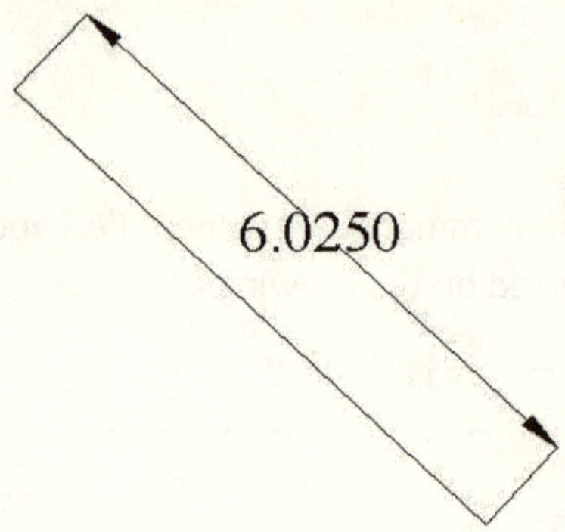

Figure 3-76

Measuring and creating dimensions of the angle between two lines

66. DIMANGULAR command with DAN shortcut

This command is used to measure the angle between two lines. To do so, run the DAN shortcut in the command line, then click on the two sides of the desired angle respectively and insert the value into a suitable location. As you can see, the value of the desired angle is both displayed in the command line and inserted on the drawing area.

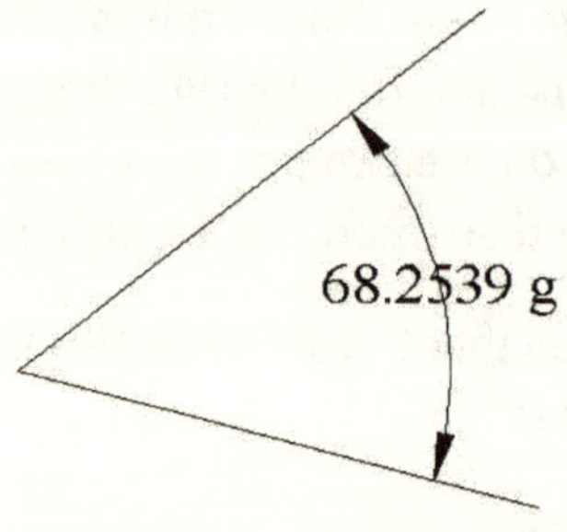

Figure 3-77

Quick measurement relative to the base point

67. DIMBASELINE Command with DBA shortcut

This command is used to quickly measure different distances from the first inserted dimension. Assume you want to insert the distances of the other points from the first inserted dimension in the

profile in Figure 3-78.

Figure 3-78

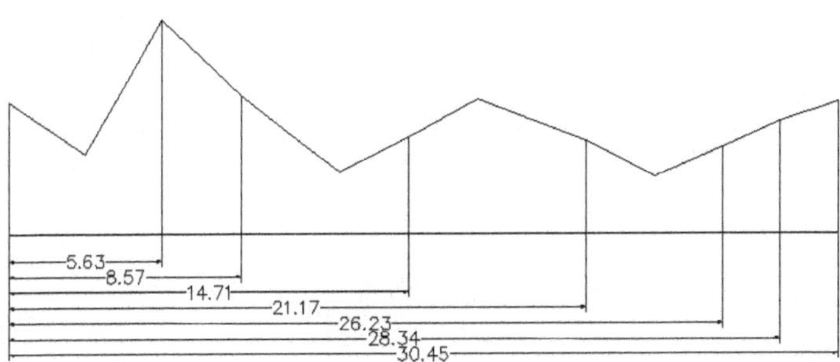

Figure 3-79

So, first insert the first dimension using the commands for creating dimensions which you have already learned. Then type and run the DBA shortcut in the command line and click on the desired dimension. Now by clicking on other points, you actually insert the dimension of those points relative to the base point on them. It should be noted that this command is used only for lines that are in the same direction.

Quick measurement relative to the previous point

68. DIMCONTINUE command with DCO shortcut

The function and the speed of creating dimensions by this command are similar to the previous command, except that the basis for the measurements in this command is its previous point. For example, as shown in Figure 3-80, if in the example of the previous command, you want to have and insert the distances between the points in the profile, type and run the DCO shortcut in the command line. Then after clicking on the first dimension, click on the other points in the section to insert the values of the distances between the points.

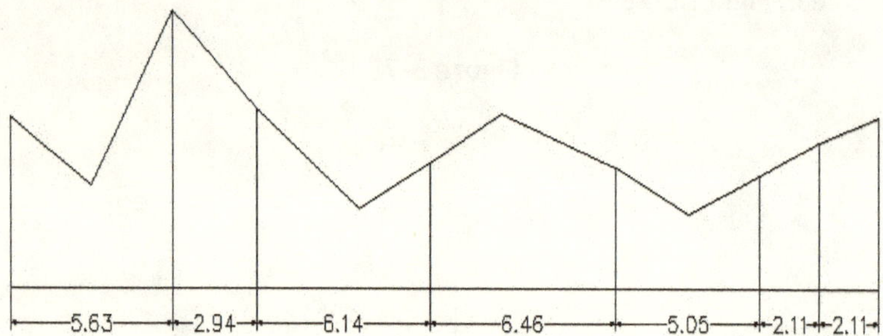

Figure 3-80

Settings for dimension texts

69. DIMSTYLE command with D shortcut

This command is used to adjust the settings for dimension texts. These settings include text size, text font, text color and text shape. To adjust the settings, run the D shortcut in the command line. As you can see, after running this command, a window like the one in Figure 3-81 pops up.

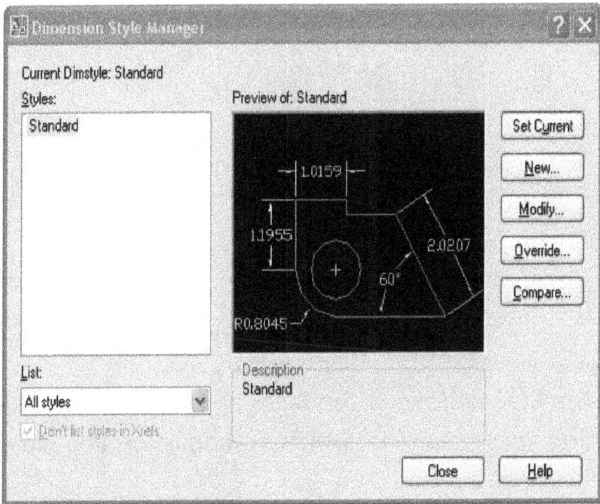

Figure 3-81

In this window, click on the Modify option to open the corresponding window. (Figure 3-82)

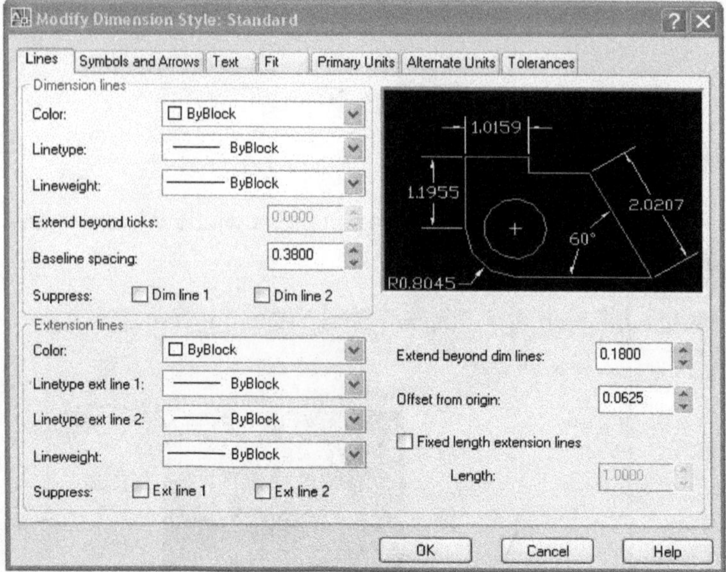

Figure 3-82

In the Modify window, in the Line tab, adjustments related to the dimension lines are made, which include color, line weight, format, and so on.

Adjustments related to the dimension arrows are made in the Symbols and Arrows tab.

In the Text tab, adjustments related to the dimension texts are made, including text color, text size, text font and text position (vertical and horizontal).

The Fit tab is related to the position of the arrows and texts.

In the Primary Unit tab, set the length and angle units of measurement. In this tab, you can set the length unit of measurement, the number of decimal places and the decimal symbol, as well as the angle unit of measurement and the number of decimal places of the angle value. It is recommended that you set this window according to Figure 3-83. It means the length unit of measurement should be Decimal with 3 decimal places and the angle unit of measurement should be Grad with 4 decimal places.

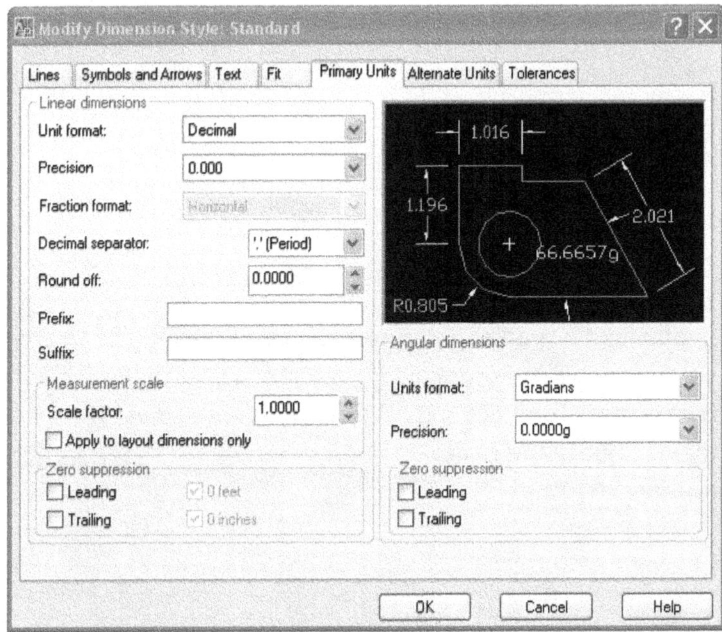

Figure 3-83

The other two tabs include other text settings which will not be explained as they are unnecessary.

Once you have made these adjustments, confirm them by clicking OK, and in the next window that opens, after clicking OK, make these adjustments current by clicking on the Set Current option.

70. DIMARC command with DAR shortcut

This command is used to measure and insert the length of an arc. To do this, type and run the DAR shortcut in the command line. Then click on the desired arc and insert its dimension wherever you want by left-clicking.

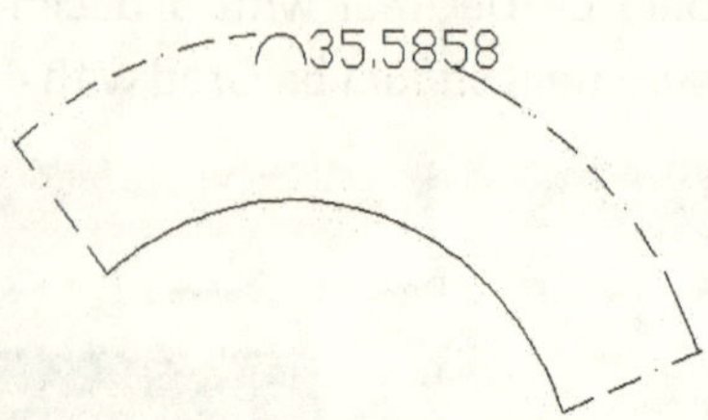

Figure 3-84

71. DIMRADIUS command with DRA shortcut

This command is used to measure and insert the radius of an arc. To do so, run the DRA shortcut in the command line, then click on the desired circle so that the software calculates its radius. Then insert its radius value in the circle.

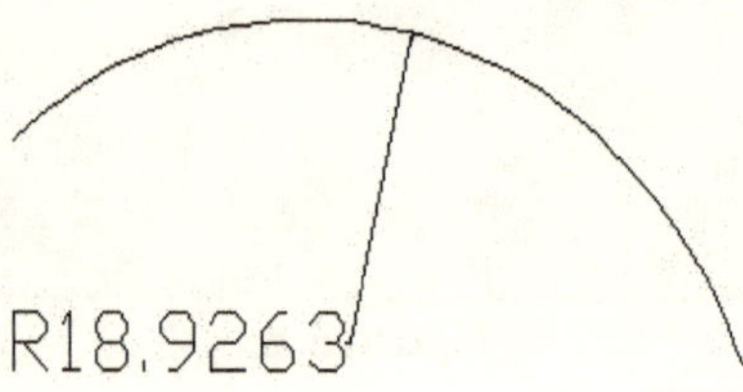

Figure 3-85

72. DIMCENTER command with DCE shortcut

This command is used to draw the center of a circle or an arc. For this purpose, run the DCE shortcut in the command line. Then click on the desired arc or circle to draw its center.

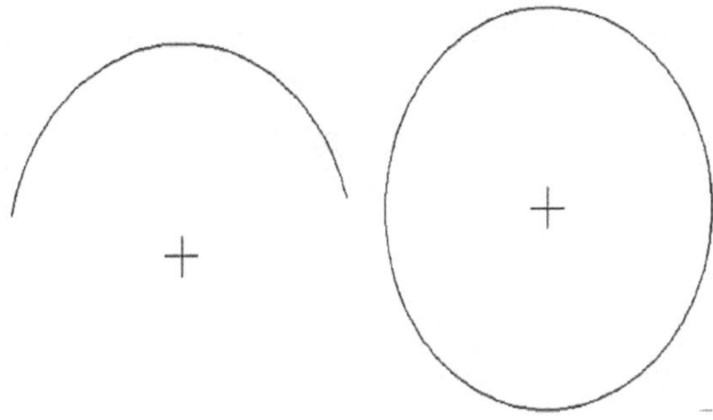

Figure 3-86

73. Quick Select command with QSELECT shortcut

You may have a large set of different objects in a drawing including lines, circles, texts and Polylines and want to work on them. For example, you have a lot of texts that you want to resize, or you want to change the color of them all, or you want to locate them in a new layer, or any other editing operations that requires selecting groups of objects. To make operations like these, first you need to select them. As you know, when you are drawing and editing a map full of features and details, selecting objects becomes very difficult. For example, if you want to edit the texts in a layer, even if you keep only that layer turned on, this is still a difficult task to do, because the layer you want may contain other objects other than texts, and the texts in that layer may have an disorganized distribution, which is the matter you will face in land surveying drawings. That is why the AutoCAD's designers have designed this tool so that the users do their editing and drawing tasks more quickly and accurately. To do so, first run the QSELECT shortcut in the command line so that the corresponding window opens up as in Figure 3-87. This window gives the user the abilities and ease of selecting objects.

Important Note:

Remember, before running this command, you need to make sure that none of the objects in the drawing are selected. To make sure, you can use the Esc key on the keyboard to make any selected object unselected.

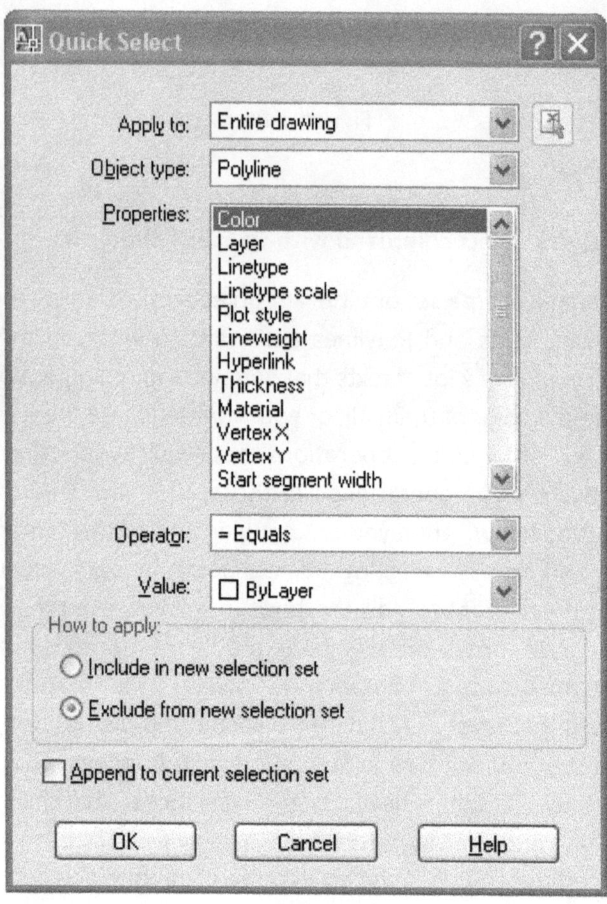

Figure 3-87

To further understand, the command will be explained using a few practical examples.

Example 1: Editing the texts in a layer

Open the Select1.dwg file. As you can see, this file contains a map of an urban region where the building blocks are displayed and the name of each building block is inserted, all of which are in a layer named Blockname. But the size and height of the text that represents the name of each building block is very small, and it is intended to triple the text height that contains the names to display it better. To do this, run the QSELECT shortcut in the command line so that a window pops up as in Figure 3-88.

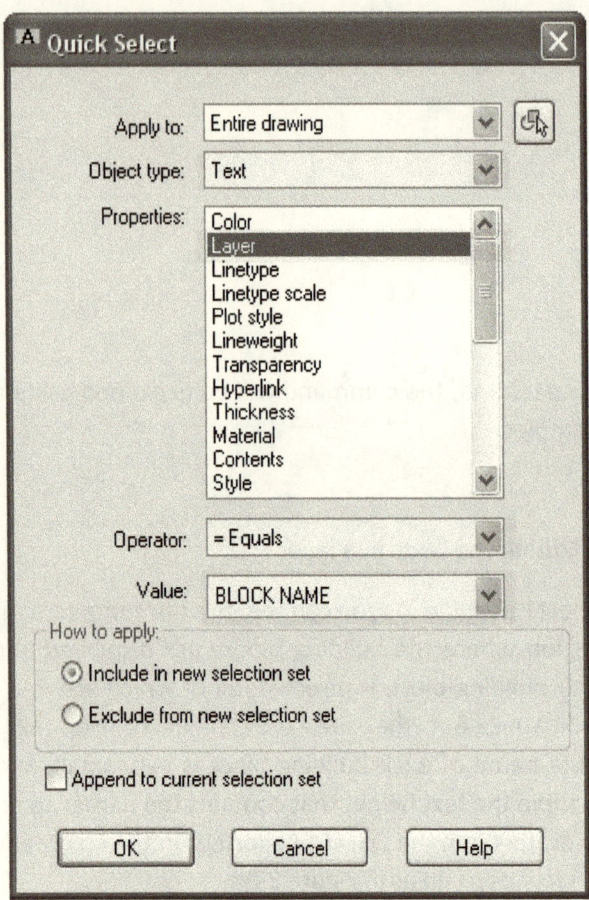

Figure 3-88

Now in the upper section of the window, in front of the Object type option, select the type of the object which is Text, set the Properties section to Layer mode, set the Operator section to =Equal which means "it equals to", and select the name of the layer in the Value section which is Blockname. And in the end, click OK to confirm all the selections that you have made. As you can see, all the texts in the Blockname layer are selected. The main problem with this task was selecting the options which was successfully done. Now, you can perform any kind of editing task. For example, if you want to move these texts to another layer, click on the layer from the drop-down menu next to the Layers toolbar to do so. Or, if you want to change their color, use the Properties menu and if you want to delete them, type and run the E shortcut in the command line.

Now, as you want to increase their height in this example, run the CH shortcut in the command line to open the Properties window as in Figure 3-89.

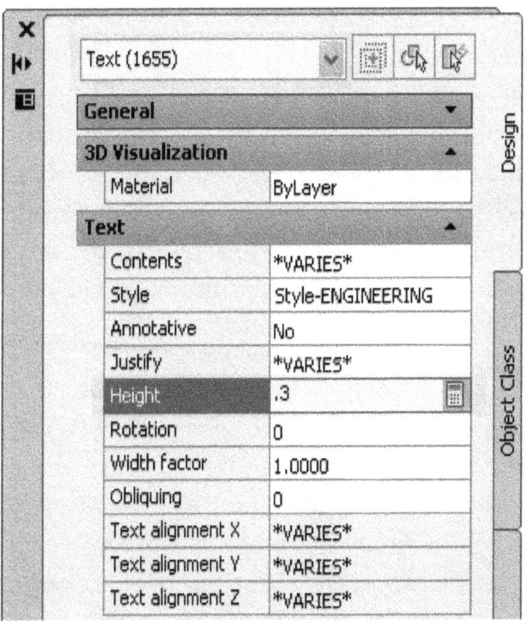

Figure 3-89

In the upper section of this window, you will see the number of selected texts which is 1655. Now to increase their height, in the Text tab, in front of the Height option, type in your desired size and press the Enter key. Here, as you intend to triple it, change the number from 0.1 to 0.3.

Example 2: Identification of open land plot polylines

When drawing cadastral maps, it is important to ensure that all land plot polylines are closed. This is important because open land plot polylines can cause error in extracting information, making measurements, adding information labels, and linking the maps to ArcGIS databases. For a small drawing, this can be done manually by checking land plot polylines one by one. But for large drawings, manual checking of all land plot polylines will be extremely difficult and time consuming. An easy way to accelerate this process is to use the *Quick Select* command. To learn this method by practice, open the file plineclose.dwg, which is a drawing of 13 land plots.

As you can see, it is difficult to visually distinguish the closed plots from the open ones. To identify the open plots, type and execute the shortcut command *qselect* to open the *Quick Select* window shown in Figure 3-90. As shown in the figure, set the *Object type* menu to *Polyline* and set the *Properties* menu to *Closed*. Since the goal is to select open polylines, set the *Operator* menu to <> *Not equal* and select the *Yes* option in the *Value* menu. After pressing OK, the polylines with the specified property will be selected.

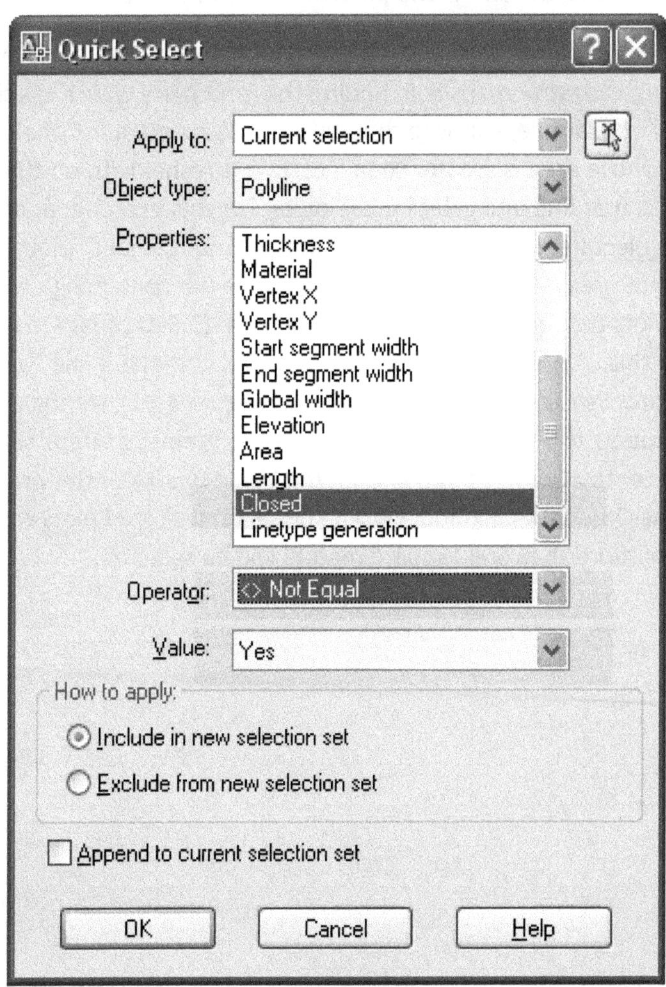
Quick Select
Apply to:
Current selection
Object type:
Polyline
Properties:
Thickness
Material
Vertex X
Vertex Y
Start segment width
End segment width
Global width
Elevation
Area
Length
Closed
Linetype generation
Operator:
<> Not Equal
Value:
Yes
How to apply:
Include in new selection set
Exclude from new selection set
Append to current selection set
OK
Cancel
Help

Figure 3-90

Example 3: Selection of land plots with a specified area

Another convenient use of the *Quick Select* command when drawing cadastral maps is in finding the land plots with a specified area. For example, suppose that we want to create a list of all land plots whose area is greater than a certain threshold. To do this, we need to first find and select those plots. For this exercise, open the file qselectarea.dwg, which is a drawing of 29 land plots with different areas. Here, the goal is to create a file containing only the land plots that are larger than half a hectare (5,000 square meters). To do this, run the *qselect* command in the command line to open the *Quick Select* window. In this window (Figure 3-91), set the *Object type* menu to *Polyline*, set the *Properties* menu to *Area*, set the *Operator* to *>Greater than*, and set the *Value* to 5000. After pressing OK, the *Quick Select* window will be closed and all land plots with an area of more than 5000 square meters will be selected.

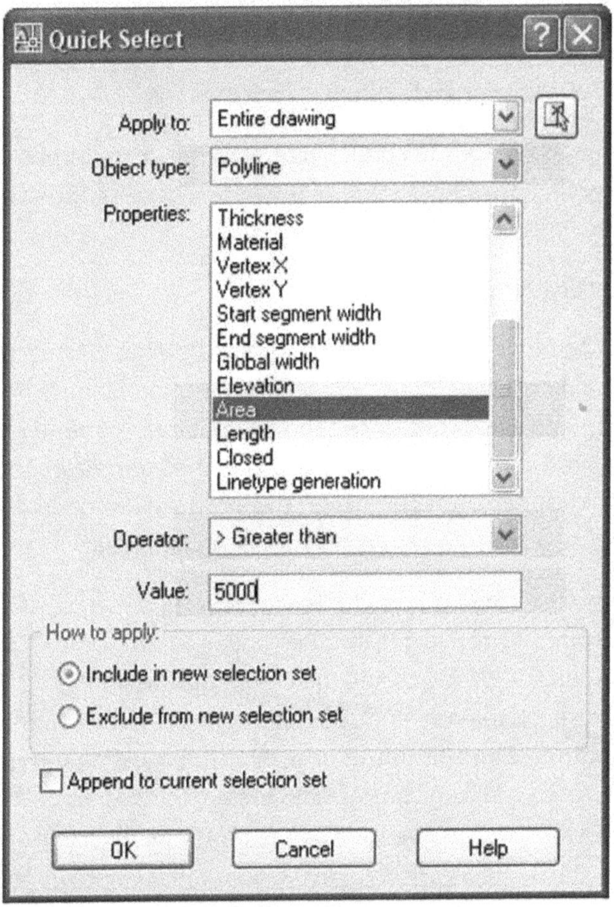

Figure 3-91

To transfer these plots to another file, simply execute the *Copy* command and paste them in the other file. Further details regarding Copy and Paste operations will be provided in the next chapter.

Please note that while advanced users may find such exercises rudimentary, the importance of this command and such simple solutions cannot be overstated. Moreover, mastering this command can assist all users to find their own convenient solutions for more complex drawing problems.

74. PEDIT command with PE shortcut

This command is used to edit Polylines and has many applications in land surveying drawings. Some of the applications of this command are:

1. Converting Line to Polyline

As mentioned before, most of the times, Polyline is used to draw lines in land surveying drawings, and the Line command is not much useful for land surveyors since the Join action is not done on Lines. You can only Join Polylines. And this is one of the major problems that cartographers face (However, this problem has been fixed and Lines can also be Joined in versions 2010 and above).

So, you should convert Lines to Polylines. Now if you only have one Line and want to convert it to a Polyline, just click on that line and type and run the PE shortcut in the command line. Then the "Do you want to turn it into one? <Y>" message appears in the command line and you can give an affirmative answer to the question by typing the letter Y, and you can cancel the messages that appear in the command line by pressing the Esc key on the keyboard. As a result, that Line turns into a Polyline. To make sure of this, simply select the line and type and run the Properties command with the CH shortcut so that it appears at the top of the Properties window. Now you can see which type of line you have. As you can see, it has become a Polyline.

But if you have multiple joined lines without breaks, you can convert them to Polylines and Join them simultaneously. To do so, click on one of the lines, then type and run the PE shortcut in the command line. Then give an affirmative answer to the message that appears in the command line by typing the letter Y, and in the appeared sections, select the Join option by typing the letter J. Then click on the other lines and press the Esc key to close the command. As you can see, your lines have not only become Polyline but they have also become Joined.

2. Adding a vertex to the drawn Polyline

In land surveying drawings, when you want to draw linear features using the surveyed points on the drawing area, you might sometimes find that the drawn line has not crossed a particular point. For example, in Figure 3-93, the drawn line should also cross point 3, but due to drawing errors, it had not happened.

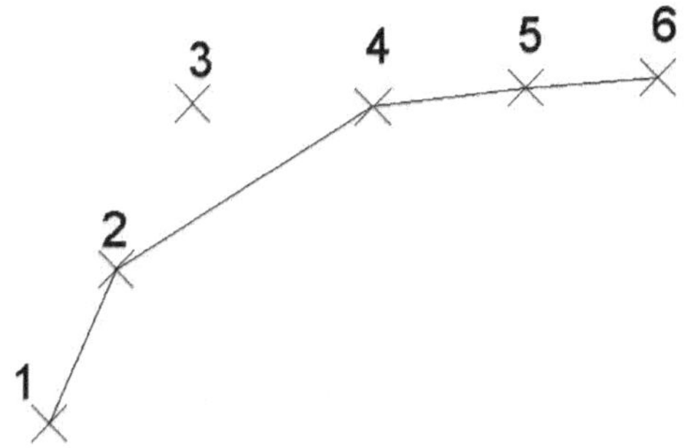

Figure 3-93

Now there are two methods to edit this line. In the first method which is using the simple editing commands, first you should break the drawn line in points 2 and 4 using the Break command and connect the broken point to point 3 using the mouse, then join the lines again using the Join command.

But as it is obvious, this method is time-consuming. The AutoCAD designers were aware of this matter and have introduced a simpler and faster method to the users which is using the PEDIT command. To do this, run the PE shortcut on the drawn Polyline and select the Edit vertex option from the appeared sections. You can type and run the letter E in the command line to select this mode. As you can see, the marker that specifies the Edit vertex option appears on point 1. After selecting the Edit vertex option, another menu will appear like the previous menu with other options, and since you want to edit the section between points 2 and 4, you should move the marker to point 2 by selecting the Next option or typing the letter N. Then to add and insert point 3, select the Insert option, then move the marker to point 3 using the mouse. As you can see, the new line also crosses point 3.

To gain more mastery, open the “Insert vertex.dwg” file and practice it.

However, in versions after AutoCAD 2009, adding a vertex is quite easy.

For this purpose, if you click on the desired Polyline and then hold the mouse for a moment on a point where you want to add a point, a menu appears as in Figure 3-94. Now if you click on the “Add Vertex” option, you can easily add another point.

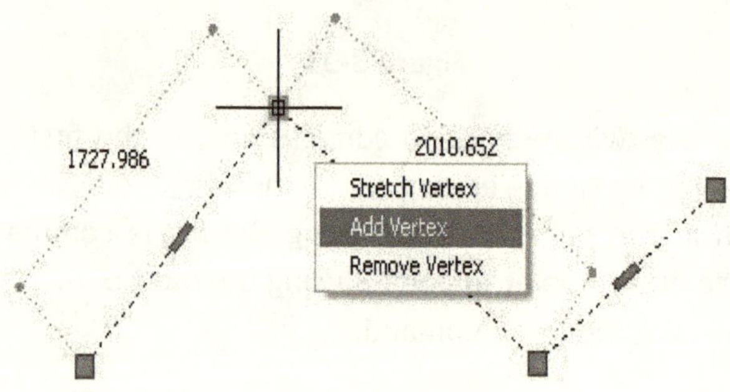

Figure 3-94

Finding a particular text and replacing it with another one

75. FIND command

Use this command whenever you want to find a particular text in a drawing. To do so, run the FIND command in the command line or select the Find option from the Edit menu so that the Find and Replace window pops up as in Figure 3-95.

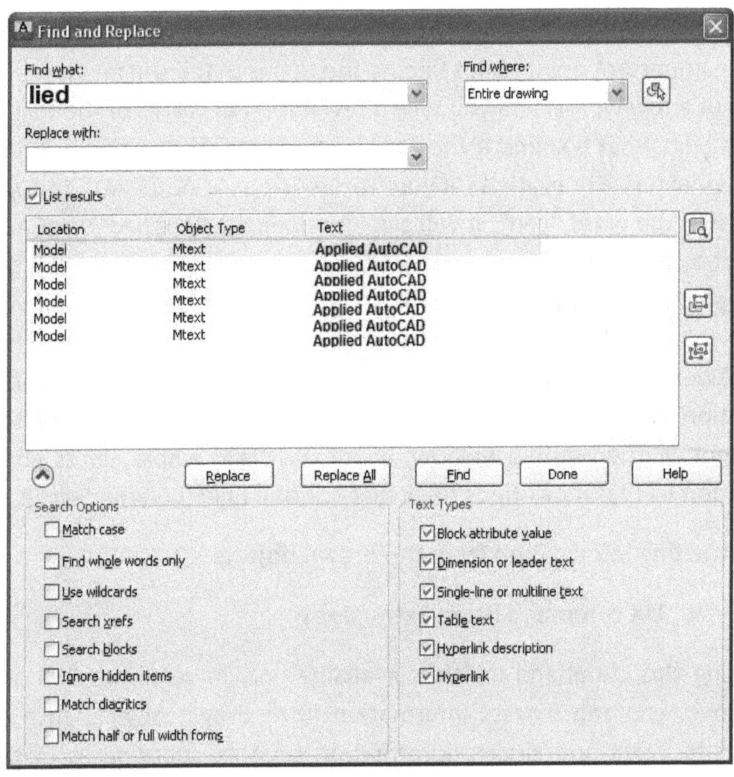

Figure 3-95

In this window, type the desired text in the "Find what" section and click on the Find option to find it. If the desired text is in the drawing area, it will appear in the List result box, and if you want to view it on the drawing area, click on the icon. Now if you want to replace this text with another one, type the desired text in the "Replace with" box and click on the Replace option, and if you want to apply the replacing action to all the texts, click on the Replace All option.

This mode can be used to change the feature descriptions in drawings.

The important point about finding the text is that if the text is made up of a few words, and you type a few letters or words of the text in the Find what box and try to Find it, it will search and find it in the original text. For example, if your text is "Applied AutoCAD" and you search the word "lied", it will also consider the "Applied AutoCAD" text as one of the found texts, because it contains the word and the Replace action will also be effective and applicable to it. Now if you only want to find the texts that contain only the word or letter that has been typed in the Find what box, you need to click on the Search option so that the search modes appear at the bottom of the window. Then in this window, check the "Find whole words only" option so that it just finds texts that contain only the typed word.

Extracting information from the drawn objects

76. DX command (Data Extraction)

Using this command which is available only in versions 2009 and above, you can extract information from drawn objects such as points, texts and circles. Information such as coordinates of the points, line angles, layers, colors and line weights, which can be saved in specific formats like txt, csv, xls, and many other supported Excell formats. The data extraction file can be saved in .dxe format so that you can edit it if needed.

To run this command, you can select the Data Extraction option from the Tools menu or run the DX command in the command line as in Figure 3-96.

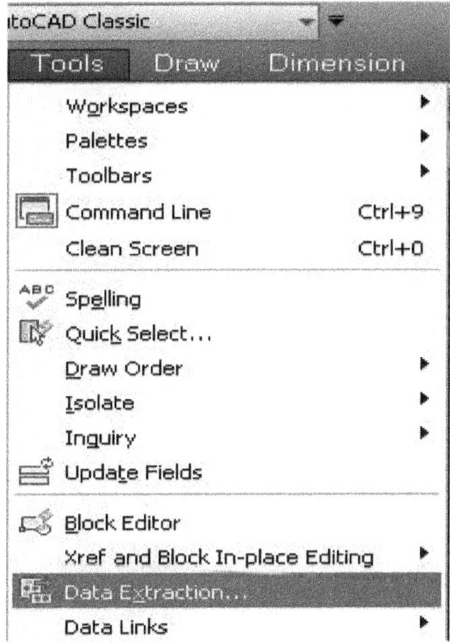

Figure 3-96

To gain more mastery over the applications of this command, it will be explained with a few examples.

Open the Extract.dwg file. As you can see, this file contains a Cadastral map of a region that contains objects such as lines, points, texts, and so on.

Assume you need to generate an export from the points inside this file that contains the position of the points X, Y and Z.

For this purpose, after using the Data Extraction option using one of the methods mentioned above, you will see that the first page (out of 8 pages) of the Data Extraction option opens up as in Figure 3-97.

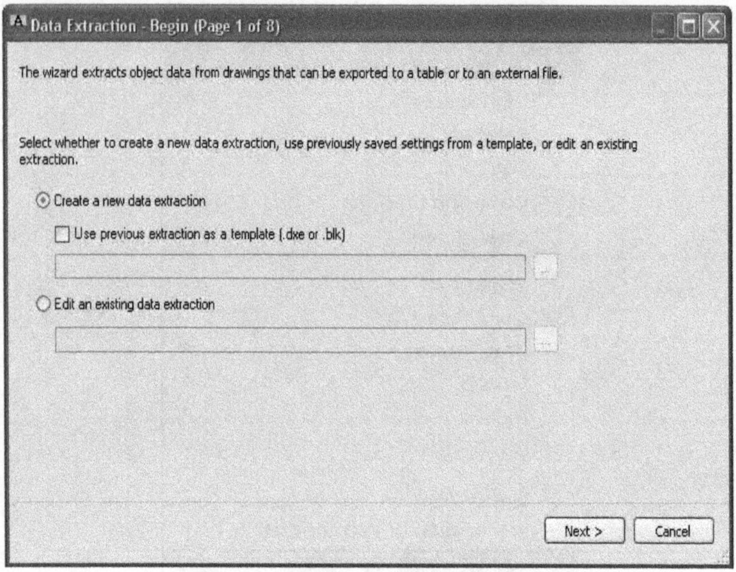

Figure 3-97

To create a new data extraction in this window, enable the "Create a new data extraction" option, and if you want to use the previous extraction, also check the "Use previous extraction as a template" option, and if you want to edit the previous extraction, enable the "Edit an existing data extraction" option.

Now to create a new data extraction, enable the "Create a new data extraction" option and click on the Next option. By clicking on this option, a window will pop up as in Figure 3-98 that asks the user for the name and the storage path for the .dxe data extraction file.

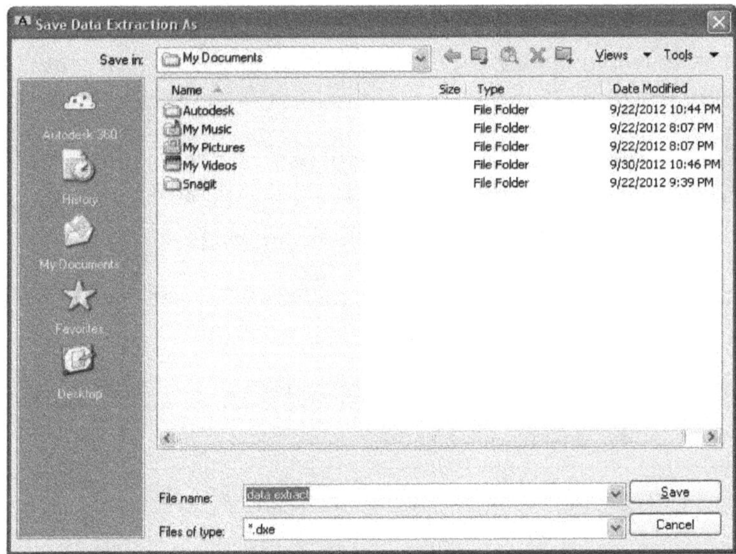

Figure 3-98

In this window, enter the storage path of the file in the "Save in" section, and enter the file name in the "File name" section, then click on the Save option to open the second page of this operation as in Figure 3-99.

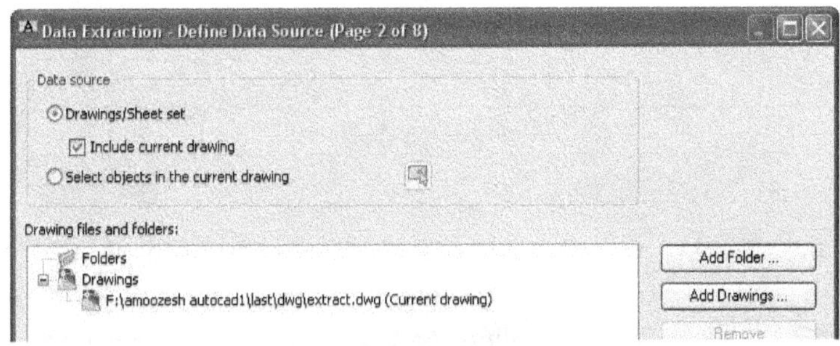

Figure 3-99

In this window, if you want to extract information from all the objects in the drawing, enable the "Drawing/Sheet set" option, and if you want to extract information from one or more specific objects in the drawing, enable the “Select objects in the current drawing” option and using the icon next to it, select the desired objects.

By clicking on the Add Drawing option, you can add another drawing to extract the information from, and by using the Add Folder option, you can add a folder containing multiple drawings.

After adjusting the above settings, click on the Next option to display the third page of this operation as in Figure 3-100.

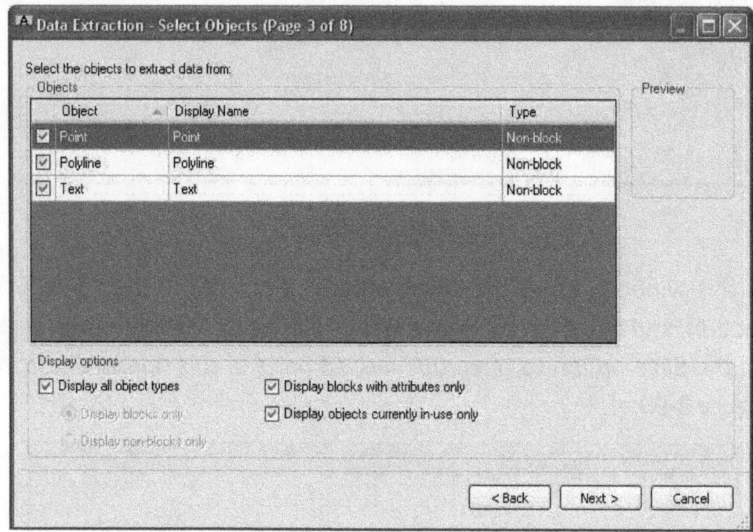

Figure 3-100

All the objects that are selected or exist on the drawing area are listed in this window. As you can see, there are three types of objects in this drawing: Points Polylines and Texts. Now since it is intended to generate an export from the points, just keep the Point object checked and uncheck the rest, then click on the Next option again so that the fourth page of the operation pops up as in Figure 3-101.

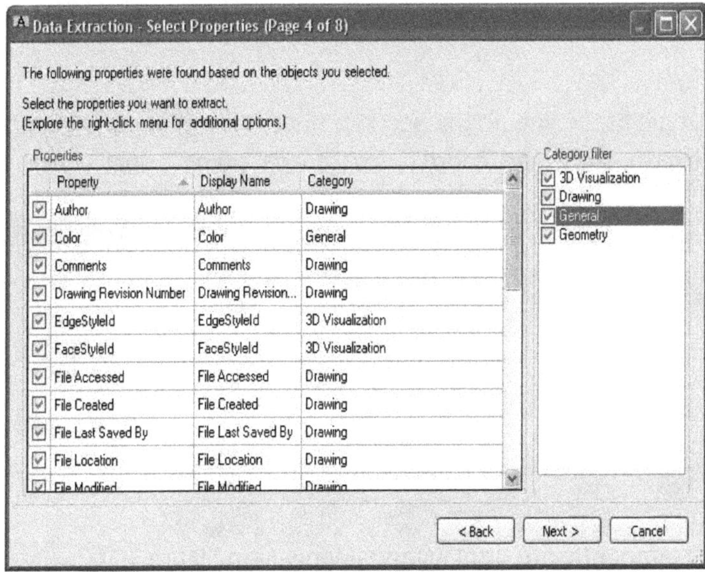

Figure 3-101

There is a box named Category filter at the right side of this window, where you can see four types of drawing information. The first category is called 3D Visualization, which is related to the 3D display information.

The second category that is called Drawing is related to drawing information such as file name, file size, storage path, map title, and so on.

The General category is related to color, layer, line weight and so on.

The last category is called Geometry, which is related to the geometrical information of the objects in the drawing, which varies depending on the type of the objects. For example, the geometrical information of a point is limited to the position of its x, y and z, and the geometrical information of a line refers to the position of x, y and z of its start and end of the line, the length of the line and also the angle of the line. In this section, since it is intended to generate an export from the coordinates of the points, only check the

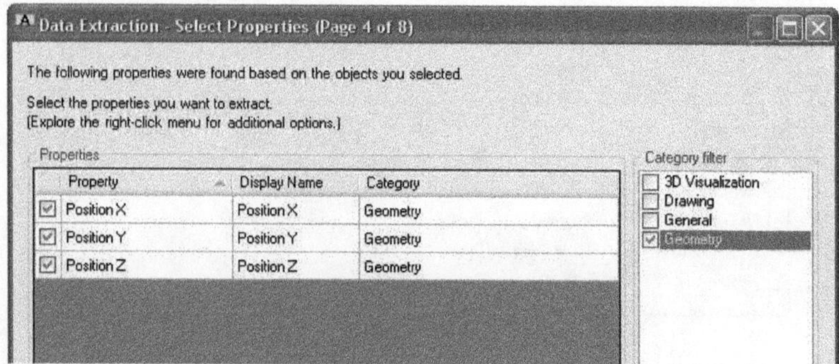

Geometry option to display this window as in Figure 3-102.

Figure 3-102

As you can see, only the position of x, y and z of the points are displayed. So, click on the Next option to open the fifth page of this operation as in Figure 3-103.

Data Extraction - Refine Data (Page 5 of 8)

In this view you can reorder and sort columns, filter results, add formula columns, and create external data links.

Count	Name	Position X	Position Y	Position Z
1	Point	379365.0000	4465987.0000	0.0000
1	Point	379366.9776	4465986.7017	0.0000
1	Point	379373.9791	4466015.8450	0.0000
1	Point	379376.1180	4466014.3938	0.0000
1	Point	379381.3124	4466048.3721	0.0000
1	Point	379383.6804	4466048.8032	0.0000
1	Point	379376.9583	4466078.3016	0.0000
1	Point	379379.5046	4466079.1114	0.0000

Combine identical rows

Link External Data...

Figure 3-103

Now for each point, the position of its x, y and z is displayed. Then click on the Next option. This will open the sixth page of the operation which is related to the method of saving the information as in Figure 3-104.

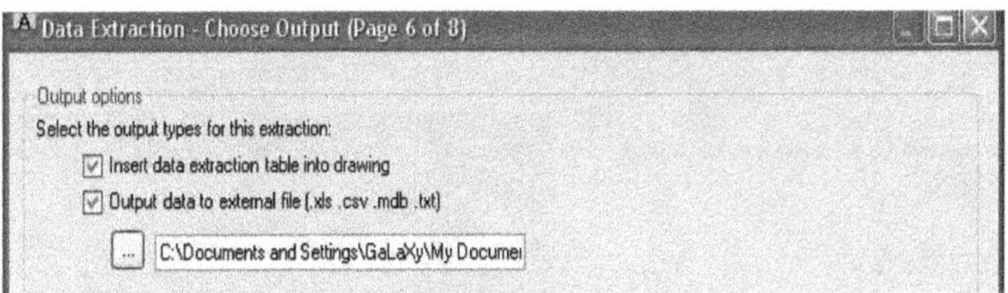

Figure 3-104

If you check the "Output data external file" option, you can select a storage path and a storage format for the information by clicking on the icon below it, and if you check the "Insert data extraction table into drawing" option, you can insert the extracted information as a table on the drawing area in the next step. Now at this step, check both options, then click on the icon below it to open the next window as in Figure 3-105.

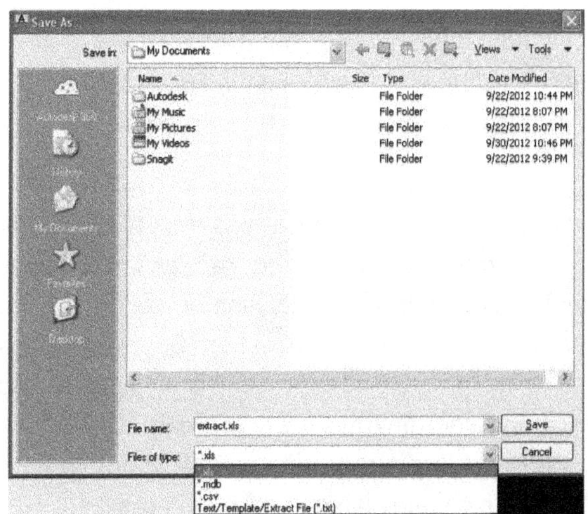

Figure3-105

In this window, select a path, a name and a format for the data extraction file, and click on the Save option, and on the same page, click on the Next option to create the file with the desired format and path. For the settings related to the insertion of the table, go to page 7 as in Figure 3-106.

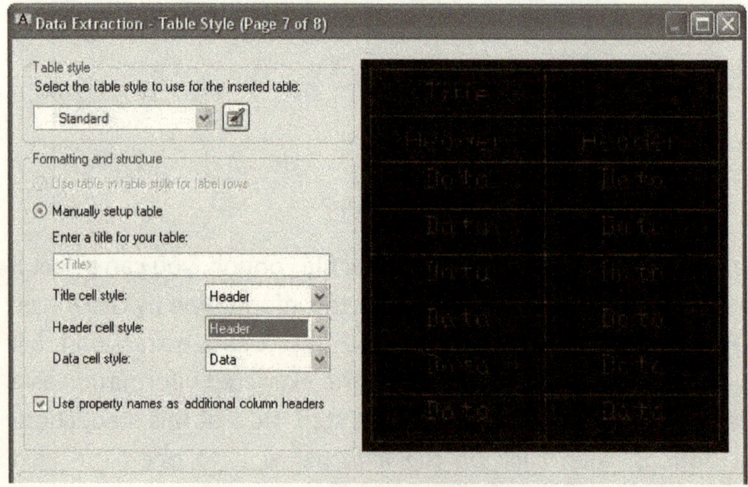

Figure 3-106

On this page, adjust the settings for the table insertion action and click on the Next option, then click on the Finish option on the eighth page, and then use the mouse to select a point on the drawing area to insert the table.

This command has many applications for land surveyors. For example, using this command, you can generate exports from parcels that have been drawn as Polyline or Region, mentioning the area, the perimeter and other information. Or you can extract a type of information from the texts inside the drawing that also contain the text insertion coordinates. Then you can edit the texts in the Excel software and insert them in their locations again using the Excel functions which is explained in the next chapter.

Eliminating duplicate and similar objects

77. OVERKILL command

In general, the basic function of this command is to eliminate objects that are similar and overlapping. For example, assume that two or more Lines are overlapping. By using this command, you can keep one of them and eliminate the rest.

To do this, run the OVERKILL shortcut in the command line. By running this command, the "Select Object" message appears in the command line to select the objects you want to eliminate their duplicates. After selecting the desired objects and pressing the Enter key, the "Delete Duplicate Objects" window will appear as in Figure 3-107.

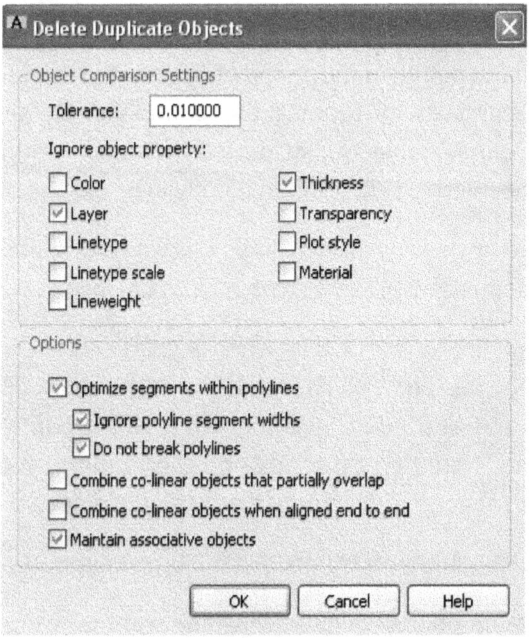

Figure 3-107

In this window, in the Tolerance section, specify the precision of the task. For example, to eliminate lines that are located 2 cm apart, a Tolerance of 0.025 that is 2.5 cm can be set, and if the Tolerance is set to less than 2 cm, these lines cannot be eliminated. In the "Ignore object property" section, it can be defined that in cases where objects are different, it does not take these differences into consideration and eliminates the extra objects.

For example, if you have defined the Tolerance as 2 cm and the line differences are shorter than this but their colors are different, those lines will not be eliminated. But by checking the Color option, it can be defined in a way that their color difference will not be taken into consideration. By selecting the "Optimize segments within polylines" option, you can also make the necessary changes to Polyline Segments.

For example, if you have Polylines that are in the same direction and there are many points in the shape of Segments, you can eliminate the extra Segments by running this command. By selecting the "Combine colinear objects that partially overlap" option, you can also omit the overlapping position of Polylines and the other lines.

For example, if there are many lines crossing along and over each other, the command will turn them all into one line.

If the "Combine colinear objects when aligned end to end" option is enabled, the lines and Polylines that are in the same direction and their start and end points are the same will become joined. By selecting the "Maintain associative objects" option, you allow the command to change or eliminate the duplicate objects.

78. OOPS command (to restore the latest deleted object)

If you delete an object while drawing and want to restore it for any reason, you can use the UNDO command, and each time you run this command, you go one step back. But if you did drawings after deleting that object, the new drawings will also be deleted using the UNDO command. Now if you only want to restore the deleted object, type and run the OOPS shortcut in the command line.

This command will only restore the latest deleted object.

AutoCAD Calculator

79. QUICKCALC command with QC shortcut

After running this shortcut in the command line, the AutoCAD calculator will appear as in Figure 3-108.

In the Number Pad section, you can perform the basic calculator operations.

The Scientific section is an engineering and scientific calculator where you can perform functions such as trigonometric functions of angles, logarithms and converting angles to radian and degree units.

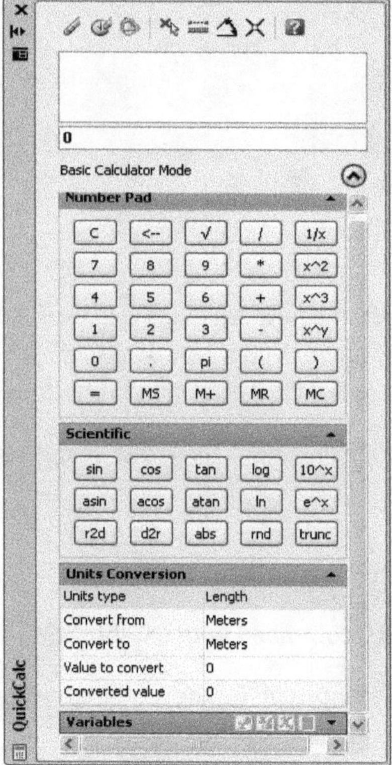

Figure 3-108

In the Unit Conversion section, you can convert units of parameters such as length, area, volume and angle to other units.

At the top of this window you will see a bar containing icons each of which provide the users with some features which are mentioned below:

This icon clears the previous calculations and makes the calculator command bar ready for the new calculations.

This icon measures a length and enters its value directly in the calculator command line.

This icon measures an angle and enters its value in the calculator command line.

This icon changes the angle measurement direction clockwise and counterclockwise.

By clicking on this icon, you can click on a point on the drawing area using the mouse and insert the coordinates of the point as a matrix in the calculator command line.

Using this icon, you can consider two intersecting lines and click on the four points at the start and end of the two lines respectively, and this will insert the coordinates of the intersection point of these two lines as a matrix in the calculator command line.

This icon enters the calculated and final results of the calculator to the AutoCAD command line.

The Variables option is for variables that can help you in some of the drawing tasks such as shortcuts and speed up the drawing operations. These variables can be defined and changed. For a better understanding, read the following example carefully.

Assume you are going to draw a circle like the one in the triangle in Figure 3-109 with a radius of 25 meters in a way that the coordinates of the center of the circle are the same as the geometric center of this triangle.

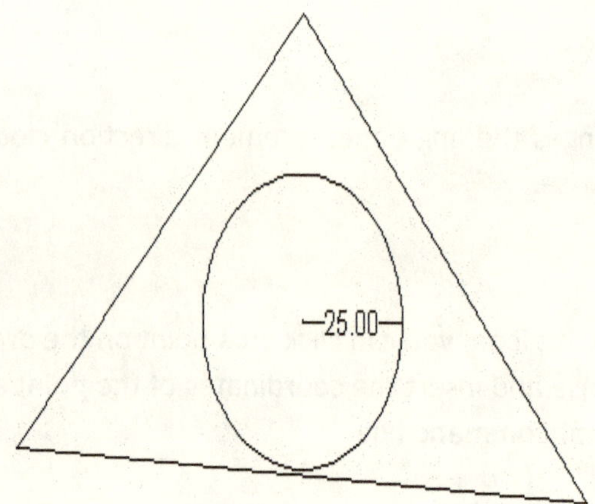

Figure 3-109

To do so, first define a function using the calculator and the Variables option so that it can calculate the geometric center of a triangle. If you define a function to calculate the average of the coordinates of the side midpoints, in fact, you have calculated the geometric center of the triangle. But how can we do it?

Using the QC shortcut, run the AutoCAD calculator, then click on the Variables option and right-click on one of the previous functions as in Figure 3-110, then click on the New Variables option so that the Variable Definition window pops up as in Figure 3-111.

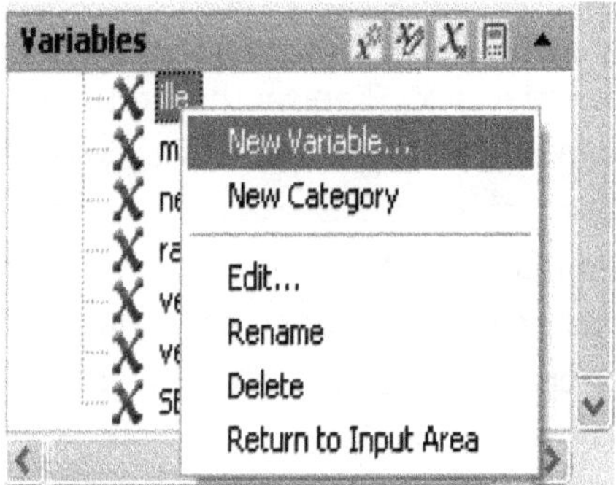

Figure 3-110

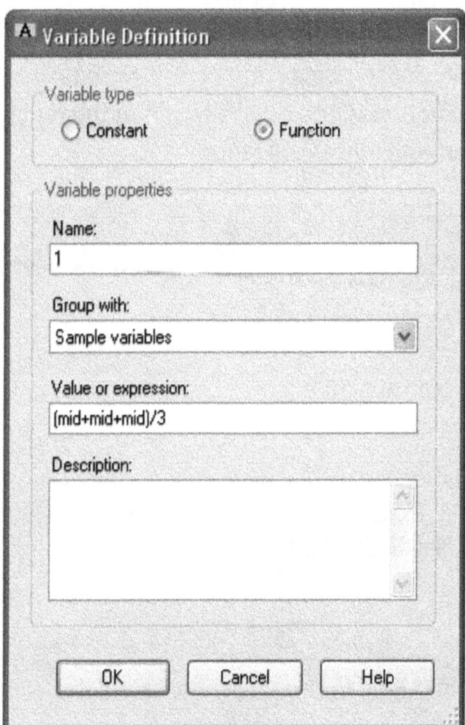

Figure 3-111

In this window, in the Variable type section, select the Function option and define a name for your function in the Name section of the Variable properties box. Then set the Group With option on the Sample Variable mode, and type the formula of the function in the Value or Expression box. In this example, since it is intended to calculate the geometric center of the triangle, and as mentioned before, it depends on the calculation of the average of the triangle side midpoints coordinates, type “(mid+mid+mid)/3”. Then click OK to save this function to add it to the list of calculator functions with the “1” name, and close the calculator window at the end.

Now to draw the circle with the coordinates of a desired center, type and run the C shortcut in the command line to draw the circle, and while the command line asks you to specify the center of the circle, launch the calculator using the Ctrl+8 keyboard shortcut. Now double-click on your defined function so that the function enters the calculator command line as in Figure 3-112.

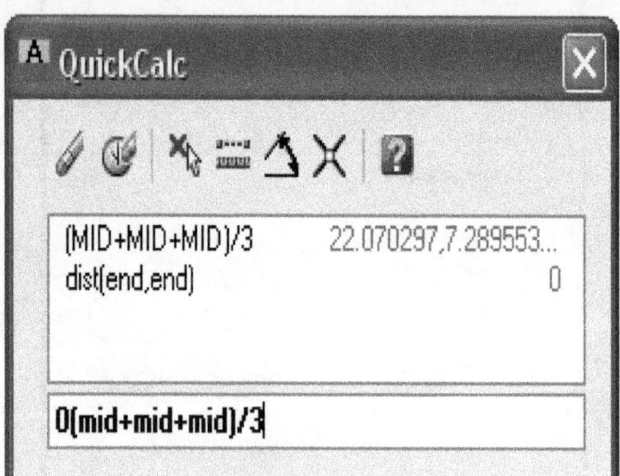

Figure 3-112

Then click on the Apply option. Now the calculator window will close and AutoCAD asks you to click on the three sides of the triangle. After doing so, the desired coordinates are calculated and considered as the coordinates of the center of the circle, and you should simply type 25 in the command line as the radius of the circle to draw the desired circle.

Using this option, you can define shortcuts to speed up your drawing operations, which has not been explained here further, and you can refer to other books or use the AutoCAD guide to become familiar with the other capabilities of this option.

But there is a faster way to use the calculator and that is using the CAL shortcut.

80. Calc command with CAL shortcut

This command is used to run the AutoCAD calculator quickly in the command line. For example, if you want to calculate the total of two numbers or sine of an angle, run the CAL shortcut in the command line. Then type in what you want using the keyboard and press the Enter key. Then you can see the results in the command line.

For example, you can see the results of several operations using this command as in Figure 3-113.

```
Command: CAL
>> Expression: 256+342
598
Command:
CAL
>> Expression: sin(30)
0.5
Command:
CAL
>> Expression: log(10)
1
Command:
CAL
>> Expression: asin(.5)
30
Type a command
```

Figure 3-113

81. LINEWEIGHT command with LWEIGHT shortcut

Sometimes you draw lines with line weight, but they look thin on the drawing area, and if you print the drawing, the lines will be printed with their own specific line weight. The point is that you can enable or disable the line weight display mode.

By typing the LWEIGHT shortcut in the command line and running it, a window appears as in Figure 3-114.

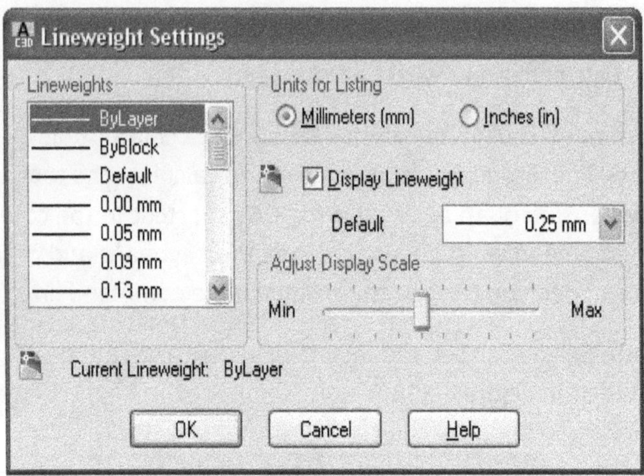

Figure 3-114

In this window, by checking the Display Lineweight option, you can enable the line weight display. From now on, each line will be displayed with its own specific line weight.

82. Menubar command

This command is used to display or hide the menu bar. For this purpose, type and run this command in the command line. By doing so, the message below will appear in the command line:

Enter new value for MENUBAR <1>

If you type the 0 value as a response to this request, the menu bar will be disabled and if you type the 1 value, the menu bar will be enabled.

83. -TOOLBAR command

This command is used to quickly display the toolbars and is mostly used when you do not see any toolbars on the drawing area, because as you know, in order to display a toolbar, you should right-click on one of the toolbar icons, then select the desired toolbar from the opened menu. But you should use this command when none of the toolbars are active on the drawing area. For this purpose, type the "-Toolbar" shortcut in the command line and press the Enter key. By running this command, the message below will appear:

-Toolbar Enter toolbar name or [ALL]

With this message, AutoCAD asks you to enter the name of the desired toolbar or select the ALL mode, which means selecting all the toolbars. As a response to this request, type in the name of one of the toolbars such as the Draw toolbar. By pressing the Enter key, the following message will appear:

Enter an option [Show/Hide/Left/Right/Top/Bottom/Float] <Show>

As a response to this request, type the letter S and press the Enter key to select the Show mode and the Draw toolbar appears. This can be done for all the toolbars.

84. Isolate command

This command is used when you want to perform an action on only one or a few objects. This command is widely used in maps full of details and features.

By typing and running this command, the command line asks you for the objects you want to isolate. After selecting the desired objects and pressing the Enter key, only those objects are displayed on the drawing area and the rest of the objects are not displayed temporarily. After finishing the work on the desired objects, you can use the Unisolate command to go back to the previous state.

85. Date command

This command is used to view the date and time.

By running this command, the following message will appear in the command line:

Initializing...**Thu2010/10/3 18:26:25.889**

which from left to right, it displays the day, the Gregorian date and the time with milliseconds precision.

86. Time command

This command allows you to view the time spent on a drawing. For this purpose, type and run the Time command in the command line. As you can see, the Text Window will appear, where the following information is reported:

Current time: **Thursday, October 03, 2013 7:20:49:875 PM**
Times for this drawing:
Created: **Thursday, October 03, 2013 6:33:46:171 PM**
Last updated: **Thursday, October 03, 2013 6:34:06:109 PM**
Total editing time: **0 days 00:46:44:609**
Elapsed timer (on): **0 days 00:00:02:625**
Next automatic save in: <no modifications yet>

Reports resulted from this command include the current time, file creation date, date of the last update, total time spent on the file, and the time elapsed since the last Reset respectively.

You can also use the “Enter option [Display/ON/OFF/Reset]” options which will appear after viewing the reports to display, turn on, turn off or reset the timer.

Chapter 4: Advanced AutoCAD settings

- Encrypting the drawings
- Professional changes to command shortcuts
- Creating new icons
- Quick settings for creating dimensions

Saving personal settings

Each user has their own set of personal settings such as page color settings, layout settings and save settings that they need in order to get started.

You can save these settings and import them when using a new AutoCAD software installed on your computer or an AutoCAD software on another computer. Using this simple method, any user can have their own settings and they do not have to reset the settings when they want to work with another AutoCAD software. They just need to import that file.

To do so, after customizing the settings, as shown in Figure 4-1, open the Option window and click on the Export option from the Profiles tab and save it in the desired location.

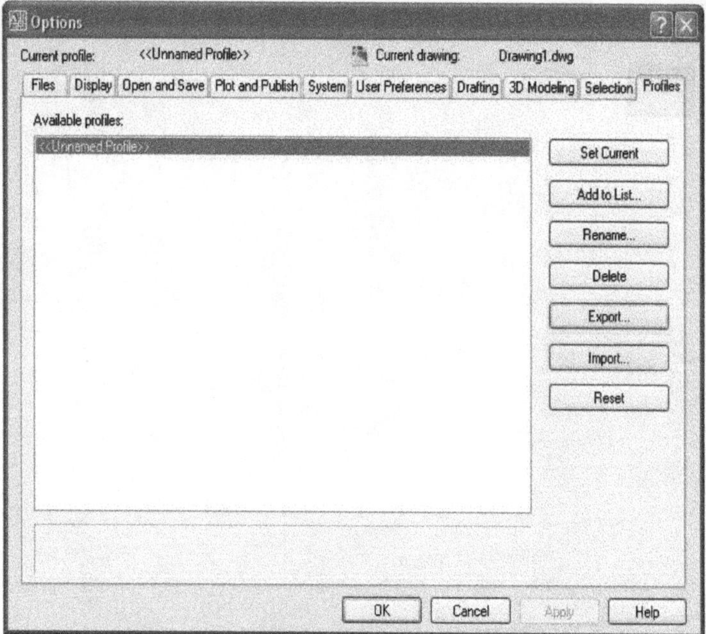

Figure 4-1

To reread these settings, open the Option window and click on the Import option from the Profiles tab and reread the settings.

Opening specific layers of a drawing

When it is intended to work on a burdensome project consisting of multiple layers, for the convenience and to speed up the operations, you can only open a set of layers that you want to work on. To do so, after selecting the Open option from the File menu and selecting your file in the window that appears, as shown in Figure 4-2, click on the arrow next to the Open option and select the Partial Open option.

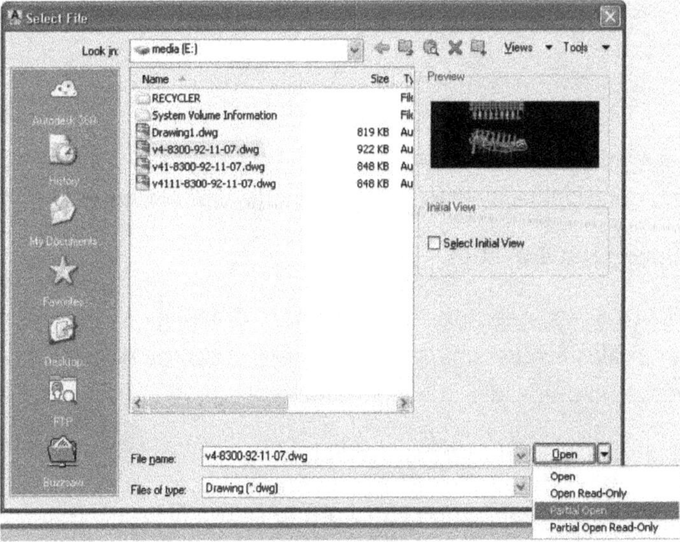

Figure 4-2

After selecting this option, a window like the one in Figure 4-3 pops up and allows the user to select the desired layers.

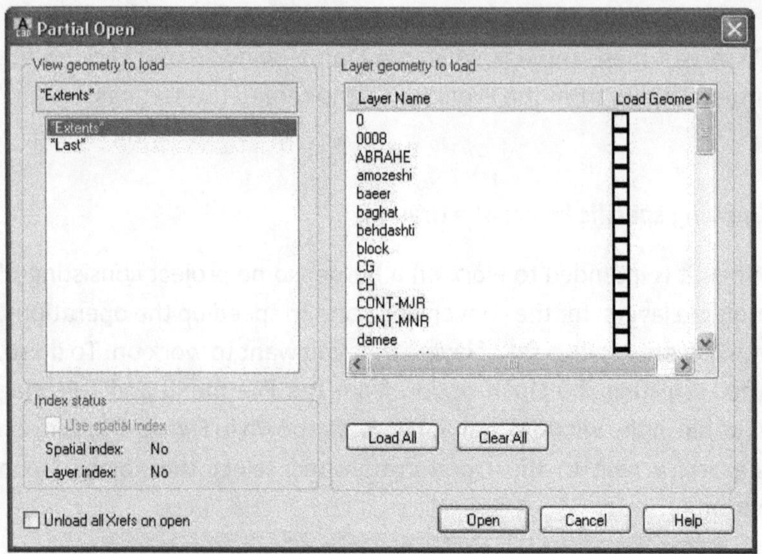

Figure 4-3

In this window, you can check and select the layers you want to work on and open those layers by clicking on the Open option.

Encrypting the drawings

AutoCAD users need to encrypt their drawings to make their personal files inaccessible to other users. It can be done using one of these two methods:

1. Via the Save Drawing As window

This window appears when you want to save a file for the first time or use the Save As command.

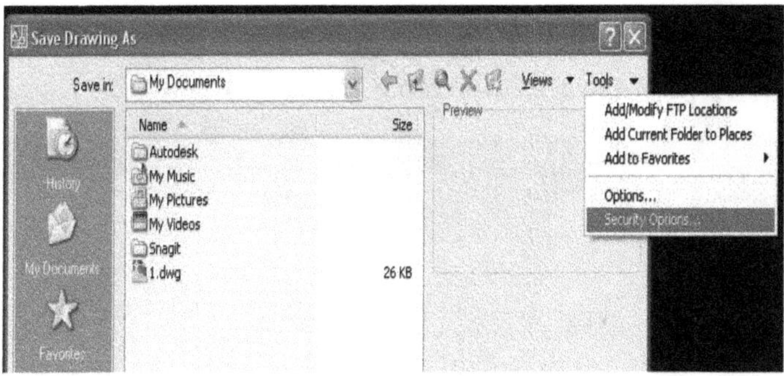

Figure 4-4

Click on the Tools option at the top right section of this window and select the "Security Options..." option.

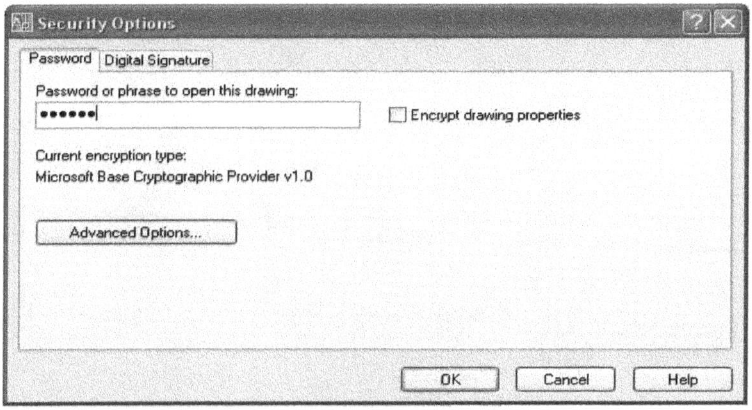

Figure 4-5

In the window that appears, type in the desired password in the Password tab and click OK. A new window will appear where you can re-enter the password and click OK and save your file.

2. Using the Option window

Open the Option window using one of the methods mentioned above, and in the Open and Save tab, in the File Safety Precautions section, click on the "Security Options..." option and continue with the process like the previous step.

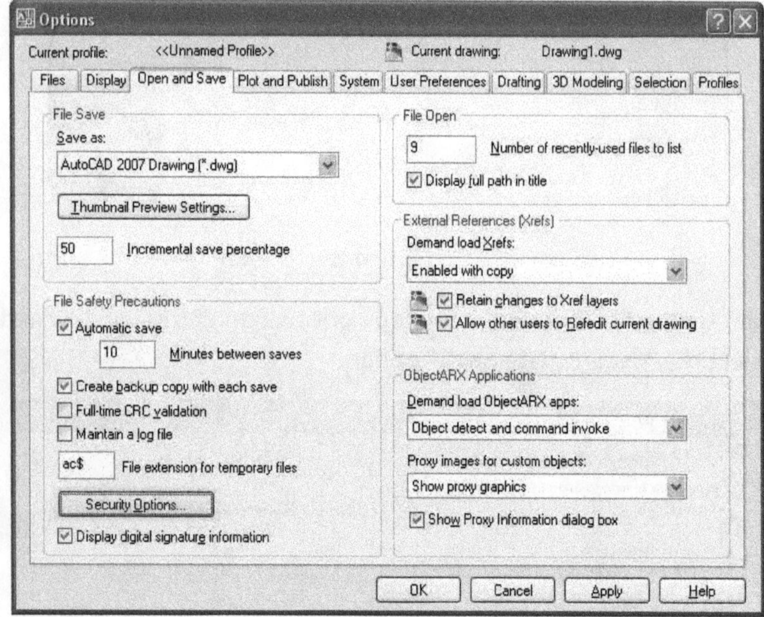

Figure 4-6

How to disable AutoCAD commands

You can use the Undefine command to disable an AutoCAD command and prevent the software from recognizing it in the future. For example, if you want to disable the *Line* command, type *Undefine* in the command line and press enter, and when the software ask you to *Enter command name*, type *line* in the command line.

Automatic repeating of commands for accelerated drawing

Perhaps you know that the command *Multiple Point* can be used to quickly create a large number of points in succession. Similarly, to create a large number of circles in succession, you can type the command *Multiple* in the command line and then add *Circle* to initiate successive execution of the *Circle* command.

Similarly, you can use the *Multiple* command to repeat any command you desire. This command is helpful in situations where a repetitive task must be performed quickly and without interruption.

Setting the Copy command

By using the COPYMODE system variable and setting it, you can define that after copying an object, you will only be allowed to paste it once or infinite number of times.

For this purpose, run the COPYMODE system variable in the command line. By running this system variable, the "Enter new value for COPYMODE <0>" message will appear in the command line, where you can choose values of 0 and 1 for this command. If you reply to this message by typing in the value of 1 and pressing the Enter key, you can only paste each object once and to paste it elsewhere, you have to run the Copy command again. But if you type in the value of 0 and press the Enter key, you can paste any object infinite times after copying it.

How to modify command shortcuts?

Professional users often execute commands with shortcuts and usually modify these shortcuts to further accelerate the process. For example, a user who has make repeated use of *Layiso* shortcut (to run the *LayerIsolate* command) may prefer to change this shortcut to a much shorter shortcut such as *01*. Indeed, the software can be modified to execute the *Layer Isolate* command whenever the user enters the shortcut 01 in the command line. The method of this modification is explained below.

First, open the *Express* menu and select *Tools* and then *Command Alias Editor* (Figure 4-5).

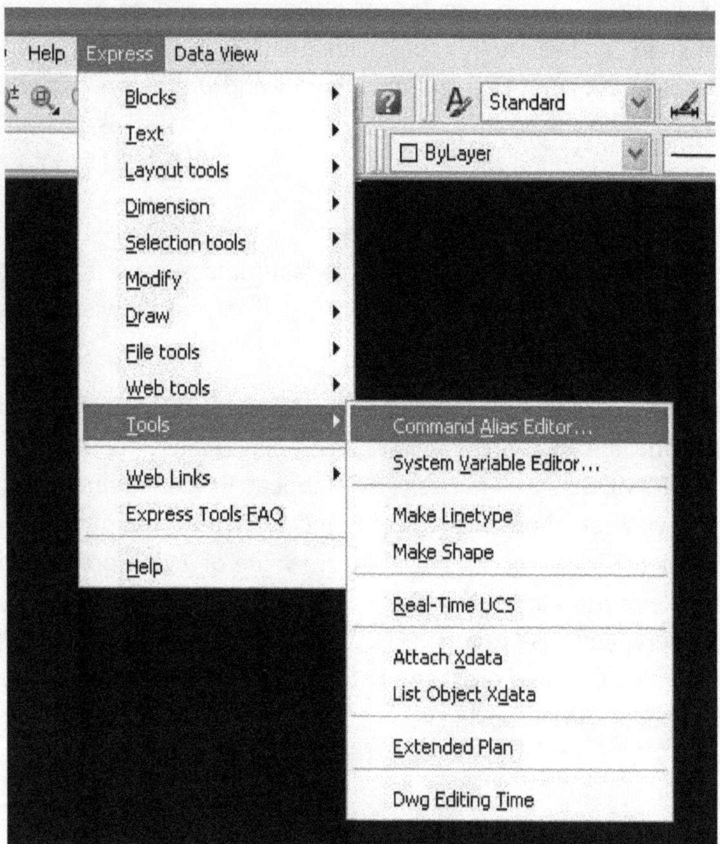

Figure 4-5

This opens a window named *acad.pgp - AutoCAD Alias Editor*, which is displayed in Figure 4-6.

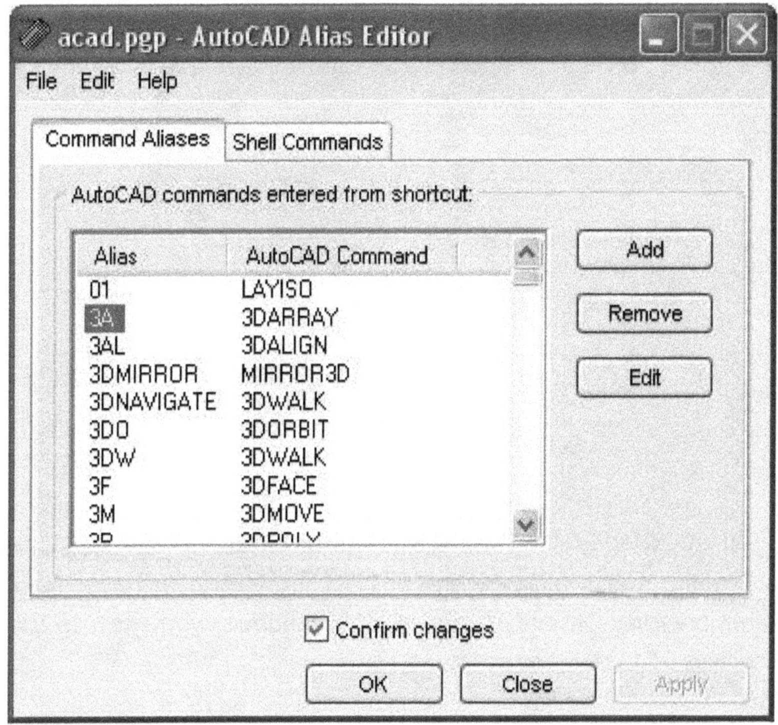

Figure 4-6

To assign the shortcut *01* to the *Layiso* command, press the *Add* button to open the *New Command Alias* window shown in Figure 4-7.

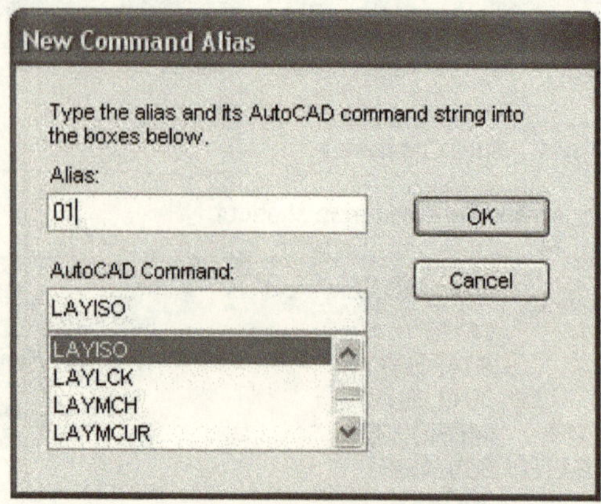

Figure 4-7

In this window, find the command of interest in the *AutoCAD Command* menu and type the desired shortcut in the *Alias* field. After pressing OK and closing all the windows, you can use the shortcut *01* to run the command *Layiso*.

How to make a new Icon?

To make a new Icon, execute the shortcut command *CUI* or open the *Tools* menu and select *Customize* and then select *Interface* to open the *Customize User Interface* window (Figure 4-8).

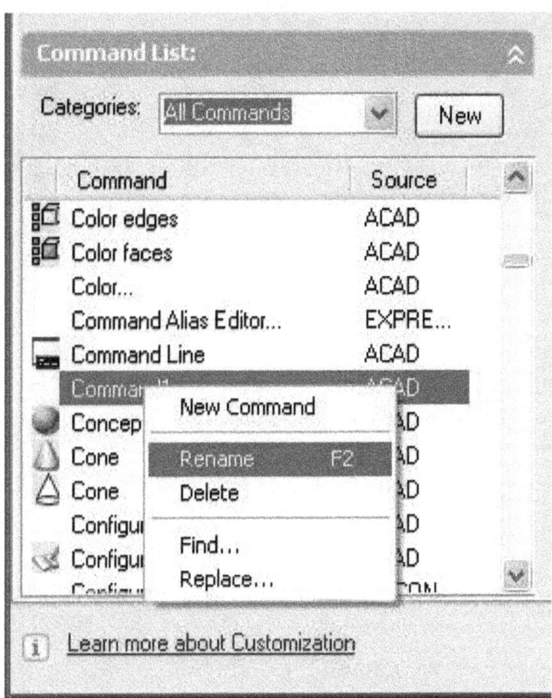

Figure 4-8

In the lower left part of this window, there is a box named *Command List* and a bottom named *New*, which you must press to create a new command (named *Command1* by default). You can right-click on the created command and select *Rename* to change its name.

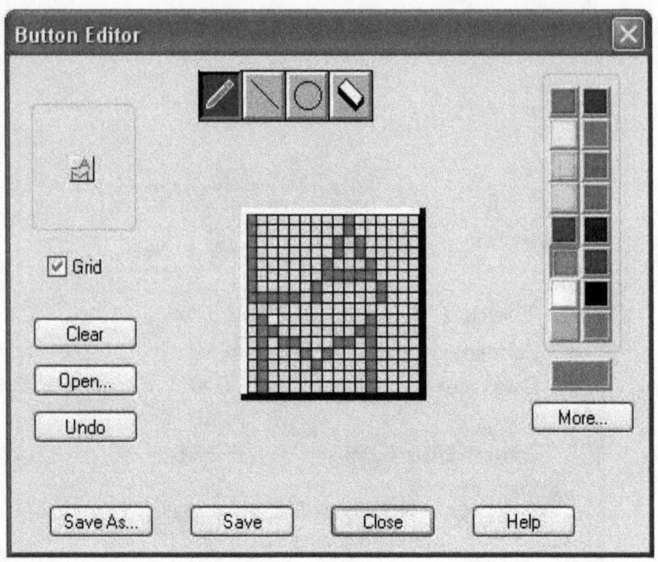

Figure 4-9

In this example, we named the command *Laymerge* (because we want the Icon to execute the *layermerge* command).

Now click on the command and press the *Edit* button in the *Button Image* section to open the *Button Editor* window shown in Figure 4-9.

Use the tools provided in this window to design an icon. Once done, press the (*Save)* button to save the icon, and assign it to the created command.

Note that if you click on any command, you will see its properties in a box named *Properties* to the right. For example, if you click on the *Ellipse* command (used for drawing ellipses), you will see the *Properties* window shown in Figure 4-10.

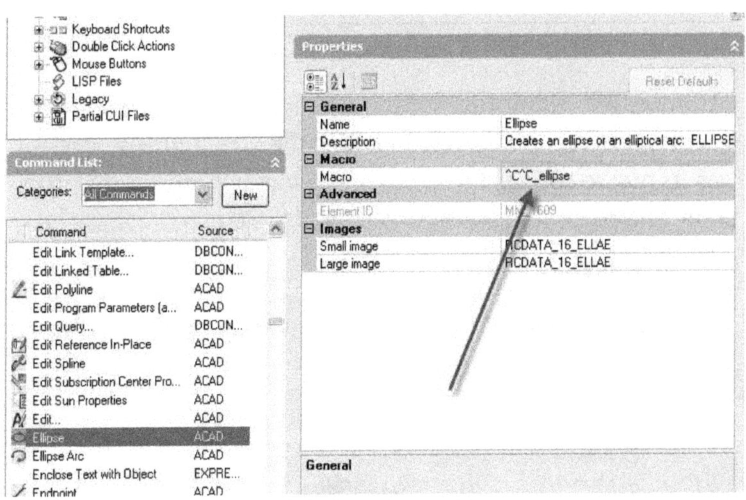

Figure 4-10

One of these properties is the macro code of the command.

As you can see, the macro code of the *Ellipse* command is ^C^C_ellipse.

If you copy this code into the macro field of the command you just created, it will function exactly the same way as the *Ellipse* command (i.e., it will draw an ellipse).

But since we want the button to execute the *Layermerge* command, we must find this command in the command list, click on it to see its macro code in the *Properties* window (Figure 4-11), copy this code, and paste it in the macro field of the created command.

Command	
Name	Layer, Layer Merge
Description	Merges selected layers into a target
Extended Help File	
Command Display Name	LAYMRG
Macro	^C^C_laymrg
Tags	
Advanced	
Element ID	ID_LAYMRG
Images	
Small image	RCDATA_16_LAYER_MERGE_2
Large image	RCDATA_32_LAYER_MERGE_2

Figure 4-11

So far, we have created a command that performs the function of the *Layermerge* command.

The next step is to place this command in the *Draw* toolbar after the *Line* command.

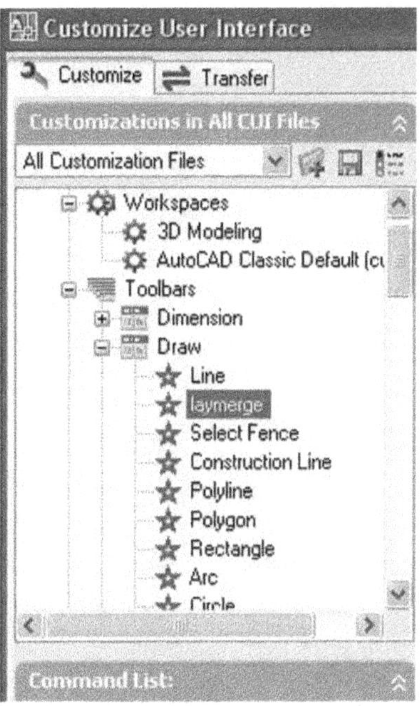

Figure 4-12

To do this, find a box named *Customizations in All CUI File* in the same window. Expand the *Toolbars* branch and then the *Draw* sub-branch. Find the created command in the box positioned below and drag and drop it below the *Line* command in the *Draw* sub-branch. After pressing OK, you must see the button appear in the defined position in the *Draw* toolbar.

This method will be especially rewarding if you master the macro codes, because then you will be able to create buttons with the codes modified for accelerated completion of repetitive tasks. For example, if you create a button with the macro *^C^C_erase all save A close*, the function of the button will be to delete all the objects in the drawing, save the file with the name A, and then close the AutoCAD.

Figure 4-13

A more practical example is to create a button with the macro *^C^C_pedit m all y j .01* for converting all *Lines* to *Polylines* and joining them together with just one click.

How to create buttons for a LISP or macro?

Before learning how to create buttons for LISPs and macros, you must learn how to load them.

To load a LISP file, open the *Tools* menu and select *Load Application* to open the window shown in Figure 4-14. Select your LISP file in the *Look in* section, press the Load button, and then close the window.

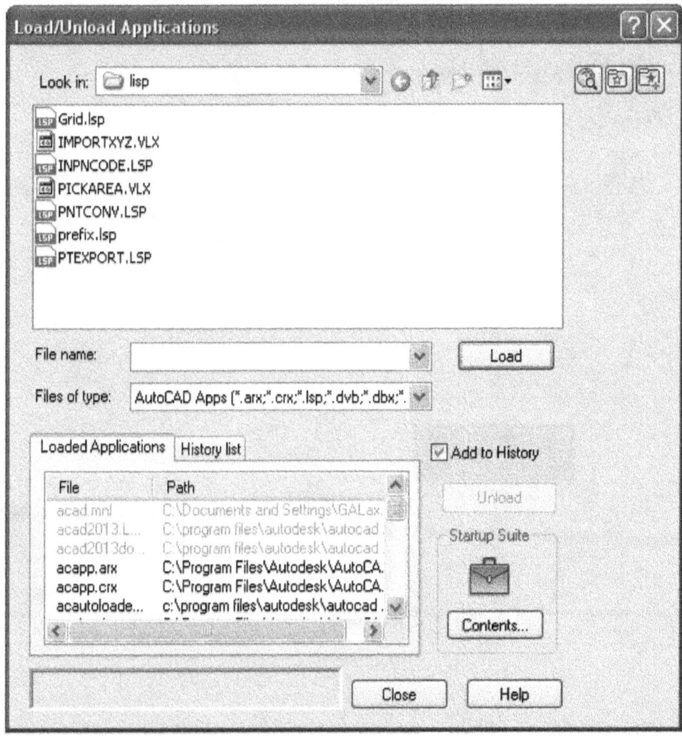

Figure 4-14

It should be noted that if you tick the *Add to History* checkbox before loading, the file will be permanently stored in AutoCAD, otherwise, you will have to reload the file every time you start the program.

After loading the LISP file, you can run it by typing its shortcut in the command line.

To load a macro file, you must open the *Tools* menu and select Macro and then *VBA Manager* to open the window displayed in Figure 4-15.

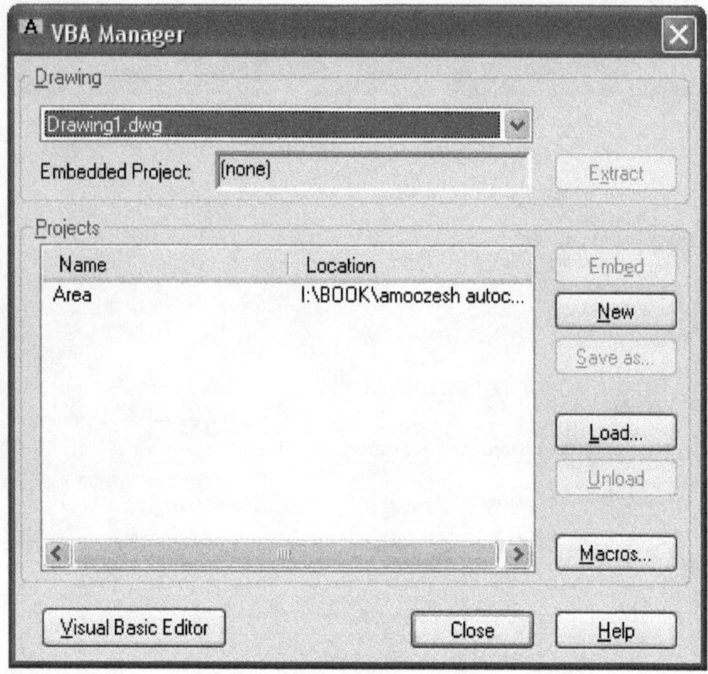

Figure 4-15

In this window, press the *Load* button and select your file. After seeing the name and path of the file in the *Projects* box, click on the *Macros...* button to open a window named *Macros*.

In this window, press the *Run* button to execute the macro.

The next step is to start creating a button for quick execution of the loaded LISP or Visual Basic program (macro). When creating a button for a LISP file, the code in the macro field should be *^C^C* followed by the shortcut name of the LIPS file.

For example, to create a button for the LISP file named *pickarea* (included in the attached disk), you have to type *^C^Cpickarea* in the macro field of the button (Figure 4-16).

Command	
Name	**pickarea**
Description	
Extended Help File	
Command Display Name	
Macro	^C^Cpickarea
Tags	
Advanced	
Element ID	MM_190_FF553
Images	
Small image	io.bmp
Large image	

Figure 4-16

But if the file is made with Visual Basic, the code in the macro field of the new button should be ^C^*Cvbarun* followed by a space and then the name of the macro. For example, to create a button for the macro *area* (included in the attached disk), the code in the macro field should be *^C^Cvbarun area* (Figure 4-17).

Command	
Name	**area**
Description	
Extended Help File	
Command Display Name	
Macro	**^C^Cvbarun area**
Tags	
Advanced	
Element ID	MM_190_18901
Images	
Small image	
Large image	

Figure 4-17

Quick adjustment of the number of decimal places displayed for length and coordinate values

You can use the command Luprec to set the number of decimal places displayed for length, area, and coordinates figures to any value between 0 and 8, without changing the AutoCAD settings or using the *Unit* window. To do this, run the shortcut command *Luprec* in the command line. The software will then ask you to *Enter new value for LUPREC <8>*. In response, you must type the desired number of decimal places, which can be any value between 0 and 8.

Note that this command does not change the actual precision of measurements, but only the number of decimal places displayed.

Quick adjustment of the number of decimal placed displayed in angle values

You can use the command *Auprec* to set the number of decimal places displayed for angle values. To do this, execute this command and then type a value between 0 and 8 as the number of decimal places you want to be displayed for angle values.

Quick adjustment of the number of decimal places displayed for a specific dimension

Using the Aidimprec command, you can change the number of decimal places displayed for a specific length or angle value. After typing and executing this command, the message *Enter option [0/1/2/3/4/5/6]* will appears in the command line. In response, type the number of decimal places you want to be displayed (could be between 0 and 6) and press enter. Then, click on the dimension you want to edit and press enter again to see the desired changes applied.

Changing how a dimension is displayed

You can use the command Aidimtextmove to change how a dimension is displayed in the drawing. This command allows you to select 3 modes of display.

After executing this command, you will be asked to *Enter option [0/1/2]*. In response to this message, you must enter 0, 1, or 2 depending on the display mode that best suits your needs. These modes are illustrated in Figure 4-18.

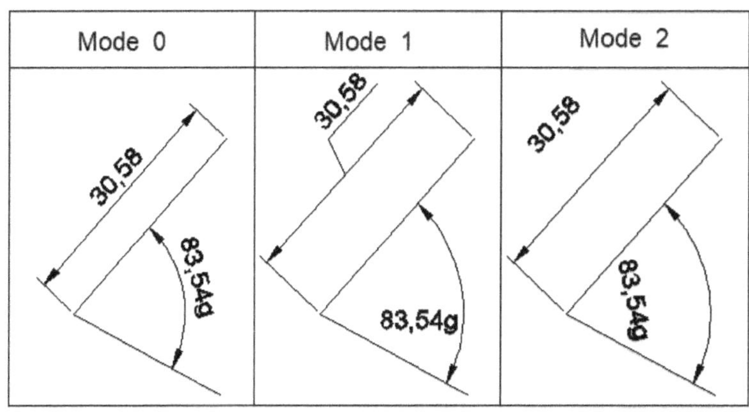

Figure 4-18

Setting the Copy command

By using the COPYMODE system variable and setting it, you can define that after copying an object, you will only be allowed to paste it once or infinite number of times.

For this purpose, run the COPYMODE system variable in the command line. By running this system variable, the "Enter new value for COPYMODE <0>" message will appear in the command line, where you can choose values of 0 and 1 for this command. If you reply to this message by typing in the value of 1 and pressing the

Enter key, you can only paste each object once and to paste it elsewhere, you have to run the Copy command again. But if you type in the value of 0 and press the Enter key, you can paste any object infinite times after copying it.

Chapter 5: Specialized land surveying exercises

- Integrating multiple drawings
- Applying transformation and drawing a traverse
- Using Excel to speed up the operations
- Drawing tunnel excavation cross sections
- Extracting layout elevation from the longitudinal section

Exercise 1

Drawing the fourth corner of a building

In land surveying, features that are either square or rectangular such as buildings, pools and ponds are usually surveyed in a way that only the three corners that are in the view of the surveying instrument would be surveyed, because the surveying instrument can only have the view of three corners of the building when it is positioned on one side of the building and the fourth corner of the building is specified using drawing software. In AutoCAD, there are different ways to draw the fourth corner of a building, and you can also write a program using programming languages such as Lisp and Visual Basic to do the task. But the fastest and easiest way to do so is using the Copy command which is described in Figure 5-1.

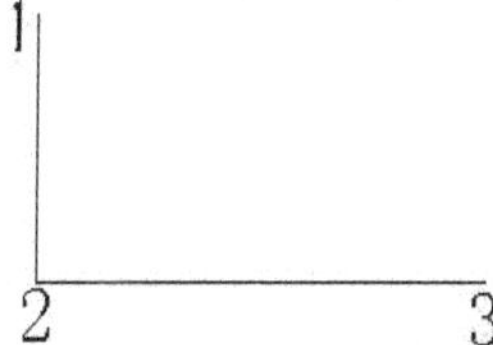

Figure 5-1

Assume that the points 1, 2 and 3 are the three corners of a building which have been drawn using the Polyline command. Now you want to draw the fourth corner and the other two sides of the building.

To do so, click on the drawn Polyline to select it, then type and run the CO shortcut in the command line. By running this command, the command line asks you for the base point of the copy action, which you provide by clicking on point 2. The command line then asks you to enter the other points for pasting. Now click on points 1 and 3 respectively. This will draw the shape in Figure 5-2.

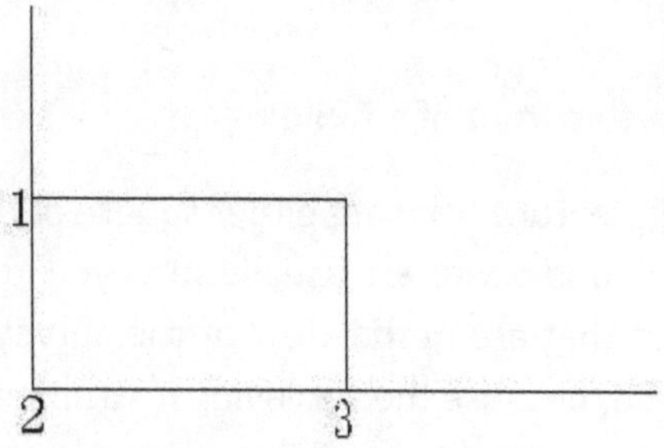

Figure 5-2

Now to eliminate the extra lines, you can use the Trim command. To do so, type and run the TR shortcut in the command line. Then to define the cutting edges, click on the two newly drawn sides and press the Enter key. Now click on the extra lines to cut them.

Exercise 2

Integrating multiple drawings

When it comes to surveying a large region, things are usually done on a daily basis. After a day's work, the file of the points that have been surveyed in that day will be transferred to the software and the drawing for that day will be done and saved as a file. And for example, if it takes 10 days to finish surveying a project, you will have 10 "dwg" files. Now if you want to have all the drawings of these 10 days in a single file, you should Merge all these files into a single file. In AutoCAD software, this can be done in two ways:

1. Using the Copy & Paste operation
2. Using Blocks

Now these two methods will be explained.

1. Using the Copy & Paste operation

To do the task via the Copy & Paste operation, you need to open all the files using the software, but before that, you need to set the AutoCAD software on the Multiple-drawing mode. For this purpose, type and run the OP shortcut in the command line so that the Options window pops up as in Figure 5-3.

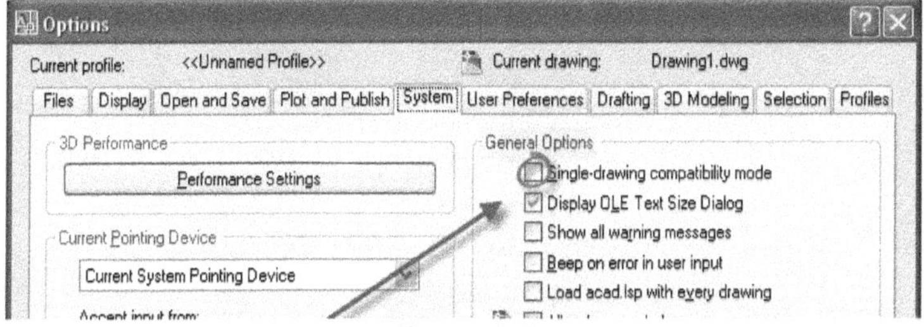

Figure 5-3

In this window, click on the System tab and in the General Options section, uncheck the “Single-drawing compatibility mode” option and then click OK. This will set AutoCAD on the Multiple-drawing mode (There is no need to go through this process in AutoCAD versions after 2008).

After that, open all the files for each day’s drawing, so that you can see the file path and the name of all the open files in the Window menu as in Figure 5-4. The check mark next to each file means that the file is already current. Then to perform the Merge operation, create a new file using the instructions below.

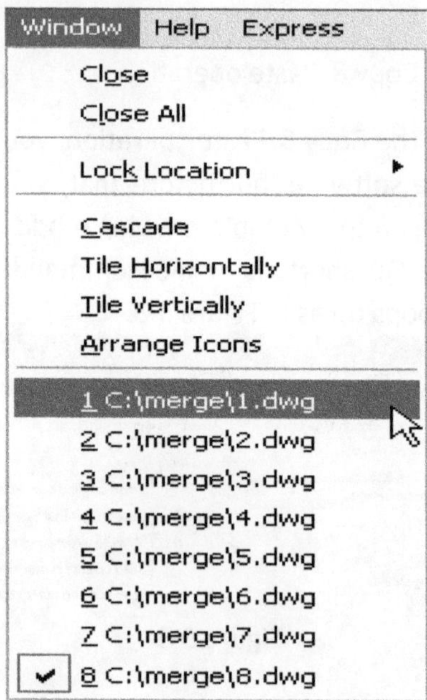

Figure 5-4

Select the New option from the File menu or use the Ctrl+N keyboard shortcut. Then in the opened window named Select Template, select the "acad.dwt" drawing template and then click on the Open option to add a new file named "drawing1" to the previously opened files. In the Window menu, you can see the name of the file with a check mark next to it. Next, you need to add these files to the newly created file using the Ctrl+Shift+C and Ctrl+V commands., the steps to do this are fully explained by doing an exercise.

In the book attachments, there is a folder names Merge, which consists of 8 drawings related to surveying a Region, which has been surveyed within 8 working days. Select these files all together using the OPEN command from the File menu and click on the Open option at the bottom right side of the window to open them all one after another. And also create a new file using the above-mentioned method. Then, from the Window menu, click on the name of one of the drawings to enable and display it on the drawing area. Then use the Ctrl+A keyboard shortcut to select all the objects in the drawing or do so using the mouse. Then use the Ctrl+Shift+C keyboard shortcut for copying. At this point, the "_copybase Specify base point" message appears in the command line which asks you for the copybase point. Specify this point with (0,0) coordinates. Therefore, you just need to type 0,0 in the command line and press the Enter key. Then enable the file you have just created from the Window menu and use the Ctrl+V keyboard shortcut in this file, then the "_pasteclip Specify insertion point:" message appears in the command line which asks for the insertion point. Here again, type in (0,0) coordinates and press the Enter key to insert that file with the same coordinates like those of the original file, in the new file. Likewise, repeat this process for the other files and paste them in the new file. After you have pasted all the files, save the new file with the desired name.

Note: You need to know that it is not necessary to type in 0,0 coordinates when specifying the copybase point, but you have to type in the same coordinates you type in when copying, in the time of insertion.

2. Using Blocks

However, the other method to Merge multiple files, as mentioned before, is using blocks. For this purpose, select the Block option from the Insert menu or use the I shortcut. In the Insert window, click on the Browse option and select one of the 8 drawing files, then click on the Open option. In the Insert window, in the Insertion point section, uncheck the "Specify on screen" option and type in 0 as the coordinates of X, Y and Z as in Figure 5-5.

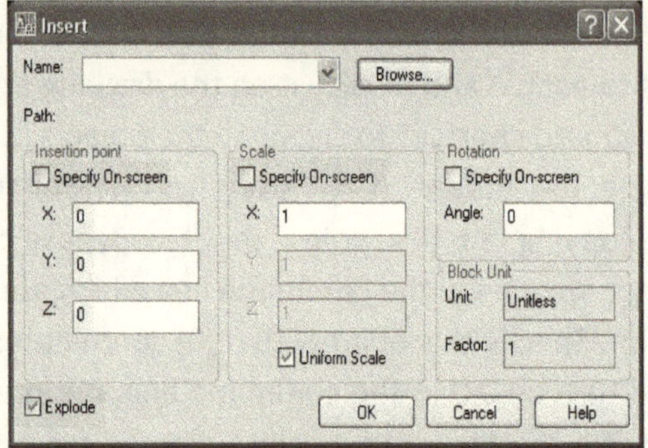

Figure 5-5

In the Scale section, type in 1 as the scale of X, Y and Z. At the bottom of the window, check the Explode option and at the end, click OK in the Insert window so that the file will be inserted in the drawing area with its own actual coordinates. Do this operation for all the files. Then save the new file with a desired name using the Save As command.

However, it should be noted that before inserting a block in the drawing, you must open the Drawing Units window using the Un shortcut, and in the Insertion Scale section, select the Unitless option in the "Units to scale inserted content" box so that the imported block in the drawing will be located in its own actual coordinates.

Exercise 3

Smoothing the contours

One of the most important tasks in cartography is to smooth the contours. As you know, contours are usually Polylines and they are usually drawn using Vertexes. But according to the definition of a "contour", you know that a contour is a smooth surface without any vertexes. The PEDIT command is used to fix the vertexes of the contour lines. Open the Contour.dwg file. This file is part of a map of contours of a Region with a scale of $\frac{1}{2500}$. If you zoom in on the contours, you will notice that the contour lines have vertexes. To smooth these contours, it is necessary to select all of them. However, since the PEDIT command differs from the other AutoCAD commands, it is not possible to select the contours first and then use the PEDIT command. Therefore, it is not possible to use the Quick Select command to select all the contours. But how can we do that?

Before using the PEDIT command, you should turn off all the layers in the drawing except the layer that contains the contours, in a way that only the contours would be there on the drawing area and no other objects would be observed. This can be done using the LAYISO command. The steps are as follows:

First, type and run the LAYISO command in the command line, then click on one of the major contours and then on one of the minor contours and press the Enter key. By doing so, only the two layers containing the major and minor contours will remain turned on and the rest of the layers will be turned off. Then type and run the PE shortcut in the command line, then type the letter M and press the Enter key to select all the contours. Then use the mouse to select all the contours and press the Enter key. To smooth them, you should select the Spline mode by typing the letter S and pressing the Enter key. After doing so, use the Esc key to close the command. Now, if you zoom in on the contours, you will notice that they do not have vertexes anymore and have become smoothed. To turn the layers on again, use the LAYUNISO command.

Another method to do this task is to first select the contours using the Quick Select command. Then display the Properties window by typing and running the PR shortcut in the command line. At the bottom section of this window, meaning the Misc section, set the Fit/Smooth option to Cubic as in Figure 5-6.

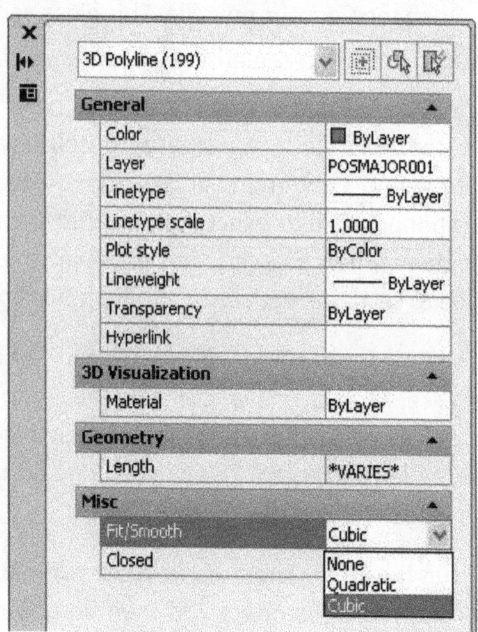

Figure 5-6

Exercise 4

Changing the elevation scale of longitudinal and transverse profiles

In road construction projects, it is typical to draw longitudinal profiles with vertical exaggeration ratios of 5, 10, or 20. In cases where surveyors need to change the vertical scale of such longitudinal or transverse profiles, this cannot be done with the *Scale* command, because this command changes the scale in both x and y directions. In order to change the scale along only the y-axis (i.e. to change only the elevation scale of a longitudinal profile), you need to use a command named *Insert Block*. Before learning how to use this command, open and see the files named *Along Section* and *Cross Section* in the folder *dwg*. In these files, longitudinal and transverse profiles are drawn with a vertical exaggeration ratio of 10 (the vertical scale is 10 times the horizontal scale). But as you know, transverse profiles should be drawn on a scale of 1:1. Thus, the vertical (elevation) scale of the transverse profiles must be decreased by a factor of 10.

To do this, open the *Insert* menu and select *Block*, or just execute the shortcut command *I* to open the window shown in Figure 5-7. Press the *Browse* button and select the file *Cross Section*.

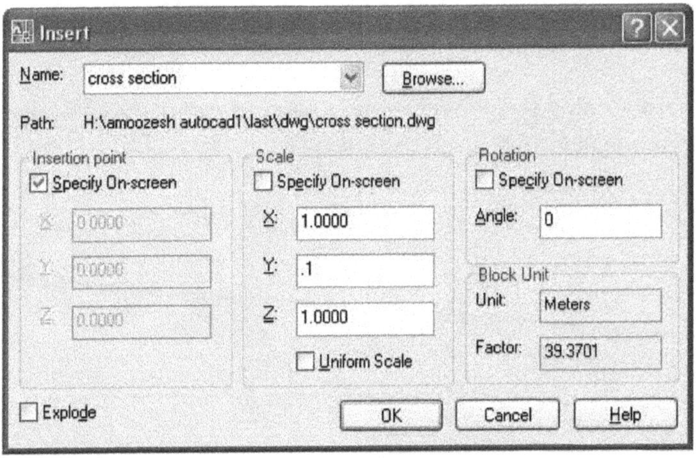

Figure 5-7

Since we need to reduce the vertical scale by a factor of 10, the *Y* field in the *Scale* box should be set to 0.1. Press OK to close the window, then click on the point where you want the block inserted. By doing this, you will insert all cross sections with a scale of 1:1.

Note that there is actually no need to open the source file and you can do this in the file on which you are currently working. Also, remember that if you adjust the scale settings as explained above, all inserted objects will be rescaled, so to avoid error, it is recommended to first isolate the profiles in another file, and then use that file for insertion.

After insertion, you will see that the inserted texts are also rescaled and thus difficult to read. Hence, the next goal is to edit these texts to restore them to their original state.

To do this, use a selection method such as Quickselect to select the texts, then execute the command *PR* to open the *Properties* window (Figure 5-8). In the *Text* box of this window, set the *Style* to *Standard*. If this does not fix the problem, return to this window and reduce the *Width factor* to one-tenth of its current value.

Before doing this, however, you need to use the *X* command to explode the inserted blocks (profiles).

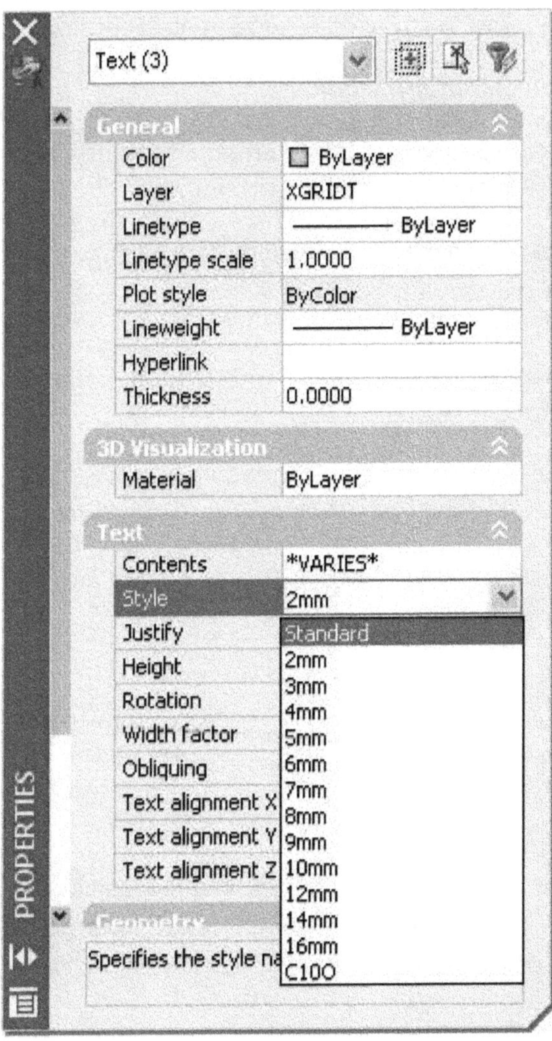

Figure 5-8

Exercise 5

Transformation of local coordinates to global coordinates

Definition of transformation:

In the field of surveying, transformation means converting the coordinate system from one mode to another.

A transformation may become necessary for two reasons:

- To convert local coordinates to UTM coordinates
- When the survey is done with a Total Station configured incorrectly for any reason.

Before explaining the transformation process, it is worth to quickly review the stage of surveying. These stages are as follows:

- Reconnaissance and marking
- Traversing and error balancing
- Levelling
- Feature surveying
- Drawing and cartography

In the traversing stage, stations can be converted to UTM coordinates based on the horizontal coordinates provided by a national mapping agency. This can be done in both land and satellite surveying.

In land surveys, coordinates are often measured with angle and distance measurement instruments. But in satellite surveys, these measurements are carried out using single-frequency and dual-frequency GPS. To accelerate the surveying operations, the steps after reconnaissance and marking, i.e. traversing, levelling, and feature surveying can be performed simultaneously by three separate teams. But how can we start surveying features before finishing traversing and error balancing, i.e. without having the exact coordinates of stations?

When the UTM and exact coordinates of two or more stations are not yet available, we can proceed to survey with local coordinates and transform the collected data to UTM once the exact and corrected coordinates of all stations are available. The standard method of transformation is to conduct separate calculations based on the raw survey data (measured distances and horizontal and vertical angles) of each individual stations with the help of standard computing software such as SDR Map and Excel. But in small projects where there is no need to produce text files for original and transferred coordinates, the whole operation can be performed faster and more conveniently in AutoCAD, where there is no need to repeat the tasks for each individual station. In computational transformation, we often use the coordinates of two points, namely the current station and the backsight point, but in AutoCAD, we use three points to ensure greater precision. It should be explained that the transformation operation in AutoCAD can be described as the combined use of three commands: *Move*, *Rotate*, and *Scale*. In the following, we explain how to perform this transformation with the help of an example.

Open the file Transfer2.dwg in the attached disk. In this example, an area has been surveyed with a local coordinate system consisting of the stations Z1, Z2, Z3, and Z4. After traversing and coordinate transfer, the UTM coordinates of the stations have been obtained as listed in Table 5-9.

Point	LOCAL		UTM	
	X	Y	X	Y
Z1	1768.9217	6490.9361	625705.7785	3077695.9900
Z2	2070.1435	5989.0668	625676.0257	3077111.5399
Z3	2861.8440	6574.9870	626658.0534	3077153.1677
Z4	2540.4905	7019.1818	626640.8143	3077701.1319

Table 5-9

Here, we use the points Z1, Z2, and Z3 for transformation and use Z4 for control. For control, the transferred coordinate of Z4 after transformation will be compared with the UTM coordinates of the same point. For transformation in AutoCAD, we use the command *Align* with the shortcut *AL*. But before doing this, we have to draw the stations with the *Point* command, so that they can be controlled after the transformation. To do so, type and execute the shortcut command *PO* and then type the UTM coordinates of Z1-Z4 to draw them. Then, select all the objects on the drawing including the station points and execute the *AL* command in the command line. The software will then ask you to *Specify first source point.* In response, enter the local coordinates of Z1. Then, the software will then display the message *Specify first destination point*, in response to which you must enter the UTM coordinates of Z1. The next two massages will ask you to *Specify second source point* and *Specify second destination point*, in response to which you must enter the local coordinates and UTM coordinates of Z2. After specifying the second point, the massage *Specify third source point or <continue>* appears. In this step, you can decide whether to specify a third pair of source and destination points or continue the process with just two points. For this example, use the local and UTM coordinates of

Z3 as the third source point and the third destination point respectively. In short, the contents typed in the command line should be as follows.

Command : al

Command : Specify first source point: 1768.9217,6490.9361

Command : Specify first destination point: 625705.7785,3077695.99

Command : Specify second source point:2070.1435,5989.0668

Command : Specify second destination point:625676.0257,3077111.5399

Command : Specify third source point or <continue>:2861.844,6574.9870

Command : Specify third destination point:626658.0534,3077153.1677

After specifying the third point, the points will be automatically transformed. If you do not see the transformed plot, use the command *Zoom All*. The next step is to use the point Z4 to control the accuracy of work. If you completely zoom on Z4, you will notice that the transferred Z4 is only slightly different (about 2 centimeters) from its UTM counterpart, which is sufficiently accurate for most projects.

To practice, repeat the transformation with the points Z2, Z3, and Z4 and use Z1 for control.

Exercise 6

Drawing traverses

First, it is important to note that AutoCAD does not have a specific command for drawing traverses, and traverse calculation and drawing are typically performed with other software such as Excel, SDR map, Survey, etc. However, you can AutoCAD commands to draw simple traverses. Also, remember that AutoCAD is not recommended for error balancing, so this exercise assumes that the error of closure is acceptably small. Rather than being focused on traverses, this exercise aims to familiarize the reader with a number of tricks and shortcuts that make it easier to work with AutoCAD.

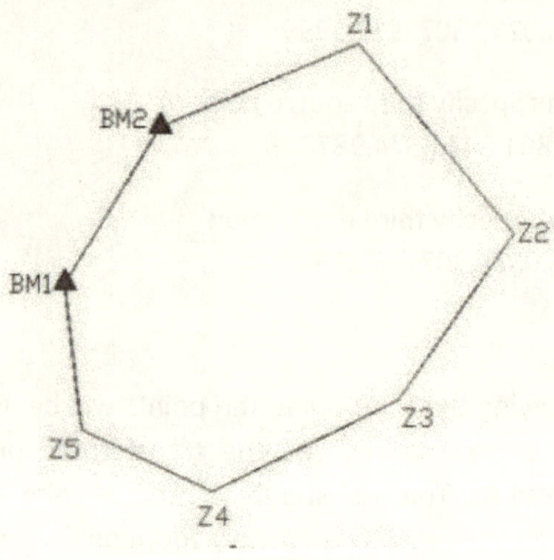

Figure 5-10

Coordinates of benchmark points			Distances		Angles	
ID	X	Y	ID	Value	ID	Value
BM1	565099.3251	4157280.6352	BM2-Z1	768.6523	BM2	160.3785g
			Z1-Z2	861.3194	Z1	120.6906g
			Z2-Z3	714.0180	Z2	115.1927g
BM2	565442.4798	4157822.6317	Z3-Z4	742.7243	Z3	167.2654g
			Z4-Z5	512.3764	Z4	145.5294g
			Z5-BM1	508..9949	Z5	134.2081g
					BM1	156.7353g

Figure 5-11

In this exercise, we draw a traverse with the general layout displayed in Figure M5-10. In this traverse, the benchmark points BM1 and BM2 have been used to measure the coordinates of unknown points Z1-Z5. All angle and distance values have been recorded with 0.0001 precision. Each angle has been measured with four repeats of double-centering and each distance has been measured eight times. The angle and length values obtained after error balancing are given in Table 5-11.

First, to plot the baseline BM1-BM2, the software coordinate system must be set to the absolute Cartesian mode (because BM1 and BM2 both have UTM coordinates, which is an absolute Cartesian system). To do this, run the shortcut command *SE* to open the *Drafting Settings* window. Go to the *Dynamic Input* tab and click on the *Setting* button in the *Pointer Input* pane to open the *Pointer Input* window. In this window, tick the *Cartesian Format* and *Absolute Coordinate* checkboxes, and press OK to confirm the selections. Next, you need to draw the benchmark points with the *Line* command. For this purpose, run the shortcut command *L* and then enter the coordinates of BM1 as the first point, enter the coordinates of BM2 as the second point, and finally press enter to draw a line between these points. If you do not see the line, run the command *Zoom Extend*.

Command: L

Command: LINE Specify first point: 565099.3251 , 4157280.6352

Command: Specify next point or [Undo]: 565442.4798 , 4157822.6317

Command:Z

Command:E

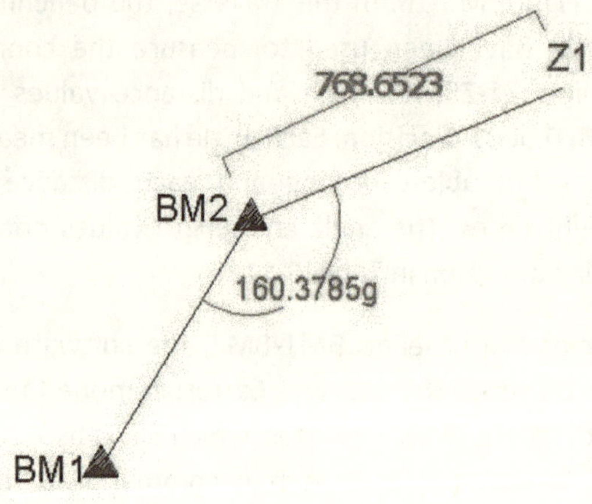

Figure 5-12

After drawing the benchmark points (BM1, BM2), you must use the collected distance and angle data to draw traverse vertices one by one. Before doing this, you have to set the coordinate system to the relative polar coordinate system. To do so, run the *SE* command, go to the *Dynamic Input* tab and enable the *Polar Format* and *Relative Coordinate* options in the *Pointer Input* pane.

Now you must use the BM2-Z1 distance and the BM2 angle to find the position of Z1 relative to BM2. Note that since Z1 should be drawn based on BM2, you have to set the reference of angle measurement to BM2-BM1 line. To do this, execute the shortcut command *UN* in the command line to open the *Drawing units* window. In this window, set the unit of angle measurement to grad with 4 decimal places (because in this exercise, angles have been measured in grads with 4 decimal places). Then, click on the *Direction* button on the bottom of this window to open the *Direction Control* window. In this window, you can set the reference direction of angles to north, east, south, west, or any direction of your choosing. Since we need to set the reference of angle measurement to a specific direction, you have to enable the *Other* option and click on the bottom below it. After pressing this button, the windows will be closed and AutoCAD will be ready to receive the direction to be used as angle measurement reference. In this step, you just have to click first on BM2, and then on BM1 to specify the BM2-BM1 line as the reference of angle measurements. When done, press OK until all windows are closed. Note that if angles were external, you had to choose the BM1-BM2 direction instead of BM2-BM1.

Now, to draw the point Z1, execute the shortcut command *L* and click on BM2 to mark it as the first point. Then, use the sign @ to inform the software that the values to be entered are relative to the first point. Next, type the measured distance between BM2 and Z1, i.e. 768.6623. Then, type the sign < to inform the software that you intend to enter the angle, and then type the BM2 angle, i.e. 160.3785. Press enter when done. Now, you must see a line drawn between BM2 and Z1.

Command: PL

Command: LINE Specify first point: (click on BM2)

Command: Specify next point or [Undo]: @768.6623<160.3785

After drawing the BM2-Z1 line, you must repeat the above process to draw the Z1-Z2 line using the measured distance between Z1 and Z2 and the measured Z1 angle (remember to change the angle reference to the Z1-Z2 line). Repeat this process until reaching the point BM1 and forming a closed traverse. Open traverses can also be drawn in the same way.

Exercise 7

Drawing the Cadastral map of a region

Project description:

We have surveyed a region using a Total Station instrument to draw the Cadastral map, then transferred the Total Station instrument data to PC and imported the transferred file to the SDR map software. Then we have saved a dxf file of those points. Now we want to do the drawings of this project using the AutoCAD software. So, first, launch the AutoCAD software and type and run the Dxfin shortcut in the command line to open the dxf file. Then open the Cadastre.dxf file from the files folder attached to the book.

Note: If you cannot see the features on the drawing area after opening the dxf file, use the Zoom All command.

To do so, first, type the letter Z and then press the Space key to run it, then type the letter A and press the Space key again to see the whole file.

In this file, you will see all the surveyed points along with their codes; codes which have been inserted with a Text type. You will also see a graded box made by the SDR map software.

First of all, to get more control and better view over the drawing, erase the drawing margin using the Erase command.

As you can see in Figure 5-13, due to the proximity of the points in some regions, the codes of the points have overlapped each other. This brings up some mistakes when drawing.

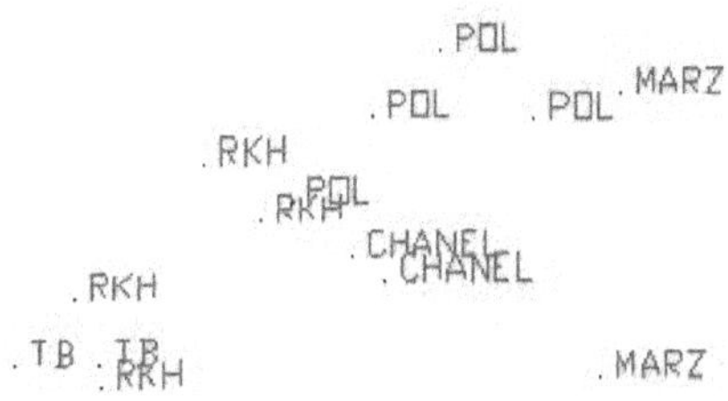

Figure 5-13

To fix this issue, you just need to reduce the size of the code texts. To do so, first you need to select all the codes. Then type and run the QSELECT shortcut in the command line so that a window pops up like the one in Figure 5-14-1.

As you know, all the codes are in the P1 layer, so you need to select all the texts in the P1 layer to select all the codes. To do this, select the Text option in the Object type section in the window that pops up as in Figure 5-14-1 and set the Properties section to the Layer mode and select the P1 layer in the box next to the Value option so that after clicking OK in the window, all the texts in the P1 layer become selected. To make sure all the texts are selected, you just need to know that all the texts are dashed. Once you have selected all the codes, you need to resize them.

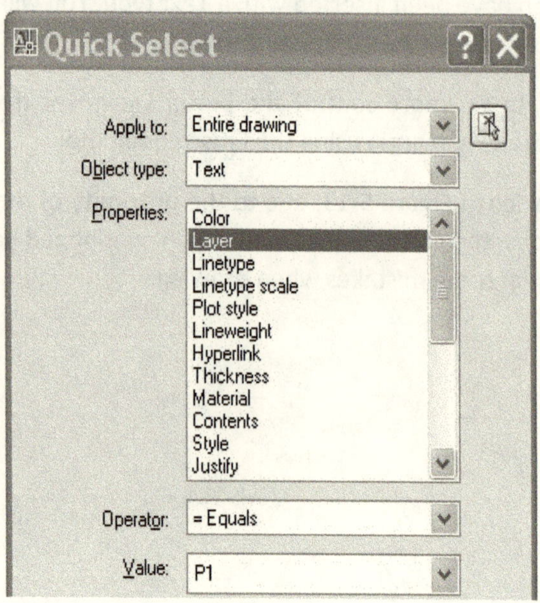

Figure 5-14-1

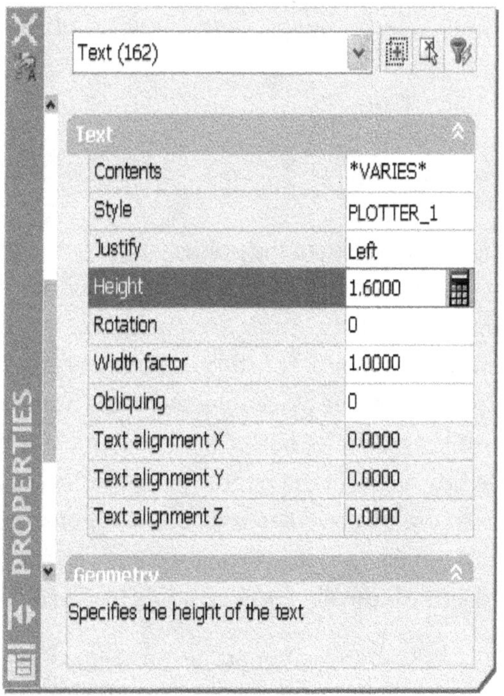

Figure 5-14-2

To do so, you should keep the codes selected, then type and run the PR shortcut in the command line so that the Properties window pops up as in Figure 5-14-2.

In this window, in the Text tab, next to the Height option, you can set the size of the texts. The number 1.6 shows the current size. To reduce the size of the texts, reduce the number. For example, if you want to quarter their sizes, type 0.4 and press the Enter key. After closing the window, you notice that their sizes are smaller than the previous size.

As you can see, the symbol selected by the SDR map software for the points is not visible and this brings up mistakes in the drawings.

Therefore, you need to change the point symbols. However, the type of the point symbols is "block reference" when entering the AutoCAD software, and the EXPLODE command must be used to convert them to "points". For this purpose, run the QSELECT shortcut again and after the quick select window appears, select the block reference option in the object type box and click on "layer" in the properties box, then set the operator box on "=equal" and select the P1 layer in the value box. Then click OK to select all point symbols that are of block reference type. Then type and run the X shortcut in the command line to convert these symbols to point.

The note that has to be mentioned here is that after running the EXPLODE command, points are moved from the P1 layer to 0. After converting the point symbols, select the Point Style option from the Format menu and select one of the point symbols in the window that pops up. Then type in a number as the size of the symbol in the Point Size box and click OK.

After doing this, when you zoom in on the points, you will find that the points are far from their codes. To resolve this issue, as mentioned above, select all the codes again using the QSELECT shortcut, then type and run the PR shortcut in the command line so that the Properties window pops up as in Figure 5-16.

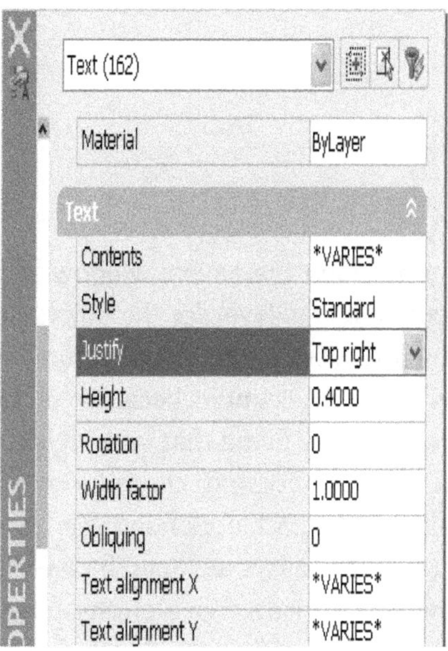

Figure 5-16

In this window, select the Top right mode next to the Justify option so that the codes of the points have a suitable position relative to the points themselves.

After making the adjustments above, you should start drawing the features. It is important to know that while drawing the map, you have to use a lot of drawing and editing commands, and while running these commands, the drawn points may be accidentally affected by these commands. In order to prevent making such a mistake and prevent your points from being eliminated or moved while running the drawing and editing commands, simply move all the points to a new layer and lock it.

By locking the points layer, no editing action will be done on the points in that layer. To do so, simply type and run the LA shortcut in the command line to open the Layers window. After opening the Layers window, create a new layer for the points by clicking on the icon or using the Alt+N keyboard shortcut, and then choose a name for the new layer. For example, because you want to move the points to this layer, you can name that layer "Points". Then next to the new layer, in the Color column, choose a color for the desired layer, and also click on the Lock option in order to lock the created layer. Then click Ok in the Layers window to save the layers and the adjustments. Now you want to move all the points to the Points layer which is locked. To do so, first you need to select all the points.

You need to use the QSELECT shortcut to select all the points in the drawing. For this purpose, type and run the QSELECT shortcut in the command line so that the corresponding window pops up. In this window, select the Point option in the Object type box, and select the Layer option in the Properties box, then set the Value box to the new name of the points layer which is 0, and then click Ok to select all the points.

After selecting all the points, to move them to the newly created layer, click on the Layers toolbar drop-down menu so that the list of the layers appears as in Figure 5-17. Then click on the Points layer to move all the selected points to the Points layer.

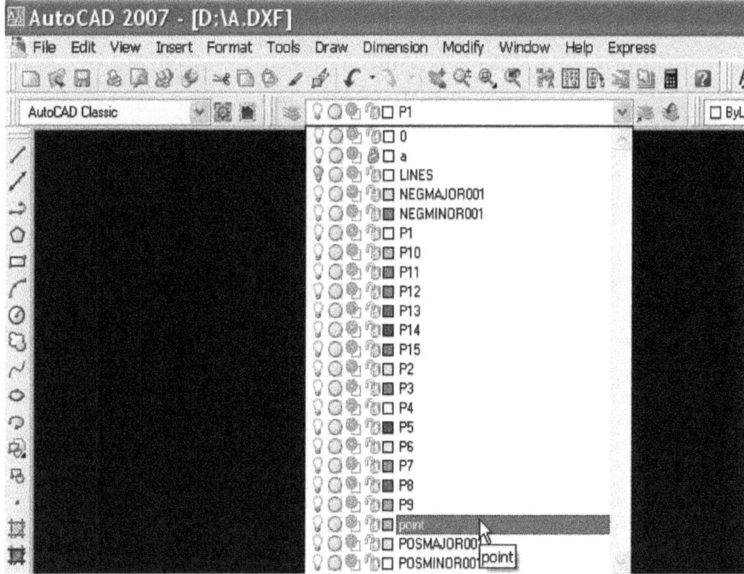

Figure 5-17

Before moving on to the next steps of the drawing, it is necessary to explain a bit about points codes to those who have not yet experienced land surveying.

In land surveying, each point has 5 parameters; three geometric parameters and two descriptive parameters. The geometric parameters, which include X, Y and Z, specify the position of the point in the 3D model space, and the descriptive parameters include point numbers and point codes. The point descriptive parameters are used for identifying and drawing. However, the code parameter is used more frequently. During land operations, define a code related to a feature when surveying each point of that feature so that it can be saved along with the geometric parameters. To make it easier and not to waste time on the land operations, make a list of the features in that region and define one or more abbreviations for each of them and give the Total Station instrument the code of that feature to survey each point of the feature. Most of the time, however, numeric codes are used. In the table in Figure 5-18, you can see the list of codes and features that has been used in this drawing.

1	BAGH	Garden
2	CHAH	Well
3	CHANEL	Channel
4	CHANEL B	Concrete Channel
5	JOY	Narrow Stream
6	MARZ	Land Border
7	POL	Bridge
8	POOL	Pool
9	RKH	Soil Road
10	TB	Light Pole
11	TREE	Tree

Figure 5-18

To draw the features more quickly and easily, define a layer for each feature and insert all the codes in that layer so that when you want to draw the dirt roads, you can turn the other codes off to avoid crowding the map and have more control over drawings. You will find out more about the importance of this matter.

Now, type and run the LA shortcut in the command line to open the Layers window as in Figure 5-19. In this window, you should create 11 layers and name each of them according to the above codes.

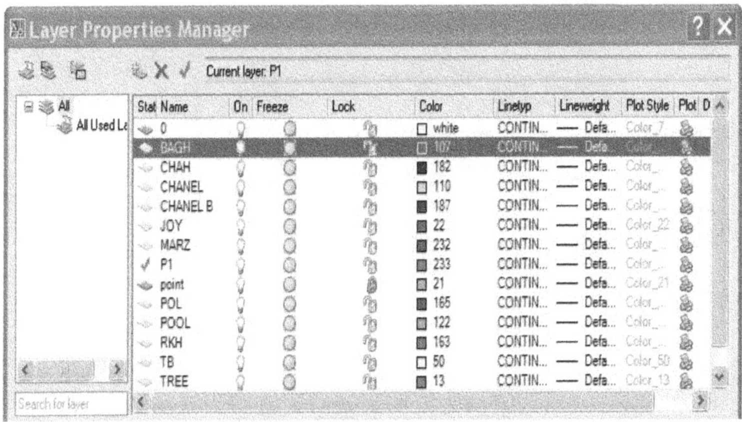

Figure 5-19

Now it is time to place the code of each feature in the layer created for that feature.

QSELECT shortcut should be used again for this purpose. For example, you want to select all the dirt road codes (RKH) and place them in the RKH layer.

So, type and run the QSELECT shortcut in the command line to open its window. In this window, as shown in Figure 5-20, select the Text option in the Object type section, and select the Contents option in the Properties section, then in front of the Value box, type the desired code which is RKH and select all of them by clicking OK. Then as shown in Figure 5-21, click on the drop-down menu next to the Layers toolbar so that the Layers list opens up. In this list, select the RKH layer so that all the RKH codes will be moved to the RKH layer.

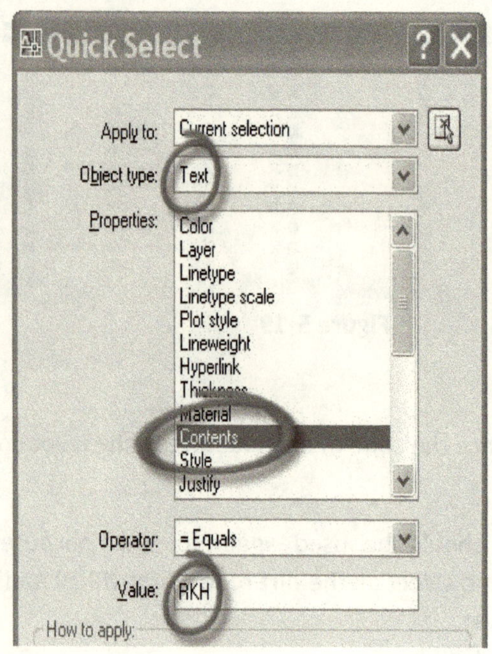
Quick Select
Apply to:
Current selection
Object type:
Text
Properties:
Color
Layer
Linetype
Linetype scale
Plot style
Lineweight
Hyperlink
Material
Contents
Style
Justify
Operator:
= Equals
Value:
RKH
How to apply:

Figure 5-20

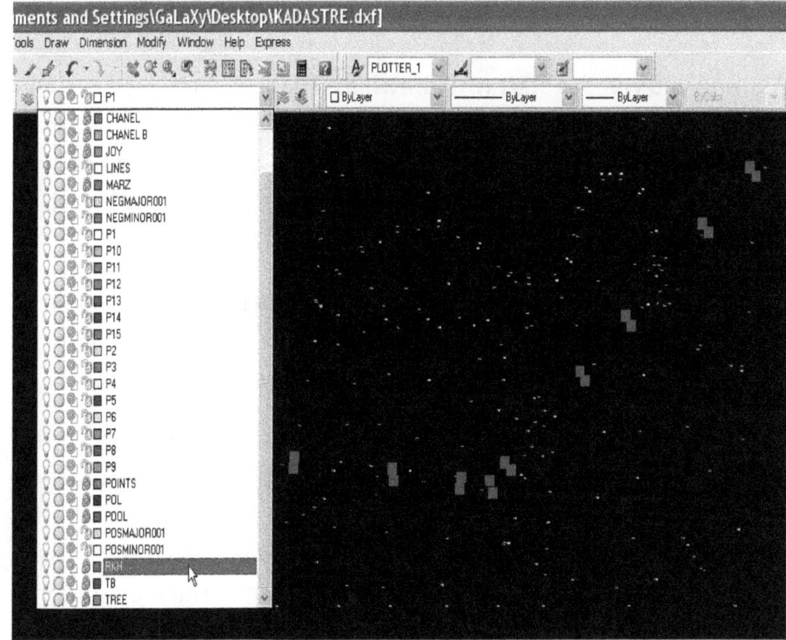

Figure 5-21

Likewise, do this for all the codes so that each code is in its own layer.

Now it is time to draw the features. As you know, in land surveying, the features are divided into three categories: Point features, Linear features and Area features. Standard symbols are used for Point features such as light poles, wells and trees. For Linear features such as dirt roads and channels, the special standard lines for that kind of feature are used. And standard hatches are used for Area features. Now, before standardizing the map, you have to draw the Linear and Area features. To do so and speed up the drawing operation, you just need to turn off the rest of the layers and just keep the layer you want to draw turned on. Of course, the points layer should always be turned on.

Assume you want to start with drawing a channel. First, type and run the LA shortcut in the command line to open the layers window. Then keep the CHANNEL layer and the POINTS layer turned on and turn off the rest of the layers. You should also make the CHANNEL layer current. But why?

Because you want to draw the lines of the channel, the purpose of making the CHANNEL layer current is to allow all the drawn lines to be placed in the CHANNEL layer after making it current.

As you can see, except for the CHANNEL codes and the points codes, the rest of the layers are turned off. This speeds up the drawing operation. Now to draw the channel lines, type and run the PL shortcut in the command line to run the Polyline command. Then, from the scene map that has been drawn during the land operations, connect the channel points to draw the whole channel as in Figure 5-22.

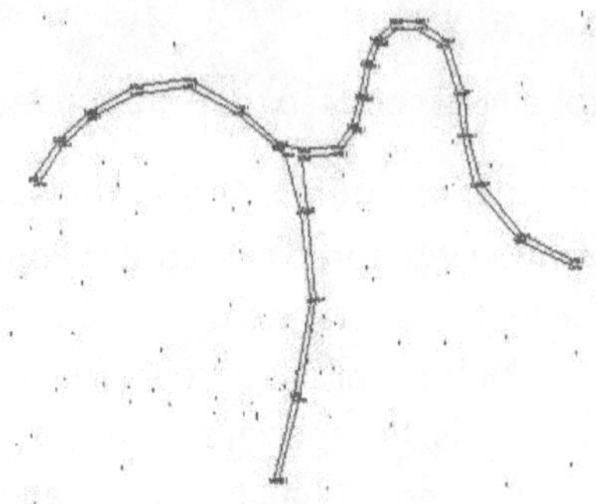

Figure 5-22

Now it is time to draw the concrete channel.

To draw the concrete channel, as in the previous case, turn off all the layers and keep only the POINTS and CHANNEL B layers turned on. Then start drawing the concrete channel. After drawing the concrete channel, you find out that only one side of the channel has been surveyed during the land operations and only one point has been surveyed from the other side as in Figure 5-23.

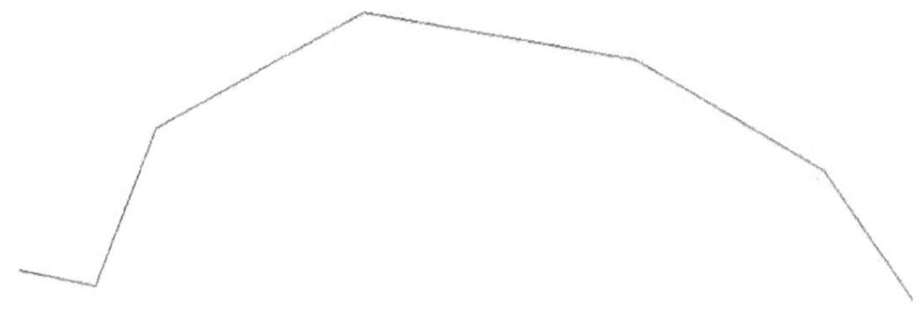

Figure 5-23

But how can you draw the other side of the channel?

Use the Offset command to do so. After drawing that side of the channel that has been completely surveyed, type and run the O shortcut in the command line. The software then asks you for the offset distance (channel width) and to provide it, click on the two starting points of the channel. Then the software asks you to specify the object that you want to Offset and you can do this by clicking on the whole channel. Then the software asks you for the side which you want the channel become Offset with that width. Do this by clicking on the point on the drawing area that is on the left side of the channel so that the right side of the channel becomes Offset to its left side and gets drawn as in Figure 5-24.

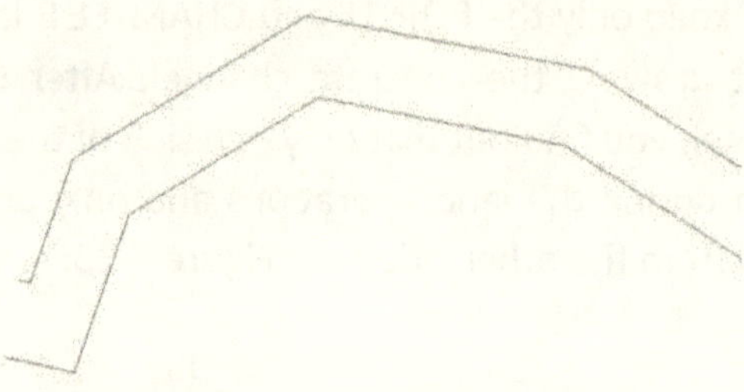

Figure 5-24

Then click on that extra part of the Offset channel and click on the end point again and connect it to the start of the left side of the channel.

Likewise, draw all the other features to have the shape in Figure 5-25 on your drawing area.

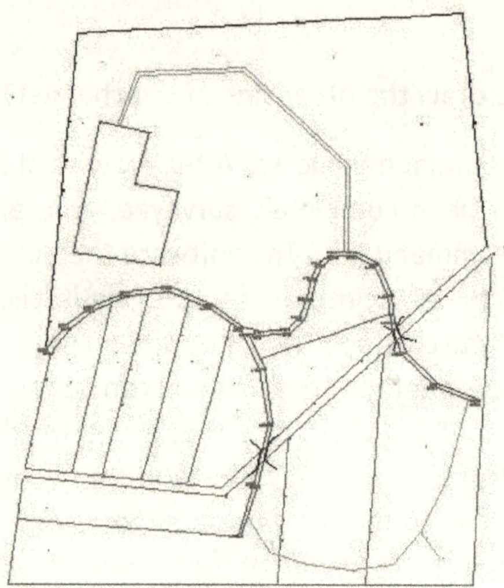

Figure 5-25

Once you have drawn the Linear and Area features of the project, it is time to standardize the map and for each feature, you should insert its own special symbol on the map.

Exercise 8

Quick insertion of feature symbols using blocks

One of the basic requirements for standard drawings is to use standard symbols for features. The standard symbols defined for features such as light poles, trees, wells, etc., are provided in the final chapter of the book.

To insert the symbol of a feature, you can simply copy the symbol and paste it at the desired points. But this cannot be done in larger drawings, where the number of features is quite high, because manual insertion of feature symbols will be extremely time-consuming.

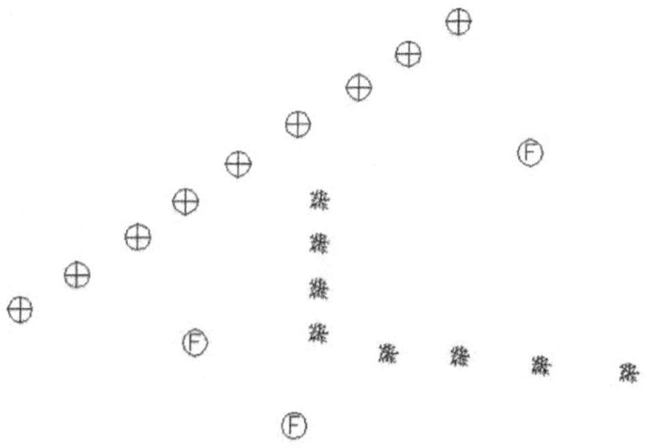

Figure 5-26

Specialized survey software such as *SDR map* and *Land* have some features for automatic insertion of these symbols. However, in cases where the symbols included in the software are not suitable for our project or the software do not allow new symbols to be defined, we have to use AutoCAD to insert feature symbols.

In AutoCAD, you can use blocks for this purpose. To do this, first, you must use the other software to insert a block for each type of feature, then change these blocks to the desired symbol in AutoCAD.

Consider the drawing shown in Figure 5-26. Produced by *SDR map*, this drawing contains 9 light poles, 3 wells, and 8 trees. In *SDR map*, each of these features has been given a Block-type symbol with the following names.

Feature Name	Symbol	Block Name
Tree		TREE_2-12
Well		SS_MANHOLE-20
Light pole		CROSS_CICLE-18

Open the file Symbole.dxf in the folder dwg in the attached disk.

This file contains the standard symbols of the above feature symbols (Figure 5-27).

Figure 5-27

These symbols are for well, tree, and light pole respectively. Now, the goal is to use these symbols in place of previous symbols.

Exercise 9

Mass importing of points into AutoCAD with the help of Excel

In this part of the book, we explain how you can use Excel to accelerate your work in AutoCAD.

It should be noted that Microsoft Excel is a very powerful and practical software with wide-ranging applications in survey computations (e.g. for traverse calculations, error balancing in levelling projects, etc.), which fall beyond the scope of this book. With that said, this section is focused on the simple solution that can be implemented in Excel to speed up the process of executing frequently used AutoCAD commands.

For example, suppose you want to create a single point in AutoCAD. To do this, you must first type the command *PO* or *Point* in the command line, press Space or Enter to execute it, then type X, Y, and Z coordinates of the point separated by a comma, and finally press Space or Enter to draw the point.

Now, suppose you want to draw two points with the following coordinates.

1	675000	3824200	1311.51
2	674960	3824200	1311.43

If you manage to produce a text or Excel file with the contents:

Point 675000,3824200,1311.508

point 674960,3824200,1311.428

You can simply copy this into the command line and create both points at once (because the text in each line satisfies the requirements for running the *Point* command).

Practice this on the file named 2point.txt provided in the data folder.

Important note

In the AutoCAD command line, *Space* key performs the same function as *Enter* key. In other words, this key executes a typed command and if no command is typed in, it executes the last command executed. Hence, we can use the *Space* character to emulate the act of pressing *Enter* after typing a command. In the above lines of text, one space character is used after the word *Point* to start executing this command and another is used after the Z coordinate to finish the command. Thus, both of them are necessary for executing the *Point* command.

The explained method can be used to draw a large number of points at once, but preparing the text needed to do this could become very time-consuming. Fortunately, we can use Excel to speed up the process and create a large body of text ready for use in the AutoCAD command line.

Note that to use Excel, you must first learn the rules that apply to writing texts and defining functions in this software. These rules can be learned, rather easily, from Excel training books available online or in paper. For example, to produce the above lines of text, you must create a function in the following form:

="point "&x&","&y&","&z

where x, y, and z are the cells containing the X, Y, and Z coordinate of the point.

Suppose you want to import the points of Figure 5-28 using the above formula.

Paste Format Painter Clipboard Font Alignment Merge & Center

CONCATENATE =“point "&B1&","&C1&","&D1

	A	B	C	D	E
1	1	675000	3825320	1312.01	="point "&B1&","&C1&","&D1
2	2	674960	3825320	1312.025	
3	3	674760	3825280	1313.96	
4	4	674800	3825280	1314.615	
5	5	674840	3825280	1315.59	
6	6	674880	3825280	1316.565	
7	7	674920	3825280	1317.54	
8	8	674960	3825280	1312.01	
9	9	675000	3825280	1312.025	
10	10	675000	3825240	1313.96	
11	11	674960	3825240	1314.615	
12	12	674920	3825240	1315.59	
13					

Figure 5-28

To do this, after inserting the points into Excel, type the above formula in the first row of a new column (in this example, the cell E1) and then replace the x, y, and z with the name of the cells containing the X, Y, and Z coordinates, which here are B1 and C1 and D1. After editing the formula, press enter to confirm it. The contents of the cell E1 should then change to:

point 675000,3825320,1312.01

Now, move the mouse cursor to the bottom right corner of the cell E1 until the cursor changes to a + sign, and then click and drag down until reaching the last row of data, that is, the cell E12. This makes the software reproduce the formula for all the subsequent rows, as shown in Figure 5-29.

Figure 5-29

F7 | fx

	A	B	C	D	E
1	1	675000	3825320	1312.01	point 675000,3825320,1312.01
2	2	674960	3825320	1312.025	point 674960,3825320,1312.025
3	3	674760	3825280	1313.96	point 674760,3825280,1313.96
4	4	674800	3825280	1314.615	point 674800,3825280,1314.615
5	5	674840	3825280	1315.59	point 674840,3825280,1315.59
6	6	674880	3825280	1316.565	point 674880,3825280,1316.565
7	7	674920	3825280	1317.54	point 674920,3825280,1317.54
8	8	674960	3825280	1312.01	point 674960,3825280,1312.01
9	9	675000	3825280	1312.025	point 675000,3825280,1312.025
10	10	675000	3825240	1313.96	point 675000,3825240,1313.96
11	11	674960	3825240	1314.615	point 674960,3825240,1314.615
12	12	674920	3825240	1315.59	point 674920,3825240,1315.59
13					

Now, to insert your points, you just have to select and copy these cells (Figure 5-30) and then paste them in the AutoCAD command line (by right-clicking on the command line and selecting *Paste* or clicking in the command line and pressing Ctrl+V)

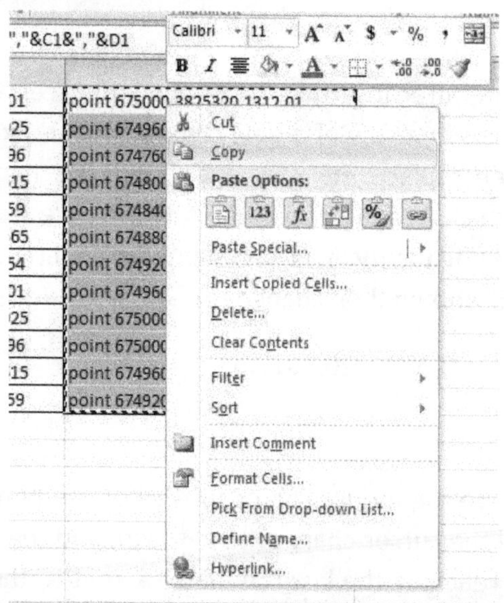

Figure 5-30

You can use the file point.xls in the folder data to practice this method.

Exercise 10

Creating texts for a multitude of points with the help of Excel

To create a text for multiple points in a drawing, we must examine how texts are created in AutoCAD, emulate the steps in Excel, and finally copy the results from Excel into AutoCAD command line.

Steps that must be taken to create a text in AutoCAD are:

1. Type the command -text

2. Type a space to execute the command

3. Enter the x coordinate of the base point

4. Type a comma character ((,))

5. Enter the y coordinate of the base point

6. Type a space to confirm the base point and proceed to the next step

7. Enter the text height

8. Type a space

9. Enter the text rotation angle (usually zero)

10. Type a space

11. Enter the desired text (can be the point elevation, code, coordinates, or any other data)

The excel formula for emulating the above steps is:

="-text "&<u>X</u>&","&<u>Y</u>&" "&<u>height</u>&" "&<u>angle</u>&" "&<u>text</u>

where *X* and *Y* are the cells containing the x and y coordinates of the point, *height* is the desired text height, and *angle* is the desired text rotation angle.

For example, to perform this process for the points of the previous exercise, you should create an excel file like the one displayed in Figure 5-32.

CONCATENATE ="-text "&B1&","&C1&" "&2&" "&0&" "&D1

	A	B	C	D	E
1	1	675000	3825320	1312.01	="-text "&B1&","&C1&" "&2&" "&0&" "&D1
2	2	674960	3825320	1312.025	-text 674960,3825320 2 0 1312.025
3	3	674760	3825280	1313.96	-text 674760,3825280 2 0 1313.96
4	4	674800	3825280	1314.615	-text 674800,3825280 2 0 1314.615
5	5	674840	3825280	1315.59	-text 674840,3825280 2 0 1315.59
6	6	674880	3825280	1316.565	-text 674880,3825280 2 0 1316.565
7	7	674920	3825280	1317.54	-text 674920,3825280 2 0 1317.54
8	8	674960	3825280	1312.01	-text 674960,3825280 2 0 1312.01
9	9	675000	3825280	1312.025	-text 675000,3825280 2 0 1312.025
10	10	675000	3825240	1313.96	-text 675000,3825240 2 0 1313.96
11	11	674960	3825240	1314.615	-text 674960,3825240 2 0 1314.615
12	12	674920	3825240	1315.59	-text 674920,3825240 2 0 1315.59
13					

Figure 5-32

Next, you just have to select and copy the created cells and paste them in the AutoCAD command line.

Exercise 11

Fast drawing of a route's axis line with the help of Excel

In many projects, you will need to draw the axis line (centerline) of a route with *Line* or *Pline* commands. In cases where the points are in correct order, such lines can be drawn very quickly with the help of Excel.

Suppose that the points with the coordinates given below constitute the axis line of a route.

1	311.072	962.631
2	361.058	961.521
3	411.057	961.43
4	461.013	963.357
5	510.74	968.439
6	559.797	977.978
7	607.333	993.367
9	651.999	1015.704
10	692.16	1045.37
11	725.865	1082.195
12	751.058	1125.263
13	766.633	1172.697
14	776.544	1221.694
15	787.185	1270.537
16	807.576	1315.878
17	849.101	1341.599
18	898.826	1345.983

19	948.79	1347.548

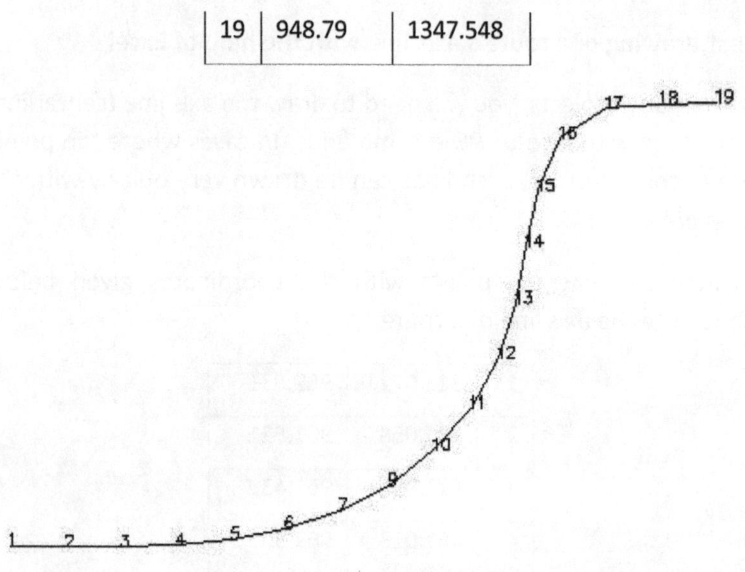

Figure 5-33

As can be seen in Figure 5-33, these points are in the correct order and are numbered 1 to 19, respectively. The Excel formula for drawing a line with these points using the *Pline* command is:

="pline "&X&","&Y

where *X* and *Y* are the cells containing the x and y coordinates of the point. The rest of the process is similar to what was explained in previous examples. As before, you must select and copy the resulting cells and paste them in the AutoCAD command line.

For more practice, use the file Ax.xls in the folder data.

CONCATENATE =“pline "&B1&","&C

	A	B	C	D
1	1	311.072	962.631	="pline "&B1&","&C1
2	2	361.058	961.521	pline 361.058,961.521
3	3	411.057	961.43	pline 411.057,961.43
4	4	461.013	963.357	pline 461.013,963.357
5	5	510.74	968.439	pline 510.74,968.439
6	6	559.797	977.978	pline 559.797,977.978
7	7	607.333	993.367	pline 607.333,993.367
8	9	651.999	1015.704	pline 651.999,1015.704
9	10	692.16	1045.37	pline 692.16,1045.37
10	11	725.865	1082.195	pline 725.865,1082.195
11	12	751.058	1125.263	pline 751.058,1125.263
12	13	766.633	1172.697	pline 766.633,1172.697
13	14	776.544	1221.694	pline 776.544,1221.694
14	15	787.185	1270.537	pline 787.185,1270.537
15	16	807.576	1315.878	pline 807.576,1315.878
16	17	849.101	1341.599	pline 849.101,1341.599
17	18	898.826	1345.983	pline 898.826,1345.983
18	19	948.79	1347.548	pline 948.79,1347.548
19				
20				

Figure 5-34

Exercise 12

Quick insertion of feature symbols with the help of Excel

Consider the following survey table.

1	384027.71	637561.75	TIR
2	384045.08	637571.98	TIR
3	384063.69	637583.14	TIR
4	384078.25	637593.67	TIR
5	384094.39	637604.83	TIR
6	384112.69	637616.61	TIR
7	384131.63	637627.45	TIR
8	384146.81	637637.37	TIR
9	384162.32	637646.97	TIR
10	384081.35	637552.08	CHAH
11	384184.75	637608.10	CHAH
12	384112.21	637527.51	CHAH

This table contains the coordinates of the points in Exercise 7, which are related to three types of feature, namely light poles (TIR), water wells (CHAH) and trees (DERAKHT). Here, the goal is to insert the symbols of each feature on the related points.

To do this, we will use the *Copy* command in AutoCAD and then using the destination coordinates prepared in an Excel file. In AutoCAD, after copying an object and pressing enter, the software will ask you to specify the point where it must be pasted, either by mouse clicking or by entering the coordinates in the command line. Hence, you can copy a symbol with the *Copy* command, then copy/paste a list of points where symbol must be pasted from an

Excel file. To prepare this list in excel, you can use the following simple formula:

=X&","&Y

Note that this process should be done separately for each feature. Thus, you must first prepare a list of points with the code representing the feature, select and copy the corresponding symbol, and paste it at the coordinates of the prepared list. To practice, use the file block.xls in the folder data, which contains the above points, and the file Symbol.dwg in the folder dwg, which contains the symbols of the features located at these points.

Using Excel's Concatenate function to construct AutoCAD commands

You can use the Concatenate function in excel to carry out the operations of exercises 8 to 11 even more quickly. Suppose we want to use with this option to complete Exercise 8, i.e., import multiple points into AutoCAD. To do this, you must open the excel file, click on the first cell of a new column, and then click on the f_x button or press Shift+F3. In this window (Figure 5-35), set the *Or select a category* menu to *All* and select the *CONCATENATE* function from the function list. Press OK to open the *Function Arguments* window displayed in Figure 5-36.

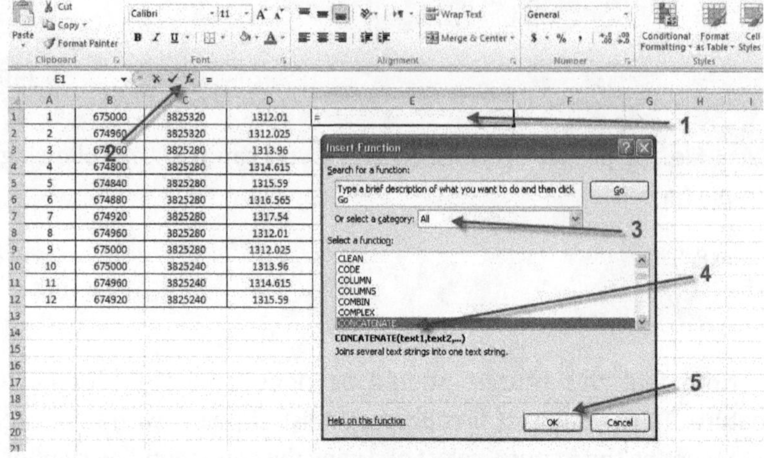

Figure 5-35

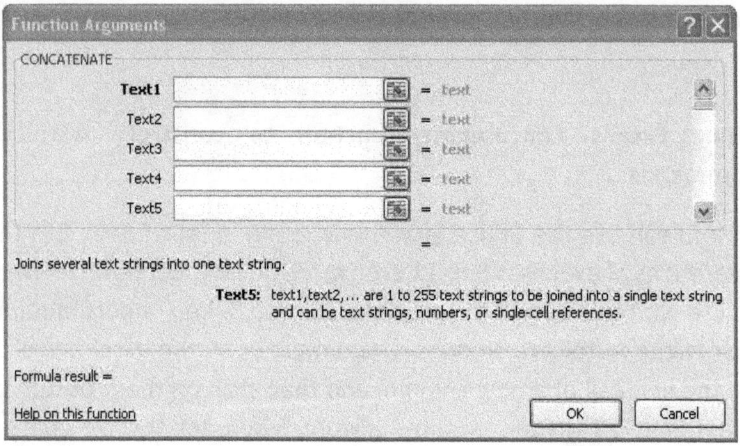

Function Arguments

CONCATENATE

Text1 = text

Text2 = text

Text3 = text

Text4 = text

Text5 = text

=

Joins several text strings into one text string.

Text5: text1,text2,... are 1 to 255 text strings to be joined into a single text string and can be text strings, numbers, or single-cell references.

Formula result =

Help on this function

OK Cancel

Figure 5-36

This window contains up to 255 boxes, named *Text1*, *Text2* .... , which can be used to construct a formula for creating AutoCAD commands. For this purpose, you must enter in the text boxes the words and components that will constitute the desired AutoCAD command. In the case of Exercise 8 for example, you must type *point* in *Text1* box, type a *space* character in *Text2* box, press the *Text3* button and select the cell holding the first x-coordinate, type a *comma* character in *Text4* box, press the *Text5* button and select the cell holding the first y-coordinate, type another *comma* character in *Text6* box, press the *Text7* button and select the cell holding the first z-coordinate, and type another *space* character in *Text8* box. When done, press OK to create the *Concatenate* function, as shown in Figure 5-37.

Clipboard | Font | Alignment

E1 | fx =CONCATENATE("point"," ",B1,",",C1,",",D1," ")

	A	B	C	D	E
1	1	675000	3825320	1312.01	point 675000,3825320,1312.01
2	2	674960	3825320	1312.025	
3	3	674760	3825280	1313.96	
4	4	674800	3825280	1314.615	
5	5	674840	3825280	1315.59	
6	6	674880	3825280	1316.565	
7	7	674920	3825280	1317.54	
8	8	674960	3825280	1312.01	
9	9	675000	3825280	1312.025	
10	10	675000	3825240	1313.96	
11	11	674960	3825240	1314.615	
12	12	674920	3825240	1315.59	

Figure 5-37

You can now drag down the created cell to let the software reproduce the function for the subsequent rows. When finished, copy the resulting column and paste it into the AutoCAD command line. To practice, redo the exercises 8-11 using the *Concatenate* function.

Exercise 13

Drawing tunnel excavation cross sections using AutoCAD

One of the most important topics in tunnel projects is drawing and representing the tunnel excavation cross sections. It can be used to calculate the volume of overbreak area, which plays a significant role in project finances.

As it is clear, the tunnel cross section is in 3D model space. But you want to see it as a 2D model space, and at the same time, from the front view, vertical to the axis of the tunnel.

For example, in Figure 5-39, you can see the coordinates of a particular cross section of a tunnel being surveyed, which appears on the map like this.

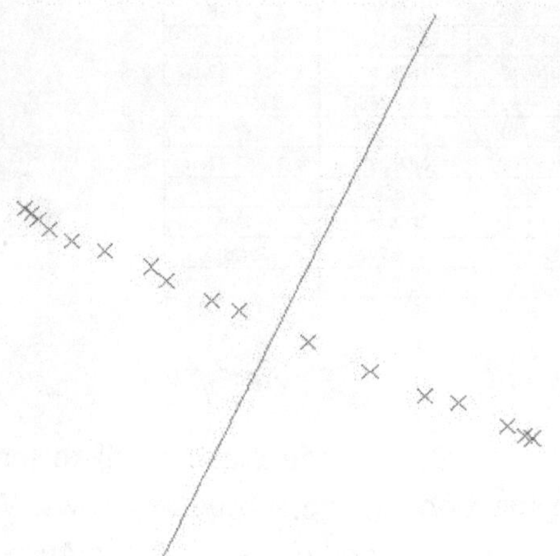

Figure 5-39

Figure 5-40

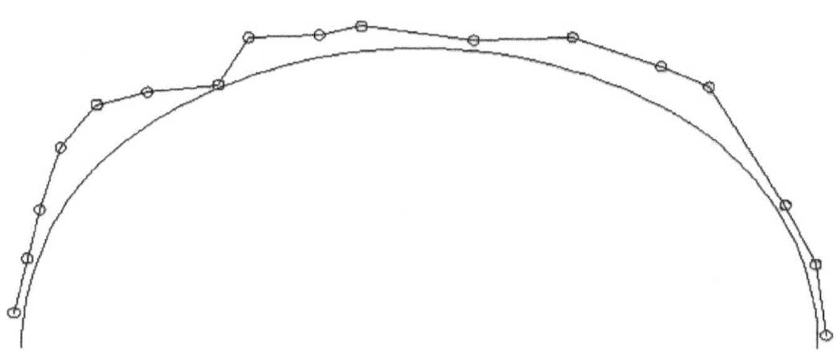

Figure 5-41

In order to view the excavated cross section and to calculate the overbreak area and underbreak area of excavation, it must be seen like Figure 5-40.

After drawing and inserting the planned tunnel profile, it will be shown as Figure 5-41.

It is now possible to calculate the overbreak area of excavation, and also calculate the volume of overbreak area according to the areas before and after this cross section.

There are many ways to do this which is possible with land surveying software such as Civil 3D and Land. But the purpose of this part of the book is to explain about how to draw cross sections using AutoCAD, which can actually be described as the fastest and easiest way to do this.

To do so, first, import the points into the AutoCAD environment using one of the point importing methods described in this book, or using other land surveying software in a way that the points have elevation.

It should be noted that if you are using a software such as Land or Civil 3D to import the points, since the type of the points in these software is civil object or cogo point, you should change their type to "point" using commands like Explode and their symbol of display should be dot (.). After importing the points, you need to place the tunnel axis on the surveyed areas, as you should make the changes relative to the tunnel axis.

After doing this, select all the points using the mouse and click on the Z Axis Vector icon from the UCS toolbar as in Figure 5-42.

Figure 5-42

Then click on the start and end of the tunnel axis to place it as the Z axis of these points. But as you can see, no changes are made on the map. Because as the Z axis of the points changes, the Z axis of the map has also been changed.

To view the tunnel cross section points as they were changed, you should select and copy the points, then paste them in a new file whose Z axis is normal and in North direction.

After doing this, connect the points using the line drawing commands, and then place the planned tunnel profile on it and calculate the overbreak area of excavation.

Exercise 14

Drawing tunnel excavation cross sections using Land

One of the most commonly used methods of drawing a tunnel excavation cross section is using the Land software and getting some help from the Excel software.

The general function of this method is to use the Offset relative to the tunnel axis and the elevation of the points. To do so, first, import the points into the Land software environment and place the axis on the tunnel on them. Then introduce the tunnel axis as Alignment to the software.

After doing this, as shown in Figure 5-43, select the Station/Offset option from the Alignment menu, then select the Display Points option. By selecting this option, the following message will appear in the command line.

Sort the points by station [Yes/No]

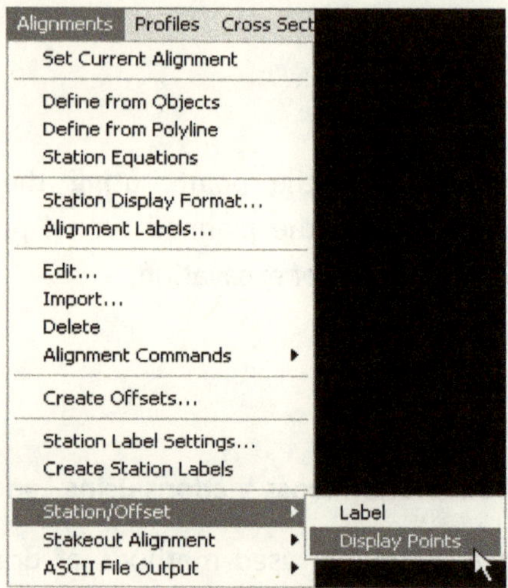

Figure 5-43

This message asks you whether the points would be arranged using the <u>points chainage</u> (low to high). So, select Yes in response.

Then another message appears in the command line asking you for the points that you want to get Offset from.

List points by [Selection/Number] <Selection

It offers two methods of selection, one with the point number and the other one selecting it using the mouse. Choose the Selection mode by typing the letter S. Then, using the mouse, select all the points and press the Enter key, and you can see that it displays the list of all the points in <u>chainage</u>, Offset and elevation forms as in Figure 5-44.

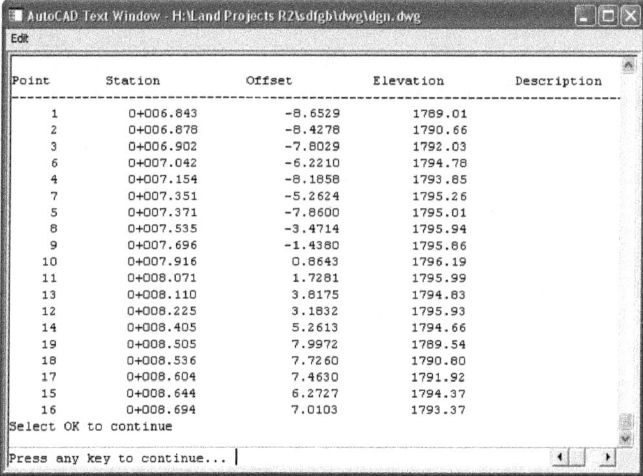
AutoCAD Text Window - H:\Land Projects R2\sdfgb\dwg\dgn.dwg

Edit

Point	Station	Offset	Elevation	Description
1	0+006.843	-8.6529	1789.01	
2	0+006.878	-8.4278	1790.66	
3	0+006.902	-7.8029	1792.03	
6	0+007.042	-6.2210	1794.78	
4	0+007.154	-8.1858	1793.85	
7	0+007.351	-5.2624	1795.26	
5	0+007.371	-7.8600	1795.01	
8	0+007.535	-3.4714	1795.94	
9	0+007.696	-1.4380	1795.86	
10	0+007.916	0.8643	1796.19	
11	0+008.071	1.7281	1795.99	
13	0+008.110	3.8175	1794.83	
12	0+008.225	3.1832	1795.93	
14	0+008.405	5.2613	1794.66	
19	0+008.505	7.9972	1789.54	
18	0+008.536	7.7260	1790.80	
17	0+008.604	7.4630	1791.92	
15	0+008.644	6.2727	1794.37	
16	0+008.694	7.0103	1793.37	

Select OK to continue

Press any key to continue...

Figure 5-44

Now, using the Copy & Paste operation, import this file into the Excel software and create a new format of the points, in a way that the first column contains the point numbers, the second column contains the Offsets, and the elevations are in the third column.

Now create an ASCII file export from this file in order to import it into the Land, in a way that the first column contains the point numbers, the second column is X, the third column is Y, and the fourth column contains the description of the points, and at the end, the P,X,Y,D text format would be generated as in Figure 5-45.

Now if you import this text file into the Land environment, it will display the tunnel excavation cross section (from the front view).

To practice more, do Exercise 13 using this method.

A	B	C	D
1	-8.6529	1789.01	1
2	-8.4278	1790.66	1
3	-7.8029	1792.03	1
6	-6.221	1794.78	1
4	-8.1858	1793.85	1
7	-5.2624	1795.26	1
5	-7.86	1795.01	1
8	-3.4714	1795.94	1
9	-1.438	1795.86	1
10	0.8643	1796.19	1
11	1.7281	1795.99	1
13	3.8175	1794.83	1
12	3.1832	1795.93	1
14	5.2613	1794.66	1
19	7.9972	1789.54	1
18	7.726	1790.8	1
17	7.463	1791.92	1
15	6.2727	1794.37	1
16	7.0103	1793.37	1

Figure 5-45

Exercise 15

Digitization of longitudinal profiles

By digitizing the longitudinal profile, we mean creating a longitudinal profile where the chainage (station) and elevation data of any point can be easily extracted with the ID command.

For example, Figure XX shows the longitudinal profile of a 360 meters long route, which involves both cut and fill operations and contains two vertical curves.

The important parameters for digitalization of a profile are horizontal and vertical scales, chainage (station), and elevation.

Horizontal and vertical scales are important because a digital profile should have a 1:1 scale in both directions. In the profile of this example, the horizontal scale is 2:1 and the vertical scale is 1:5 and, hence, the horizontal scale should be doubled and the vertical scale should be divided by 5 (or multiplied by 0.2).

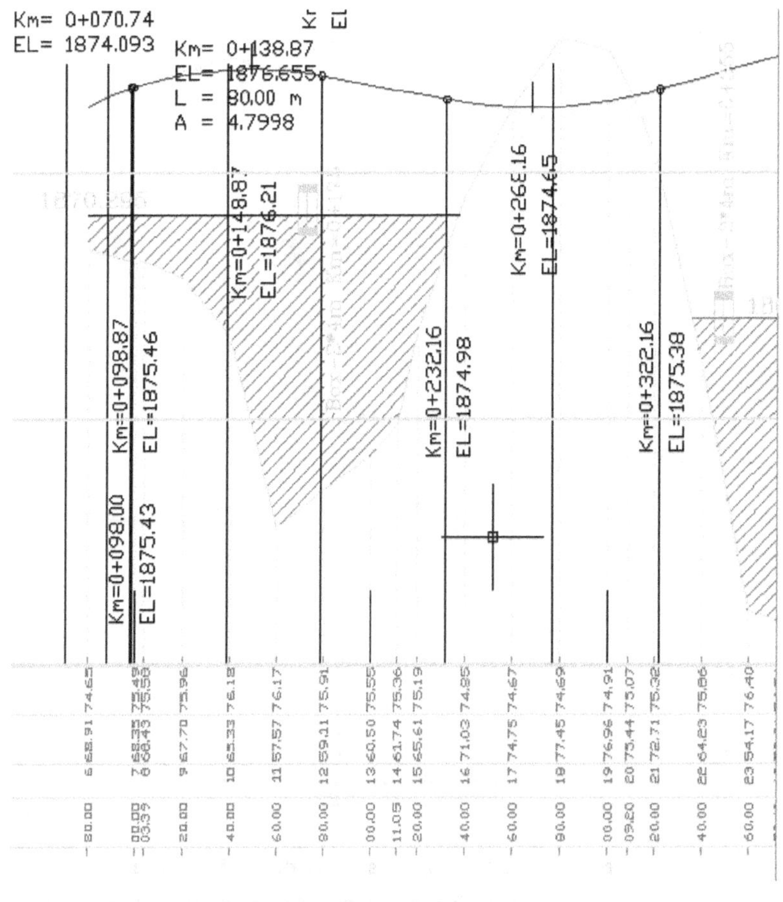

Figure 5-46

The point of all of this is to relocate the entire profile such that the X and Y coordinates of the points become equal to the route's chainage and elevation values. For example, the station 0+200 of the profile displayed in Figure 5-46 has an elevation of 75.55. Thus, if we transfer the profile such that this point fall on the coordinates (200, 75.55), then we have created a digital profile where station and elevation of any point can be easily determined by checking its X and Y values.

This can be done faster and more conveniently with the help of blocks. For this purpose, execute the shortcut command B in the command line to open the *Block Definition* window (Figure 5-48).

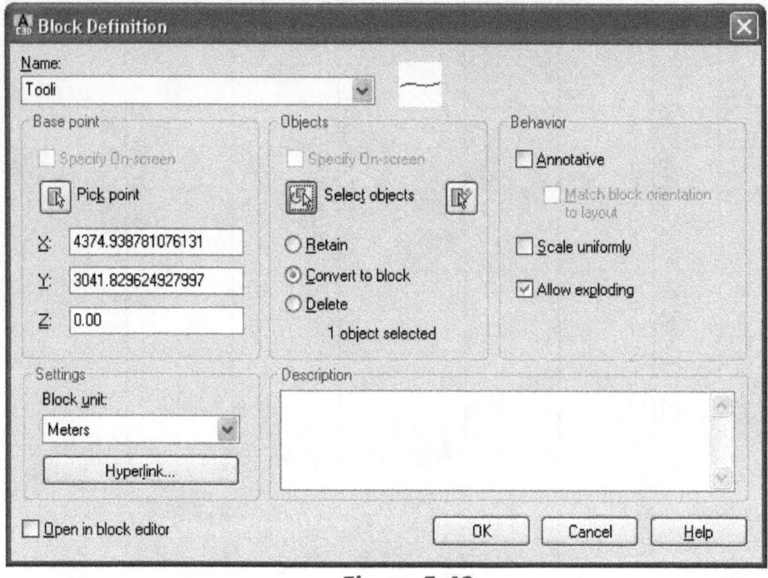

Figure 5-48

In this window, first type a name for the block, then use the *Select objects* button to select the project line (the blue line). After selecting all project lines, press the *Pick point* button, click on the 0+200 station on to the project line. In this step, make absolutely sure to click exactly on the point on the route, because the entire profile will be transferred based on this point. For an easier selection of this point, you can mark it in advance with a circle or with a colored point.

When done, press OK to make the profile into a block with the base point at (200, 75.55). Note that this point will now have a different coordinate.

The next step is to insert this block on the target point and change its scale. For this purpose, you must use the command *Insert Block* with the shortcut *I*. After executing this command, you will be directed to the *Insert* window shown in Figure 5-49.

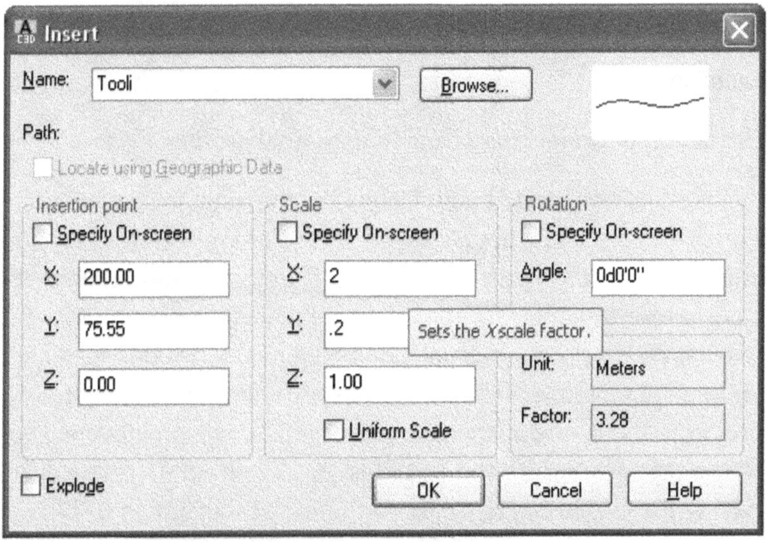

Figure 5-49

In this window, select the block you just created. In the pane *Insertion point*, you must enter the coordinates (200, 75.55). In the *Scale* pane, the horizontal scale should be doubled and the vertical scale should be multiplied by 0.2.

When finished, press OK to insert the profile at the target point.

Now, you can run the ID command on any point of the profile to determine its station and elevation values.

The files related to this exercise are located in the folder named Long section.

Note that it is customary to use the first point of the profile as the insertion point, but to avoid confusion, here we used an arbitrarily selected point (200, 75.55).

To better understand the process, try to transfer the profile using the coordinates of the first point (80, 74.65).

Exercise 16

Extraction of project data from longitudinal profiles

In many longitudinal profiles, like the one in the previous exercise, project data are displayed at regular intervals (usually 20m intervals). But to obtain project data from any other station, you have to calculate them for the target point. In straight segments, this calculation is a simple interpolation between the stations positioned immediately before and after the target point. In the longitudinal profile of the previous exercise, for example, the project elevation at the stations 0+160 and 0+180 is 76.17 and 75.91 respectively. Having these values, the project elevation at the station 0+170 can be easily interpolated to 76.04. However, if the road segment is not absolutely straight, we cannot use interpolation in this way and have to conduct curve calculations. Moreover, in cases where the route is long and contains multiple vertical curves, it would be very difficult, time-consuming, and error-prone to manually calculate project elevations at small intervals (sometimes the interval has to be 1 meter or even half a meter, particularly in tunneling projects). AutoCAD does not contain an explicit feature for dealing with this issue, but the problem can be solved by using a combination of AutoCAD commands.

But first, you need to digitize the longitudinal profile as explained in the previous exercise.

After digitizing the profile, use the *Line* command to draw a line below the profile. Then draw another line vertically such that its extension would cross the first point of the profile (see Figure 5-50).

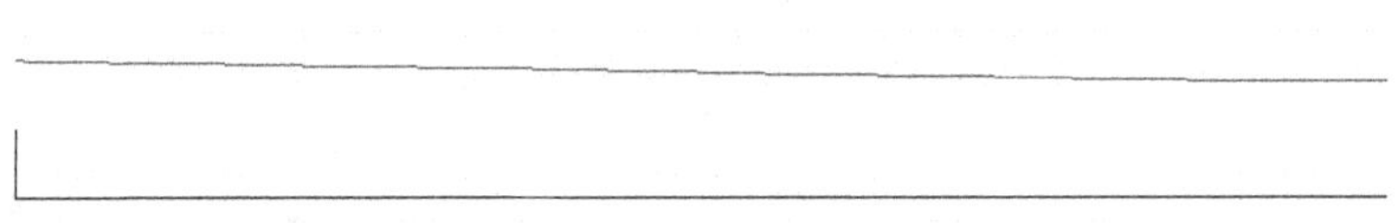

Figure 5-50

Make sure to draw the vertical line drawn with the *Line* command and none other. It is also recommended to position the line in such a way as to obtain round stations. For example, if your profile starts at a non-round chainage like 0+57.5 and you want the stations to be round, then you must relocate the line by 2.5 meters to make it match the 0+60.0 station.

The next step is to copy this line at the desired station or intervals. Here, we use the *Array* command to accelerate this operation. Executing the *array* command opens the *Array* window displayed in Figure 5-51 (If you are using 2009 or later versions of AutoCAD, execute the *Arrayclasic* command).

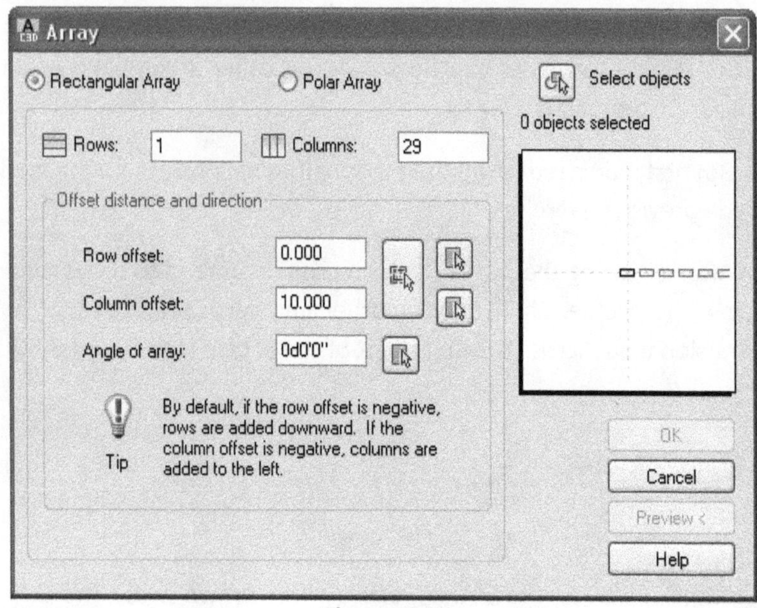

Figure 5-51

Press the *Select object* button in the upper right part of this window, click on the vertical line you drew earlier, and press enter to reopen this window. Then, use the *Rows* and *Columns* fields to set the number of rows to 1 the number of columns to 29.

The choice of the number of columns depends on the total profile length and the intervals at which we need project data. For example, since this profile is 290 meters long and we want data at 10-meter intervals, the number of columns is set to 290/10=29. Similarly, to have data at 5 meters and 1-meter intervals, this number should be set to respectively 290/5=58 and 290/1=290.

Next, set the *Row offset* to 0 and the *Column offset* to 10 (i.e. the length of each interval). After pressing OK, the lines will appear as shown in Figure 5-52.

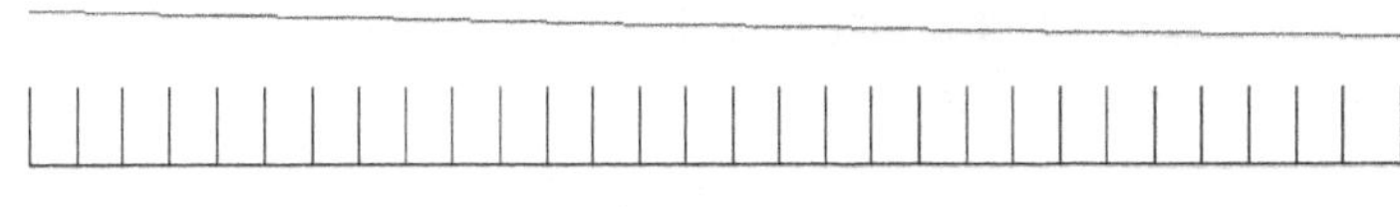

Figure 5-52

The next step is to use the *Extend* command to connect these lines to the longitudinal profile (Figure 5-53).

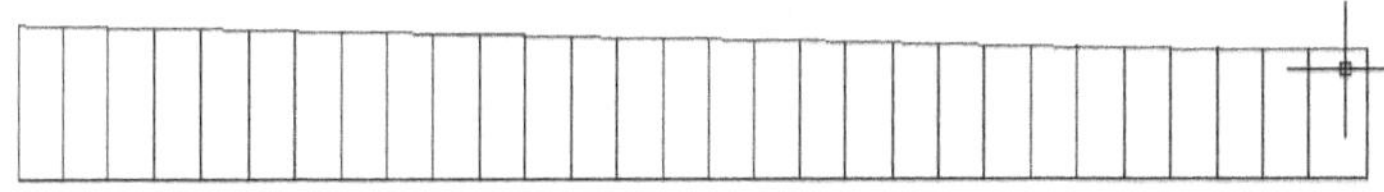

Figure 5-53

Now, since the profile is digital, the project station and elevation can be obtained by using the *Data Extraction* command to extract the coordinates of the end of the lines. This command is described in Chapter 3 and Exercise 73, so in the following, we will briefly explain the method.

After executing this command and completing its initial steps, use the *Select Objects* button to select all vertical lines. In the following steps, select only the *End X* and *End Y* options in the *Geometry* pane, and finally, save the file in .csv or .xls format. This file will be used to prepare the IDX files of the route.

During exporting, remember to check whether the profile points are the start or the end of the lines. Because if they are at the start of the lines, you should select the *Start X* and *Start Y* options from the *Geometry* pane.

Exercise 17

Extraction of texts from a drawing

Sometimes, it is necessary to extract the texts of a drawing for use in other software such as Excel.

For example, the drawing illustrated in Figure 5-54 is a plot of a wall consisting of 53 piles, with the coordinates of every pile displayed at the bottom. The goal is to extract these coordinates for use in Excel.

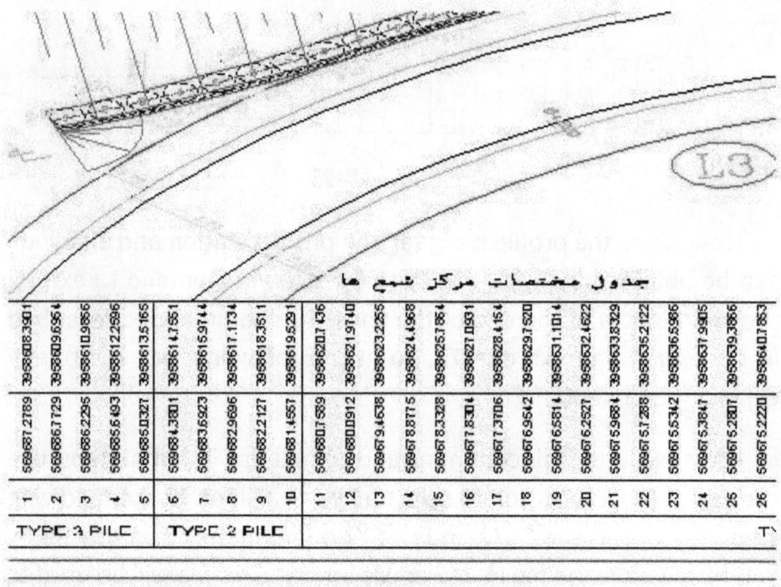

No.	X	Y
1	5696687.2789	3958608.3901
2	5696686.7729	3958609.6964
3	5696686.2295	3958610.9856
4	5696685.6493	3958612.2596
5	5696685.0327	3958613.5165
6	5696684.3801	3958614.7551
7	5696683.6923	3958615.9744
8	5696682.9696	3958617.1734
9	5696682.2127	3958618.3511
10	5696681.4557	3958619.5291
11	5696680.7589	3958620.7436
12	5696680.0912	3958621.9740
13	5696679.4638	3958623.2255
14	5696678.8775	3958624.4968
15	5696678.3328	3958625.7864
16	5696677.8304	3958627.0931
17	5696677.3706	3958628.4154
18	5696676.9542	3958629.7520
19	5696676.5814	3958631.1014
20	5696676.2527	3958632.4622
21	5696675.9684	3958633.8329
22	5696675.7288	3958635.2122
23	5696675.5342	3958636.5986
24	5696675.3847	3958637.9905
25	5696675.2807	3958639.3866
26	5696675.2220	3958640.7853

Figure 5-54

This drawing is named Pile.dwg and can be found in the folder dwg.

Open this file, and then execute shortcut command *dx* in the command line to open the *Data Extraction* window. In the first page of this window, select a name for the file and click *Next*.

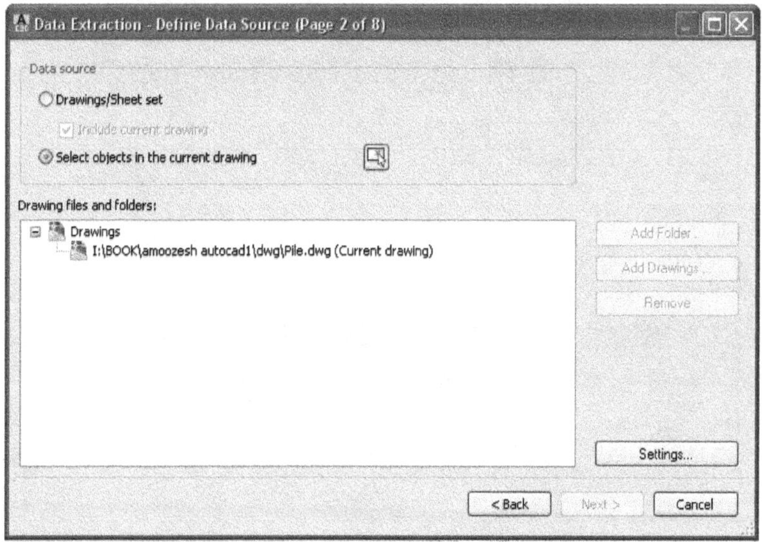

Figure 5-55

In the second page, choose *Select objects in the current drawing* (Figure 5-55), then use the button in front of it to select all the texts related to pile coordinates. After selecting all texts, press enter to reopen the window and then click *Next* to proceed to the next page

In this page, you will see a list of selected objects. As shown in Figure 5-56, check the *text* option and unchecked the rest.

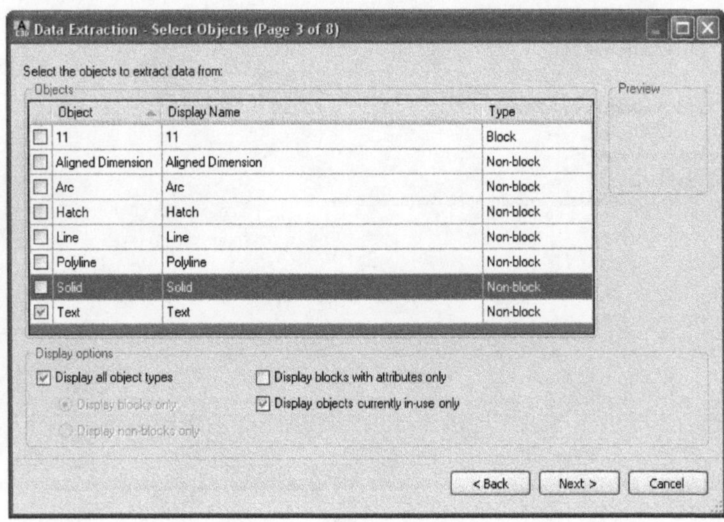

Figure 5-56

When done press Next to proceed to the fourth page of this window.

In the page, you should enable the *Text* option in the *Category filter* box and only the *Value* option in the *Properties* box (Figure 5-57). Press next when done.

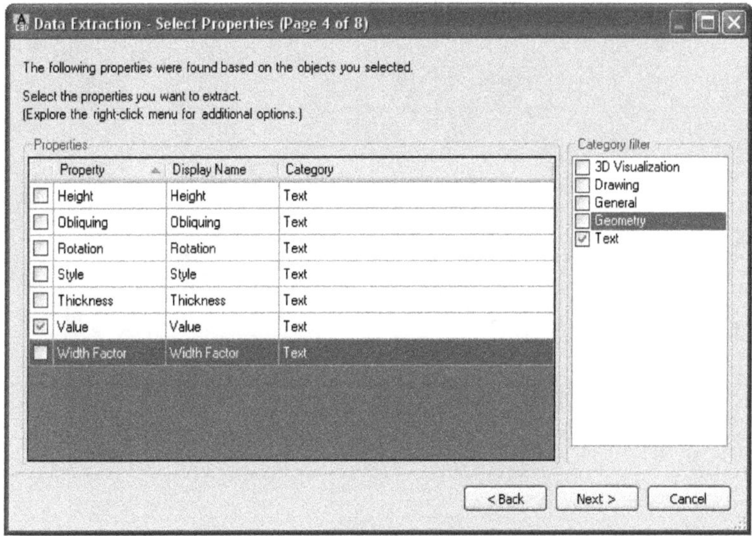

Figure 5-57

The next page will show you the selected texts. Click *Next* to go to the next page.

In this page, select the *Output data to external file* option and press the button below it to select a name and a path for the output file. When done, press *Next* in this page and *Finish* in the final page to finish the work. Now, the exported file can be opened with Excel, where you can perform the desired operations on the exported data

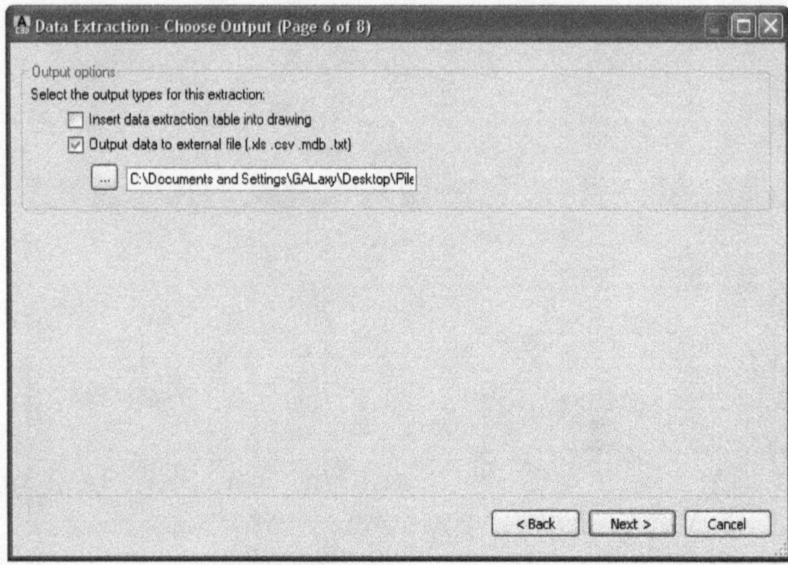
Data Extraction - Choose Output (Page 6 of 8)
Output options
Select the output types for this extraction:
Insert data extraction table into drawing
Output data to external file (.xls .csv .mdb .txt)
...
C:\Documents and Settings\GALaxy\Desktop\Pile
< Back
Next >
Cancel

Figure 5-58

Chapter 6: Answers to frequently asked questions

- In this chapter, we aim to answer the questions that users are often faced with. The subject and number of these questions vary depending on the user experience. These are usually less frequently encountered by professional users. This chapter has attempted to answer the questions that cover up the answers to other questions as well. Study and practice them carefully and try to learn the cause of the problems in a conceptual way so that you can find the answers to similar questions.

1. **Why the software may stop displaying Open and Save menus and ask for the file path in the command line**

Sometimes, when you try to save or open a drawing file, the software does not open the corresponding windows and instead asks you to enter the file name and path in the command line (for example see Figure M6-1).

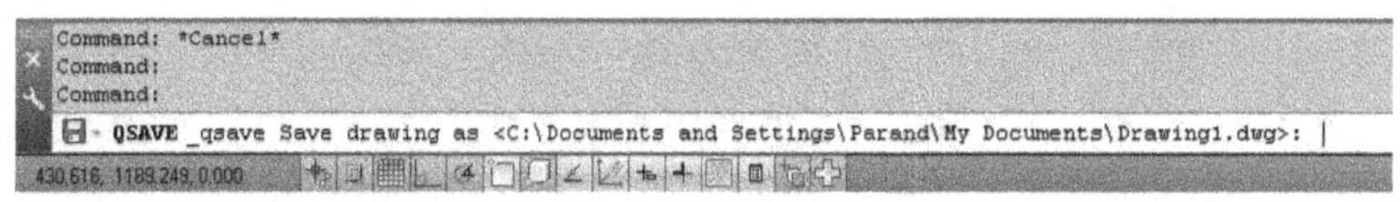

Figure 6-1

This is while most users prefer to open or save their files through the dedicated menus.

To resolve this issue, type the shortcut command *Filedia* in the command line and press enter. As shown in Figure 6-2, the software will then ask you to enter a value for the *Filedia* variable in the command line.

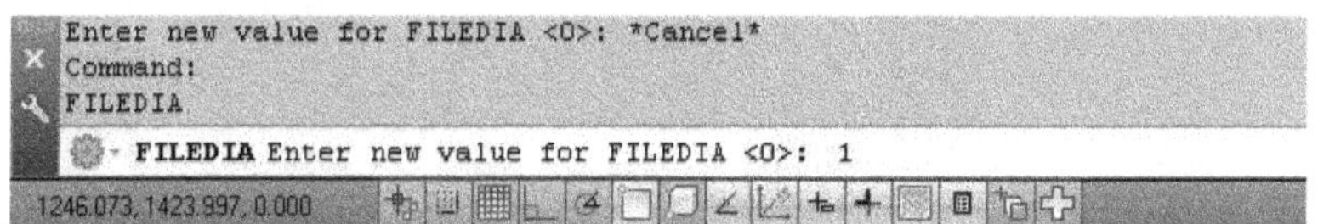

Figure 6-2

Filedia is one of the AutoCAD system variables that can be set to either 0 or 1.

When set to 0, this variable forces you to use the command line for saving and opening files, but setting this variable to 1 enables you to use dedicated menus for this purpose.

2. Why you may not be able to Zoom and Pan with the mouse wheel

By default, you can use mouse wheel as a replacement for Zoom & Pan commands. More specifically, you can roll the mouse wheel up to zoom in and roll it down to zoom out, and move the mouse while pressing the wheel button to pan around the drawing. But sometimes the mouse wheel does not perform these functions, and pressing the wheel button opens the *osnap* menu shown in Figure 6-3. To enable the pan function of the mouse wheel, execute the shortcut command *Mbuttonpan* in the command line.

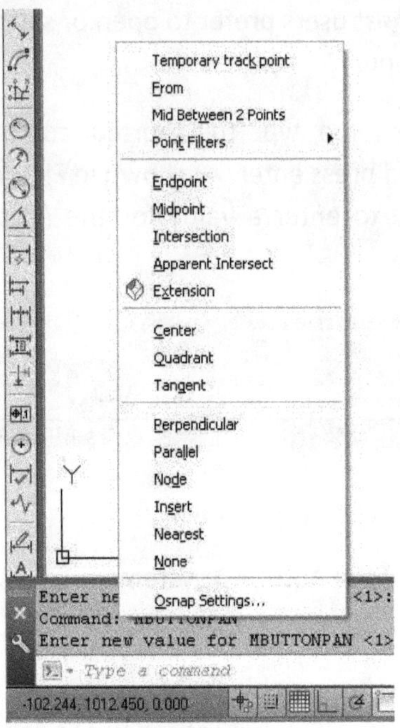

Figure 6-2

Mbuttonpan is also another AutoCAD system variable, which must be set to 1 to enable the pan function, otherwise, the software just opens the menu shown in the above figure

You can use another system variable called *Zoomwheel* to adjust the zoom function of the mouse wheel. When *Zoomwheel* is set to 0, rolling the mouse wheel up causes the view to zoom in and rolling it down causes the view to zoom out, and when it is set to 1, the wheel functions in the opposite direction.

3. Why doesn't the corresponding window sometimes appear when using the ARRAY command?

In pre-2008 versions of AutoCAD, when you type and run the AR shortcut in the command line, the Array window appears and you can adjust your settings. But in AutoCAD 2008 and the versions after that, by typing this command, the corresponding window will not appear and the adjustments must be made in the command line.

The Arrayclassic command should be used to display this window.

However, using the Aliasedit window described in Chapter 4, a shorter desired shortcut can be set for this command.

4. Why sometimes Join command cannot be used to integrate two lines

It is not uncommon to come across two lines that cannot be integrated with *Join* and *Pedit* commands.

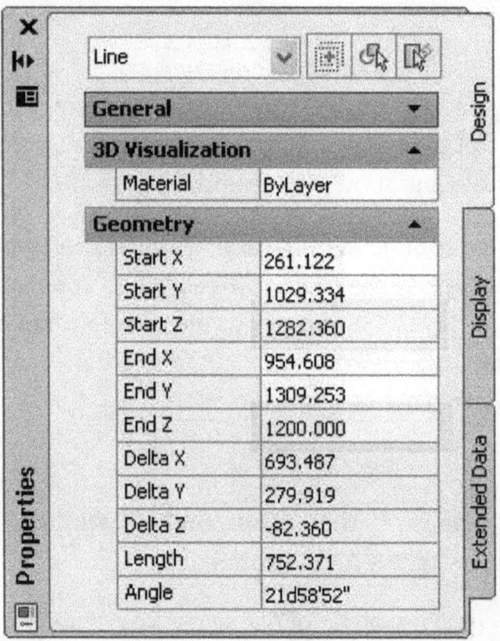

Figure 6-3

This problem may have different causes. For example, one of the lines could be a mistakenly created block. But the main reason for this problem is the difference between the elevations of the lines at the supposed point of intersection.

If you click on a line with explicit *Line* format and run the *PR* command to open the *Properties* window, you will see two parameters called *Start Z* and *End Z* (in the *Geometry* pane), which show respectively the elevation of the start point and the end point of that line.

In contrast, if you click on a *Polyline* and open the *Properties* window, you will find a parameter called *Elevation*, which shows the elevation of the entire line. The difference between these elevations is the main reason why sometimes two lines, two polylines, or a line and a polyline cannot be joined.

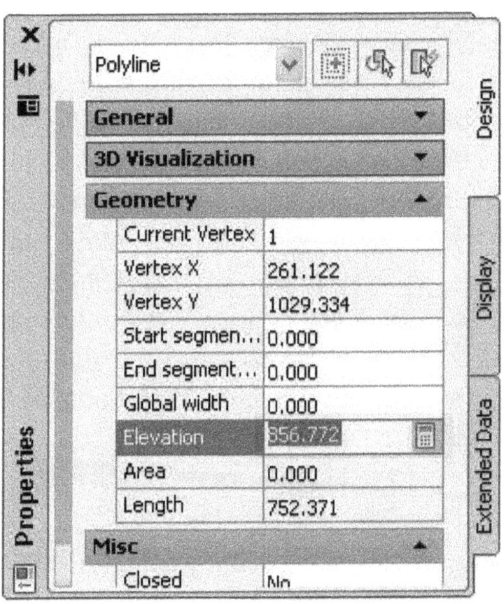

Figure 6-4

Hence, before integrating such lines, we must modify their elevations so that they match each other, albeit provided that their elevation difference is indeed small.

5. Why are blocks sometimes inserted in places other than their preferred place when inserting the blocks using the INSERT command?

Perhaps you have encountered this issue. The reason for this problem goes back to the process of creating blocks.

When you intend to create a block, you can specify a point from the drawing area as the base point of the block by typing in the coordinates or clicking on the Pick point icon in the Base point box from the Block Definition window. If not, AutoCAD will consider the 0,0,0 coordinates by default. Now if the actual coordinates of the objects that form the blocks are very different from 0,0,0 coordinates, this difference is kept and will be applied when inserting. For example, if you click on a point on the drawing area when inserting a block and that point has 100,100,100 coordinates, the value of difference between the objects that form the block and 0,0,0 coordinates will be added to 100,100,100 coordinates and the block will be inserted in another location rather than the desired insertion place.

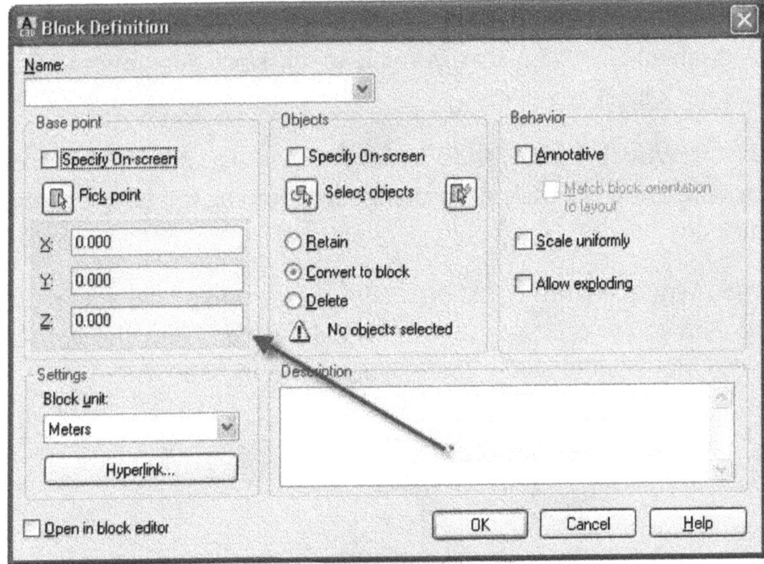

Figure 6-6

So, note that 0,0,0 coordinates should not be selected as the coordinates of base point of the block when creating it, and also use the Pick point icon to select a point close to the objects that form the block as the base point of the block.

6. Why don't blocks sometimes explode with EXPLODE command?

This case goes back to the block creation step as well. If you check the Allow exploding option in the Behavior box when creating a block, you can explode it after the block is created, otherwise the user will not be allowed to do so.

7. Why can't we sometimes insert blocks with different scales in X and Y directions?

If you check the Scale uniformly option in the Behavior box when creating a block, you cannot enter different scales after creating the block when inserting, and usually, setting the scale in Y direction will be disabled. So, keep that in mind to uncheck this option when creating a block.

8. Why are the sizes of the point symbols sometimes variable? Why do their sizes change by zooming the image in and out?

If you type the DDPTYPE shortcuts in the command line and press the Enter key, or select the Point Style option from the Format menu, the Point Style window will appear as in Figure 6-7.

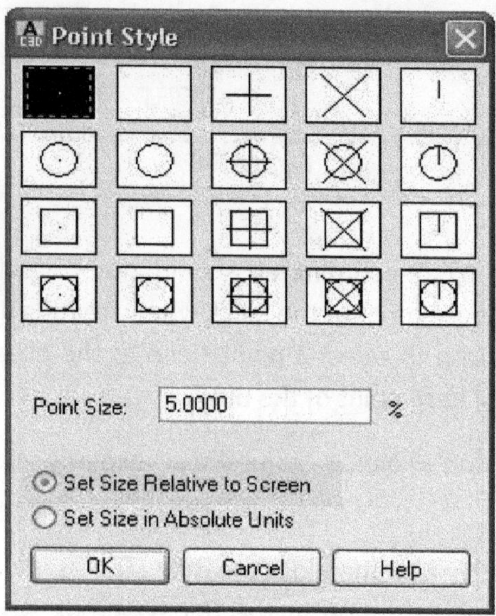

Figure 6-7

If you check the Set Size Relative to Screen option in this window, the size of the point symbols will change by zooming in and out on the drawing area. To fix this issue, you need to check the Set Size in Absolute Units option instead.

9. Why sometimes a layer cannot be deleted

Sometimes, when you delete a layer from the *Layers* window, a message like the one shown in Figure 6-8 informs you that the layer cannot be deleted. This can happen because of four reasons:

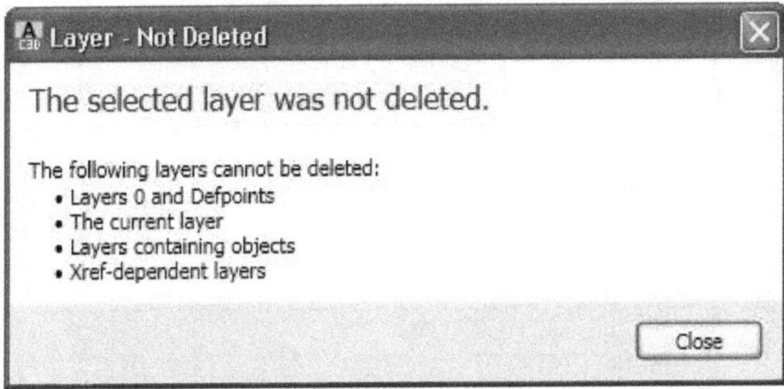

Figure 6-8

1- The selected layer is layer 0.

2- The selected layer is the current layer.

3- The selected layer contains object(s).

4- The selected layer is X-ref dependent.

If any of the above is true, AutoCAD will not be able to delete the selected layer. The best way to remove layers is to use the shortcut command *Laydel*. After executing this command, a message like the one shown in Figure 6-9 will be displayed on the command line.

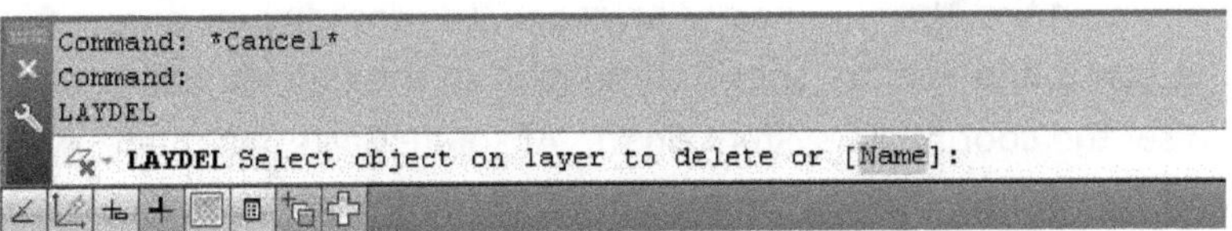

Figure 6-9

After viewing this message, you can delete that layer by clicking on one of its objects. You can also type *N* in the command line to view a list of all layers in the drawing (Figure 6-10), and then select the layer to be deleted.

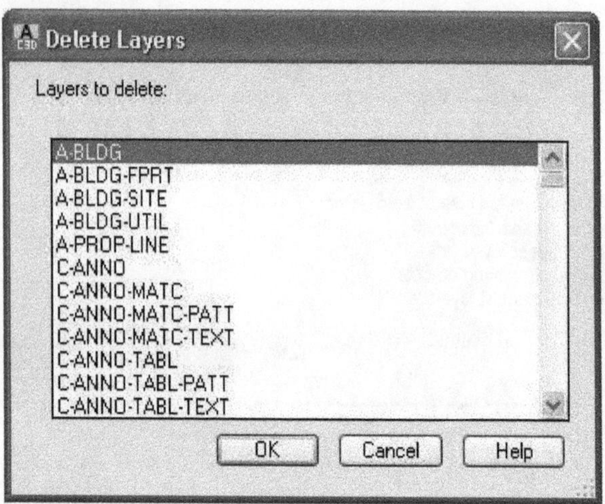

Figure 6-10

10. Why sometimes when we are drawing an object with desired coordinates, it isn't drawn in that location and is given different coordinates?

This issue occurs because the AutoCAD coordinate system is not adjusted. It occurs when copying, moving, inserting objects with coordinates, and generally, when you have selected the base point by clicking on the drawing area to run a command and then intend to select the insertion points. If the AutoCAD coordinate system is not set on the Absolute Cartesian mode, the coordinates entered in the command line are specified relative to the defined base point. To set the coordinate system on the Absolute Cartesian mode, type and run the ds shortcut in the command line, then in the window that pops up, click on the Dynamic Input tab and click on the Settings option in the Pointer Input box and in the next window, enable the Cartesian format and Absolute coordinates radio buttons.

11. Why isn't the command line sometimes visible?

If you cannot see the command line at the bottom of the AutoCAD software, you can open the command line using the Ctrl+9 keyboard shortcut.

12. Why doesn't the corresponding window sometimes pop up when you right-click?

Likewise, this issue occurs because the AutoCAD right-click settings is not set as desired. Some of the AutoCAD users set their right-click to repeat the last command ran. Some others set it to open a menu like the one in Figure 6-11.

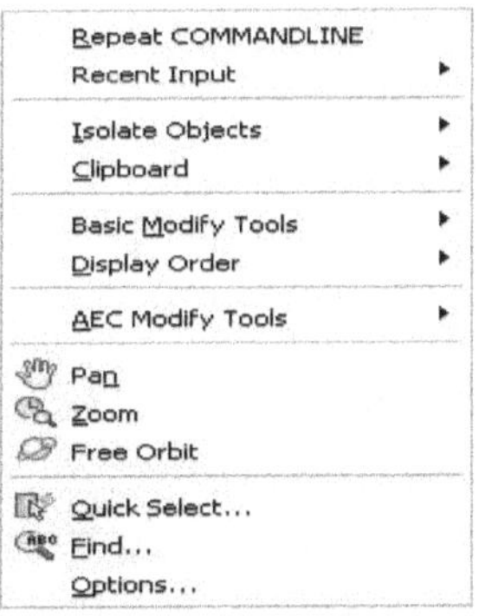

Figure 6-11

Right-click settings have been explained in detail in Chapter 2.

13. Why don't the shapes we draw sometimes appear?

This issue which you may have encountered is due to the current layer being turned off. Whenever the current layer of AutoCAD is turned off, not all the drawn objects will be displayed. Some amateur users may assume that objects are not drawn, but they are actually drawn, although because their layer is turned off, they are not visible. To fix this issue, you should simply turn the current layer on.

14. Why are lines and objects sometimes drawn with line weight?

This issue may have two reasons:

1. The default Lineweight mode is not set

2. The default Width mode of the Polyline command is not set

In the first case, if you run the LWEIGHT shortcut in the command line and select one of the line weights in the Default box in the window that pops up as shown in Figure 6-12, then all the objects will be drawn with that line weight. So, to fix this issue, you should simply set the default objects line weight to 0.00.

But in the second case, only the Polylines are drawn with a lineweight. And to set it, simply run the PL shortcut in the command line, then click on a point on the drawing area as the start of the line, then type the letter W to select the Width mode from its submenus and press the Enter key. In response to the “Specify Starting width <0.000>:” message, type in a number as the line weight of start of the line and press the Enter key. Then the “Specify ending width <2.23>:” message appears that asks the user to specify the line weight of the end of the line. By typing a number and pressing the Enter key, specify the line weight of the end of the line. Now to draw lines without line weight, enter 0.00 as the line weight of the start and end of the line.

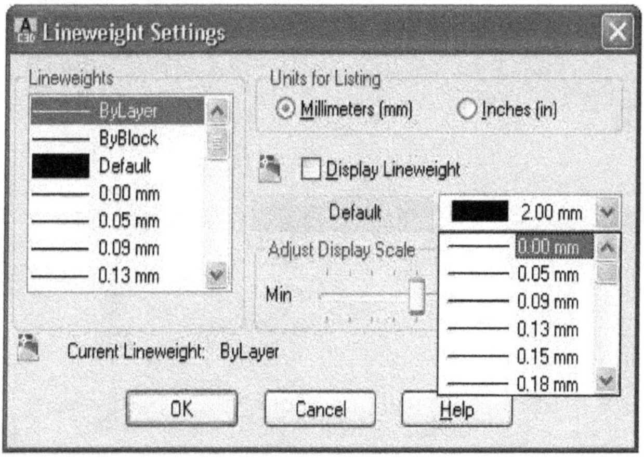

Figure 6-12

15. When we copy objects, why can't we sometimes paste them more than once?

In AutoCAD, there is a system variable called COPYMODE and if this variable is defined 1, after running the Copy command, the Paste operation can be done only once, and if it is defined 0, the Paste operation can be done infinite number of times.

To do so, type and run the COPYMODE system variable in the command line, then type 1 and press the Enter key.

16. Why can't we sometimes create a Boundary out of a closed area?

This cause of this issue is that the constituent lines of that area may have different heights. For example, in Figure 6-13, point 1 in the first line has 101.00 height and in the second line has 200.00 height. Therefore, you can never create a Boundary for this area and the height of the lines have to be equal at the overlapped points.

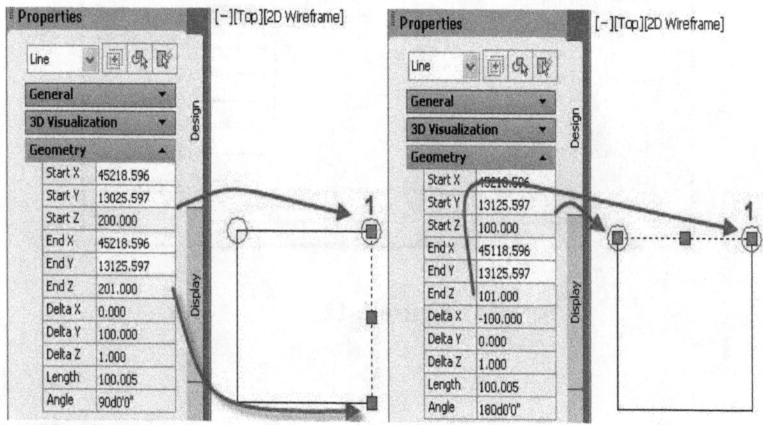

Figure 6-13

17. Why isn't the line weight sometimes visible?

The reason why the line weight is not displayed is because the Display mode of the LWEIGHT command is not set.

So, run the LWEIGHT command in the command line. Then in the window displayed as shown in Figure 6-14, check the Display Lineweight option. By doing so, all the objects that have line weight will be displayed with their own specific line weight.

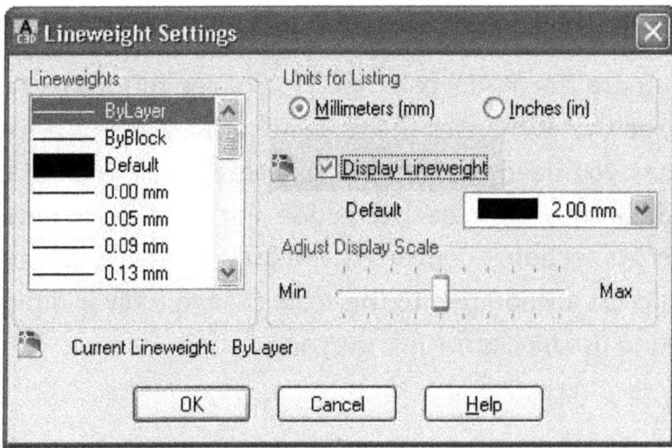

Figure 6-14

18. Why sometimes objects are missing from the plot

Often, objects do not appear in the printed plots because their plot mode is set to off.

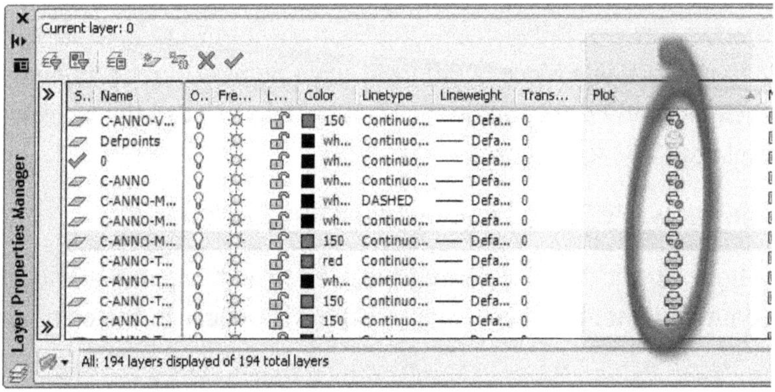

Figure 6-15

If you open the *Layers* window, you will see a column called *Plot,* where can decide which layers will appear in the printed plot.

19. How can we scale objects in just one direction (X or Y)?

When you use the SCALE command to change the scale of objects, you will see that it changes the scale in both X and Y directions. But sometimes you need to change the scale in only one direction or apply a different scale in each direction. For example, in Figure 6-16, the left cross section is converted and drawn two times longer than the right cross section due to the scale change (only in Y direction). You need to use blocks for this purpose.

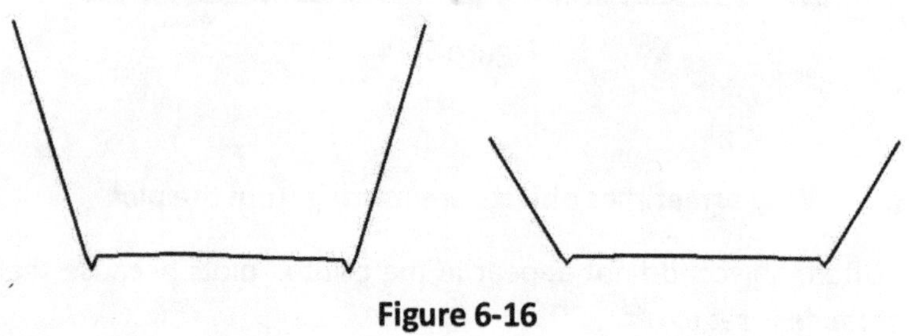

Figure 6-16

When inserting a block, a different scale number can be applied to each of X and Y directions in the Scale section to insert the block with those specific scaling properties.

Another way to do this is to use the BSCALE command.

When you click on the desired block and run this command in the command line, the following message will appear in the command line:

Specify type of scaling [Absolute (final)/Relative (multiply)] <Relative>:

This message asks the user about the relativeness or absoluteness of the scale change. So, choose the Absolute mode by typing the letter A. After pressing the Enter key, several messages are displayed respectively that ask you for the scale changes in X and Y directions, and after entering the desired numbers and pressing the Enter key, you will see the scale changes in the desired block.

20. Why doesn't the background sometimes appear while Dragging?

Most users tend to have a background of the object before insertion while dragging it (operations like copying, transferring, inserting, etc.). Because this helps to get tasks done easily. But sometimes this mode gets disabled. You must change another command to enable this mode. Type and run the DRAGMODE command in the command line. Then the command line asks the user for the value of this command.

The value of this command can be selected from one of the On, Off and Auto options.

This mode would always be enabled by selecting On.

This mode would always be disabled by selecting Off.

This mode would be enabled and displayed only when necessary by selecting Auto.

21. Why doesn't the hatches window sometimes appear for creating or editing a hatch?

You may have encountered this issue, that sometimes the hatches window does not appear after running the HATCH command.

A system variable named HPDLGMODE sets whether or not to display the hatches window in 3 modes by assigning the numbers 0, 1 and 2 to it.

By assigning 0 to this variable, the hatches window will not be displayed.

By assigning 1 to it, the hatches window will be displayed.

By assigning 2 to it, the hatches window will be displayed when the ribbons are disabled, and if the ribbons are enabled, this window will not be displayed.

22. Why aren't hatches sometimes created?

The main reason that sometimes prevents the hatches from being created is that the area is not closed. You should close that area first in order to create a hatch.

But there is a command that helps AutoCAD draftsmen a lot to create hatches.

By running the HPGAPTOL command you can define a tolerance that creates the hatch without any error messages if the length of the line that does not let the shape to be closed is less than that of the tolerance.

For example, in Figure 6-17, a 12-cm gap makes it impossible to create a hatch for this shape.

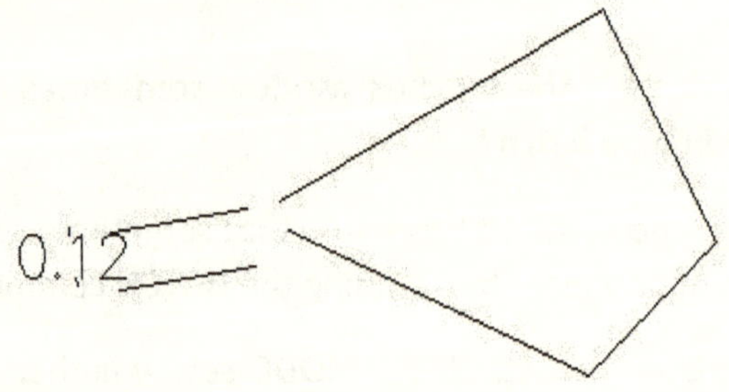

Figure 6-17

But if you use the HPGAPTOL command to set the hatch tolerance at 13 cm, you can create a hatch for this shape without removing this gap.

Another reason for not being able to create a hatch is that the height of the hatch boundary components may be variable which is described in this chapter through questions 4 and 16.

23. Why sometimes zooming is too fast or too slow

You can use the *Zoomfactor* command to set how fast the view will zoom in or out when you roll the mouse wheel. This variable can be set to any value between 3 and 100 (3 for the slowest zooming and 100 for double zooming with each roll).

24. Why don't texts sometimes appear after being moved?

You may have encountered this matter that you cannot see a text after moving it, or that you cannot see a text after typing it.

This occurs because the QTEXT command is not set. If this command is On, it does not allow the user to view texts, and only the text box can be viewed, and this will be resolved if the command gets turned Off.

25. Why doesn't the Quick Properties window sometimes appear after selecting objects?

The Quick Properties window is a window like the one in Figure 6-18, which displays a brief overview of the most important properties of objects immediately after selecting them. But whether or not to display this window is specified by the QPMODE system variable.

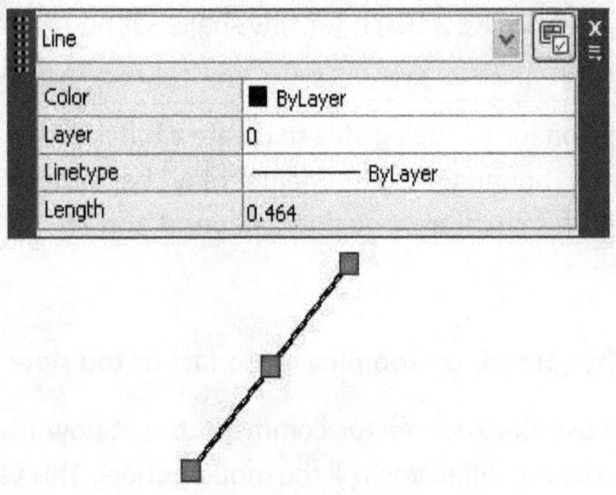

Figure 6-18

If you assign the value of 0 to this variable, this window will not be displayed and if you assign the value of 1 to it, it will be displayed after selecting each object.

It can also be defined by assigning the value of 0 to the QPLOCATION system variable so that the window will always be displayed in the middle of the screen, and by assigning the value of 1 to this variable, the window will appear near to the selected objects.

26. Why you may not be able to select an object first and then execute a command

For an operation such as erasing, you can first select an object and then execute the *Erase* command, or first execute the *Erase* command and then click on the object. The system variable that decides whether the first option is available is called *Pickfirst*. After running this command, you can set its value to 0 or 1 to disable and enable the option of selecting the object first and then executing the command.

Note that disabling *Pickfirst* can prevent error, because when enabled, it allows the users to run commands on accidentally or unknowingly selected objects. In contrast, when this option is disabled, executing any command will unselect any currently selected object, thus forcing the user to specify the objects that will be affected by the command.

27. Why sometimes hatchworks are missing from the drawing

A system variable called *Fillmode* determines whether hatchworks appear in the drawing. After running the command *Fillmode*, you can set this variable to 0 or 1 to disable or enable all hatchworks in AutoCAD.

28. Why can't we sometimes save the drawings?

One of the most important reasons that prevents the drawings to be saved is opening the file in the Read Only mode. If a file like the one in Figure 6-19 is opened in Read Only mode, it cannot be saved.

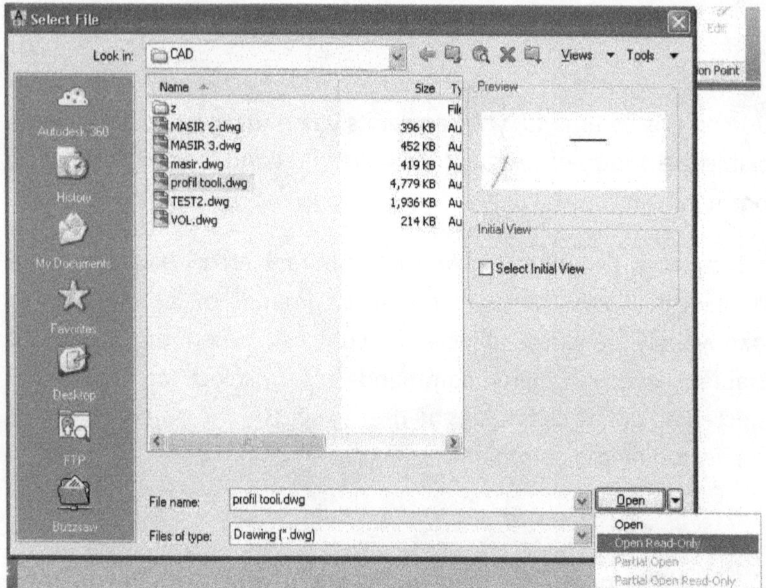

Figure 6-19

29. Why are some of the objects sometimes uneditable?

The reason behind the fact that sometimes, some of the objects are not editable or even selectable, is that their layer is locked.

Therefore, it can be unlocked through the Layers window or using the LAYULK command and afterward you can perform the editing tasks as desired.

30. Why sometimes only one object can be selected by each mouse click

AutoCAD has a system variable called *Pickadd*, which when set to 0, prohibits each mouse click from selecting more than one object.

To restore the normal mode of selection, execute this command and set it to 1.

31. Why sometimes the properties of objects cannot be changed from the Properties menu

In general, the *Properties* window allows us to change some properties of objects such as the layer, line thicknesses, line type, and even some geometric properties. But sometimes, AutoCAD does not allow us to change the properties from the *Properties* window and displays the message shown in Figure 6-20.

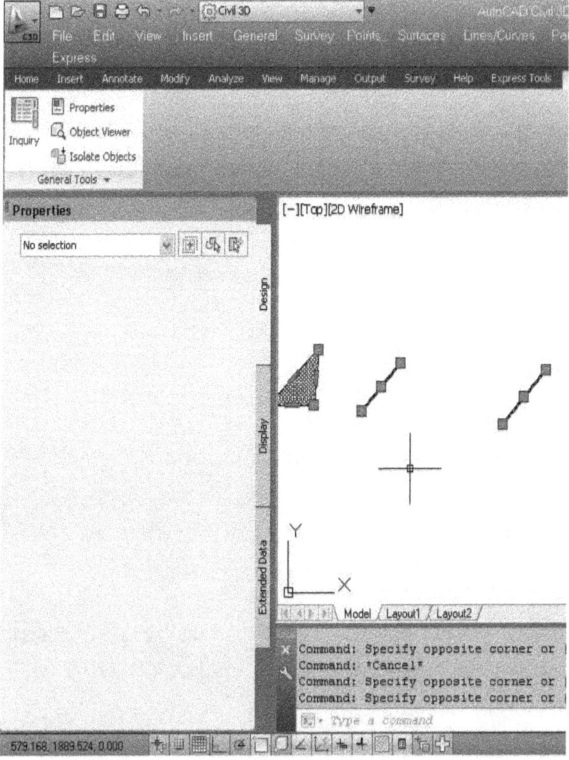

Figure 6-20

In AutoCAD, there is a variable called *Propobjlimit*, which determines the maximum number of objects whose properties can be changed simultaneously (it can take values between 0 and 32767).

In Figure M68, we have set this variable to 2, so the software cannot change the properties of three selected objects simultaneously.

32. Why can't we sometimes move the toolbars?

Sometimes, the toolbars cannot be moved in the drawing area, and as shown in Figure 6-21, a ⊖ sign is displayed next to the toolbars that prevents them from being moved.

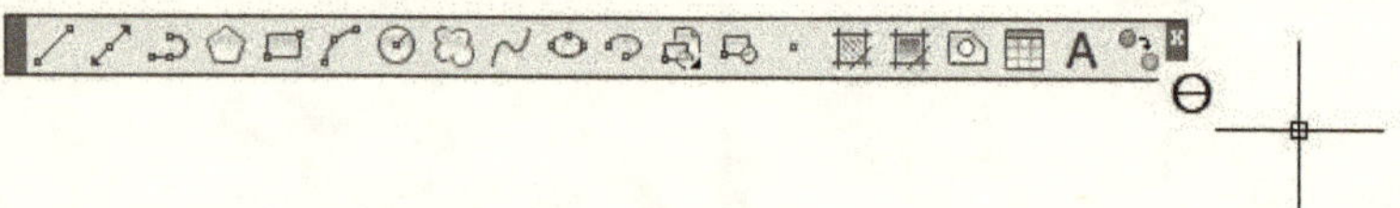

Figure 6-21

This mode of toolbars is adjustable. This means they can be set to be locked or unlocked. For this purpose, at the bottom of the drawing area, click on the icon to display the corresponding menu as in Figure 6-22.

In the menu, if you check the Floating Toolbars/Panels option, the toolbars cannot be moved and if you uncheck it, they will be able to be moved.

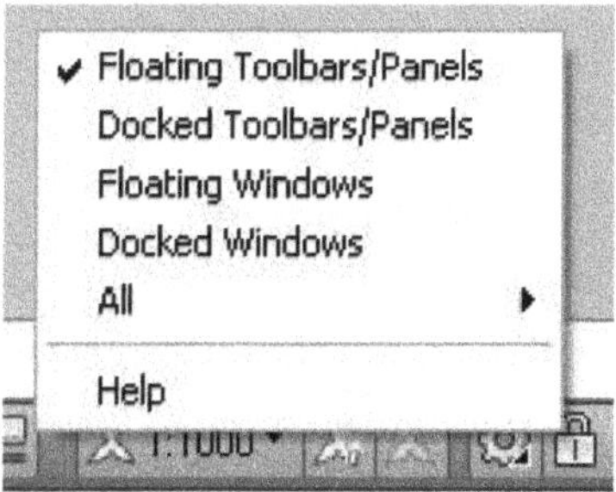

Figure 6-22

33. Why are the contours files that are made by Civil 3D or Land Desktop sometimes not visible in AutoCAD and often appear in form of rectangles?

You may have encountered this issue that when you open the contours files using AutoCAD, they are displayed in form of some shapes like rectangles.

It is because the type of contours made by software such as Land Desktop and Civil 3D cannot be identified by AutoCAD.

To fix this issue, before saving them and opening them in AutoCAD, you should change their type to Polyline or Line in the software contours are created, which is recognizable by AutoCAD. The simplest way to change the type of these contours is using the EXPLODE command.

By using Explode once, the contours will convert to Block References, and by using this command again, their type will change to Polyline.

34. What is the use of a backup file in .bak format that is created while creating a file?

The use of this file is that if inadvertently or for any reason the original file of a drawing is deleted, it can be recovered by changing the backup file format from .bak format to .dwg.

35. Why does it happen that sometimes the name and the path of the file are printed out along with the name of the printer device when printing out?

When using the Print command, in the window that pops up, you will see the Plot stamp on option in the right side of the Plot options box as in Figure 6-23. By using the icon next to it, you can set anything you want to be printed along with each file on the print page.

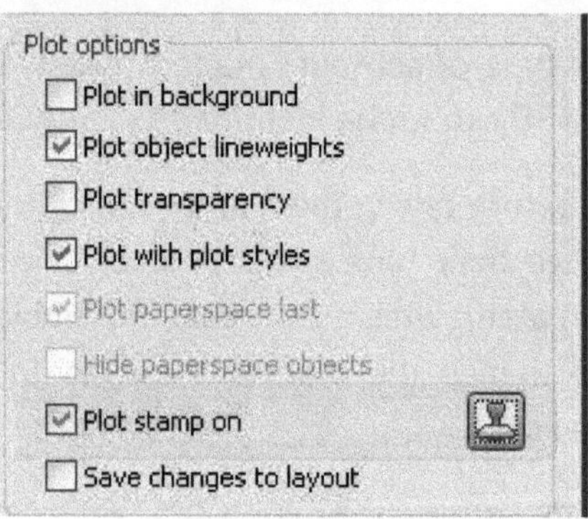

Figure 6-23

By clicking on the icon next to this option, the Plot stamp window will be displayed as in Figure 6-24.

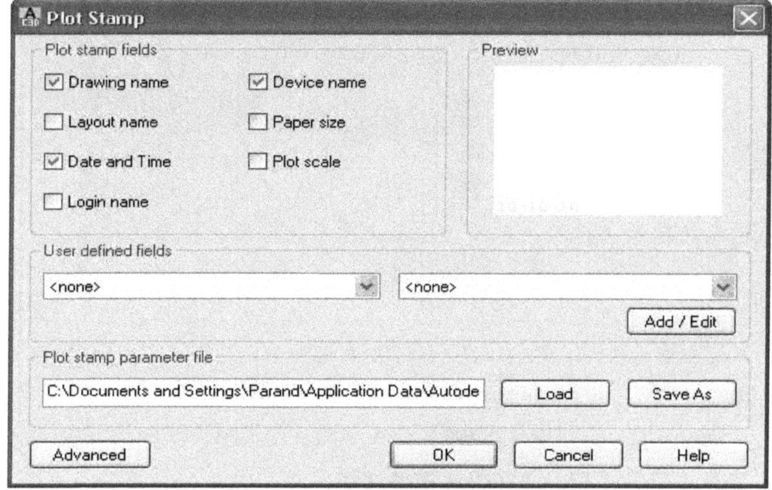

Figure 6-24

In this window, by checking each item such as drawing name, printer device name, date and time and paper dimensions, you can see them when printing out.

Now if you uncheck the plot stamp on option on the previous page, none of the above will be printed out on the sheet of paper even if they are checked.

36. How can we change the settings in a way that all the objects in a drawing get printed out without line weight?

In the print window in the right box, by unchecking the Plot object lineweights option, you can set it to print out all the objects without line weight.

And if you check this option, each object will be printed out with its own particular line weight.

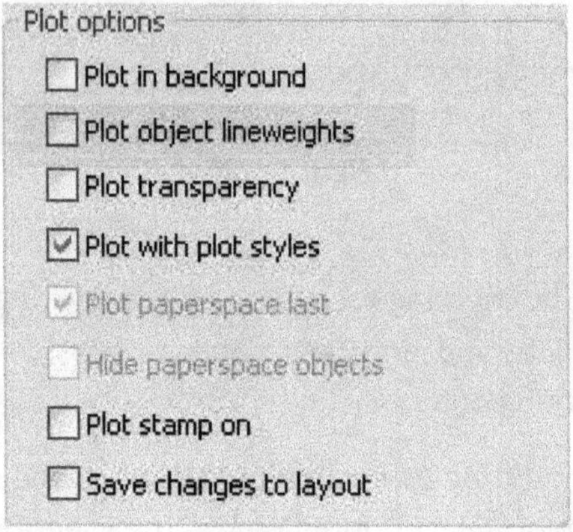

Plot options

- [ ] Plot in background
- [ ] Plot object lineweights
- [ ] Plot transparency
- [x] Plot with plot styles
- [x] Plot paperspace last
- [ ] Hide paperspace objects
- [ ] Plot stamp on
- [ ] Save changes to layout

Figure 6-25

www.ingramcontent.com/pod-product-compliance
Lightning Source LLC
LaVergne TN
LVHW041208050326
832903LV00021B/528

* 9 7 9 8 6 5 5 9 5 0 7 5 7 *